INTRODUCTION TO THE CASINO ENTERTAINMENT INDUSTRY

Vincent H. Eade
UNLV International Gaming Institute
W. F. Harrah College of Hotel Administration
University of Nevada/Las Vegas

Raymond H. Eade
Resort and Gaming Management Program
Community College of Southern Nevada

Prentice Hall
Upper Saddle River, New Jersey 07458

Library of Congress Cataloging-in-Publication Data

Eade, Vincent H.
    Introduction to the casino entertainment industry / by Vincent H. Eade,
Raymond H. Eade.
        p.   cm.
    Includes bibliographical references and index.
    ISBN 0-13-400177-X
    1. Casinos—United States.   2. Gambling—United States.   I. Eade, Vincent H.
II. Title.
HV6711.E23   1997
338.4'7795'0973—dc20   96-22263
                                                                           CIP

Acquisitions Editor: Neil Marquardt
Editorial Assistant: Rose Mary Florio
Editorial Production Services and Interior Design: WordCrafters
    Editorial Services, Inc.
Cover Designer: Miguel Ortiz
Prepress Manufacturing Buyer: Ed O'Dougherty
Managing Editor: Mary Carnis
Director of Production and Manufacturing: Bruce Johnson
Marketing Manager: Frank Mortimer, Jr.

© 1997 by Prentice-Hall, Inc.
A Simon & Schuster Company
Upper Saddle River, NJ 07458

Printed in the United States of America
10   9   8   7   6   5   4   3   2   1

ISBN 0-13-400177-X

Prentice-Hall International (UK) Limited, *London*
Prentice-Hall of Australia Pty. Limited, *Sydney*
Prentice-Hall Canada Inc., *Toronto*
Prentice-Hall Hispanoamericana, *Mexico*
Prentice-Hall of India Private Limited, *New Delhi*
Prentice-Hall of Japan, *Tokyo*
Simon & Schuster Asia Pte. Ltd., *Singapore*
Editora Prentice-Hall do Brasil, Ltda., *Rio de Janeiro*

This book is dedicated to our parents,
Henry and Albedia Eade,
both dearly loved and missed.

CONTENTS

PREFACE

As the casino entertainment industry continues its expansion across the United States, the need for gaming education is growing at an unprecedented rate. A record number of community colleges, universities, and training institutions have recognized this need and have added casino management courses to their curriculum. As is the case with any new academic discipline, there are multiple instructional needs to include the availability of textbooks on the new topic. This is especially true when planning casino management courses. It has been our observation that the meteoric rise of gaming has resulted in widespread interest by students contemplating a possible career in this exciting business; individuals seeking a beginning understanding of casino operations; employees currently in the gaming industry wishing to expand their knowledge of casino operations; newly appointed gaming regulators charged with the responsibility of overseeing this very complex business; and the general public wishing to learn more about this newest form of entertainment. *Introduction to the Casino Entertainment Industry* has been written to help fill these needs.

As an introductory textbook, and by design, concepts discussed in the various chapters are fundamental and should be viewed as a first-step process in comprehending the operations and managerial nuances of this truly unique business. It is our hope that this book casts the casino entertainment business in its proper light as one of the rising stars in the hospitality industry and helps explain the reasons for the phenomenal growth of casino-style gaming. We also believe this book's appendix, which includes a series of job descriptions, and the organizational charts found in many chapters will help profile the myriad employment opportunities available within a typical casino. In the final analysis, we trust that our readers will enjoy learning about one of the fastest growing businesses in America today.

ACKNOWLEDGMENTS

The writing of any book not only requires the efforts of the author or authors but also a multitude of support personnel and this particular textbook is no exception. The authors would like to especially thank and acknowledge the following companies, individuals, friends, and family members for their support and special contributions to this book:

Prentice Hall, for giving us the opportunity to publish this book with a special thanks to Neil Marquardt and Rose Mary Florio for their patience and diligence throughout the publication process. Thanks also to Frank Mortimer, Jr. for working with our book in a marketing capacity.

International Game Technology, for providing support material critical to the chapter on slots management.

Vic Traucer, Director of the Gaming Resort Management Program at the Community College of Southern Nevada and author of *Craps: Dealing and Supervision; Blackjack: Dealing and Supervision; Roulette: Dealing and Supervision; Baccarat: Dealing and Supervision*.

Jack McGinty, Director of Casino Operations, Sheraton Casino/Nova Scotia.

Leo Lewis, General Manager, Barbary Coast Hotel/Casino, Las Vegas, Nevada.

John Brewer, reviewer for table/card game and race/sports book chapters.

Robert K. Johnson, Cape Cod Community College, and Rhonda J. Montgomery, Ph.D., William F. Harrah College of Hotel Administration, general reviewers for this textbook.

The numerous casino operations that provided the graphics and photos displayed throughout the book.

And finally, and most importantly, to the members of our families who demonstrated their constant patience, love, and understanding throughout this long process.

Vincent H. Eade, Associate Professor/Director
UNLV International Gaming Institute
William F. Harrah College of Hotel Administration
University of Nevada, Las Vegas

Raymond H. Eade, Instructor
Community College of Southern Nevada

1

INTRODUCTION

 ## LEARNING OBJECTIVES

This chapter will enable the reader to:

- Discuss reasons why casino gaming is one of the fastest-growing segments of the U.S. entertainment industry.
- Identify segments of the gaming industry other than casinos.
- Understand the nature of a full-fledged casino and the types of wagering conducted.
- Explain the metamorphosis of the gaming industry.
- Realize that the casino entertainment industry is not only big business but also a successful business.
- Understand how expansion of riverside, dockside, and Native American tribal casinos have impacted the industry.
- Discuss the socioeconomic and psychological reasons why people visit casinos.

> Gambling will be the fastest-growing industry of the Nineties. That may surprise you. Many people don't even consider it an industry, but it is . . . a BIG industry. Legal betting of over $330 billion a year from lotteries, *casinos*, tracks, etc. . . . $30 BILLION after paying winners . . . It'll expand by 10% a year. (*The Kiplinger Washington Letter*)[1]

> *Casino gaming* is one of the fastest-growing and largest segments of the United States entertainment industry. The amount of total *casino wagers* has grown at a 9.57% annual rate since 1982. (*National Gaming Review*)[2]

Harrah's Shreveport Casino, Shreveport, Louisiana

In 1993, Americans lost $31.1 billion gambling, which was about what they spent on cable television, movie admissions and video rentals combined.[3]

In analyzing post–World War II economic trends in the United States, only a select number of ventures have been able to successfully combine a great business concept with nationwide entertainment appeal. The gaming and casino entertainment industry represents the latest entry into this elite group; it has not only captured the imagination of the business world and the consumer, it likely also represents *the* growth industry for the next decade. This business was restricted to Las Vegas and Atlantic City until the late 1980s when it exploded across the United States, surfacing on Native American tribal reservations, riverboats, and dockside locations, as well as making its debut in such cities as Windsor, Ontario, and Sydney, Australia. To put the phenomenal growth and proliferation of gaming in the United States in perspective, it is noted that casinos retain more revenue annually than money spent at the box office, on books, or on attractions and recorded music. Casino entertainment is the new American pasttime, according to *The Harrah's Survey of U.S. Casino Entertainment*. Its interactive, equal-opportunity nature sets it apart from many forms of entertainment.

Thus, the casino entertainment industry is experiencing unprecedented growth and has become a major business enterprise. The legitimacy of this business is further illustrated by the number of casino companies now traded on Wall Street.

This book will provide an overview of the casino entertainment industry in order to introduce readers to perhaps the most exciting business to emerge in America in recent history.

SIZE AND SCOPE OF THE INDUSTRY

Casinos are just one segment of the gaming industry. Gaming includes:

- **Horse and dog track racing.** Pari-mutuel betting is the most common form of wagering with track racing. The term "pari-mutuel" is derived from the French system developed in the 1860s and means "betting among ourselves."[4] Wagering odds are based on the amount of money bet on various horses, and a tote board is used to inform visitors at the track of established odds on each horse. Many U.S. states have legalized off-track betting (OTB) which allows wagering at locations other than the racetrack. Additionally, numerous casino operations now feature live race wagering in their race book operations. Typically, these race books have electronic or manually simulated tote boards; televisions featuring races at multiple tracks; racing forms and trade journals with the latest information on track conditions and jockey records; and food and beverage amenities to enhance the viewing experience for patrons.

Some state-of-the-art books now offer computerized wagering whereby betting is done without transactions being handled by a sports book writer/employee.

- **Lotteries.** State and national lotteries have long been popular forms of gaming and lucrative forms of tax revenues for governments. By the mid-1990s, approximately 40 states in the United States were offering some type of lottery advertising multimillion-dollar payoffs. Much like OTB wagering, two of the great attractions of lotteries have been the ease with which a lottery ticket can be purchased and the low price for playing the lottery.

- **Card rooms.** Throughout the United States, gaming operations known as card rooms can be found as part of the gaming industry. As the name suggests, card rooms feature card games (e.g., poker) in which the house, unlike with casino table games, does not gamble against the player. Rather, card room employees merely act as the neutral dealer, with the house taking a "rake" or percentage of player money wagered.

- **Charitable games.** Churches, religious organizations, and nonprofit organizations have offered bingo games, raffles, and "Vegas Night" promotions as a means of raising money. As casino gaming continues to proliferate, many government regulatory agencies require specifics in their requests for proposals (RFPs) from potential licensees dealing with how new gaming operators will avoid creation of an adverse impact or unfair competition with these charitable organizations.

- **Slot/video operations.** Slot/video operations represent a limited form of casino-style gaming. These businesses only offer slot machines, video slot machines, or VLTs (video lottery terminals), which may feature such games as pull tab or video bingo.

- **Bingo parlors.** As the name would suggest, bingo parlors exclusively offer bingo games. A distinction should be made between charitable bingo games (i.e., sponsored by a church or nonprofit organization) and proprietary bingo parlors such as those owned by Native American tribes.

- **Miscellaneous.** Miscellaneous types of gambling include operations featuring pull tabs, sports tabs, punch boards, bowling sweepstakes, wagering on snowmobile races, and social games such as dominoes, backgammon, checkers, chess, and darts.

As can be noted, then, the gaming industry encompasses multiple components; casinos, although only one segment of this business, have recently attracted major investors and captured the headlines, becoming the shining star of the gambling business world. Let's take a closer look at the phenomenon known as . . . the Casino Entertainment Industry.

OVERVIEW OF THE CASINO ENTERTAINMENT INDUSTRY

Casinos may be defined as gambling operations that at the minimum feature table games and card games and normally include slot operations as well as other games of skill or chance and amenities marketed toward customers seeking gaming activities or entertainment. A full-fledged casino would offer the following types of wagering and other facilities:

- **Table games.** Table games involve wagering between the casino and customers and include blackjack/twenty-one, dice/craps games, roulette, the Big 6 (aka the wheel of fortune or money wheel), baccarat, mini-baccarat, pai-gow poker, and any other type of gaming where wagers are placed on a table or a table layout as an integral part of the game. A layout (aka "felt") explains the rules of the game, has locations where bets can be placed, and acts as an ornate cover for the table. Figure 1.1 is an illustration of a blackjack/twenty-one layout.

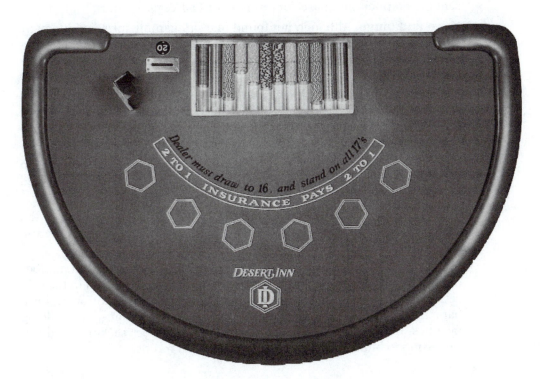

Figure 1.1
Blackjack/Twenty-One Layout (From "The Sheraton Gaming Guide," courtesy of the Sheraton Desert Inn, Las Vegas, an ITT Sheraton Resort & Casino)

- **Card games.** Casino card games are differentiated from table games in that the casino does not wager against the player but merely offers games in which players can gamble against each other with the casino providing or dealing the games. Poker is an excellent example of this situation. The casino provides a dealer for the game as well as all of the accoutrements required by the players (i.e., poker chips, cards, etc.), and the casino relies on a fixed percentage taken from each hand played as its source of revenue. Some casinos employ proposition players who do wager against the players but use their own money.

- **Slot machines/video games.** A distinction is made between slot machines, featuring simulated or actual spinning reels that are activated by the pull of a handle or the push of a button, with payoffs based on a computerized random number generator program or the alignment of the same graphics or symbols on each reel (e.g., "three cherries across"), and video games, which may include video poker, video keno, video bingo, or video lottery terminals. Once regarded as a diversion for the companion whose partner was doing the "real" gambling at the dice or blackjack game, slots have become a major source of casino revenue and now represent the number one source of revenue for Las Vegas casinos.

- **Keno and bingo.** Although not found in every gaming jurisdiction, many major casinos offer these games. Both are based on random number selections; each of these games will be addressed in greater detail later in this book.

- **Race and sports books.** A visit to a Las Vegas casino would reveal a significant amount of floor space dedicated to race and sports books. Race books feature wagering on horse track betting, while sports books take action on professional and collegiate sporting events.

- **Casino cage.** The nerve center for the entire casino operation is the casino cage. Financial customer transactions and accounting for monies handled on the casino floor represent integral activities for the cage.

- **Surveillance.** Also known as the "eye-in-the-sky," this component of the casino maintains a careful watch on all gaming activities through the use of high-tech cameras and video recording devices.

- **Ancillary departments.** Although not part of the casino *per se*, a number of support or ancillary departments are now considered critical in the success formula. Some of these departments include restaurant operations, bars, entertainment centers such as lounges or showrooms, and lodging facilities. In fact, Las Vegas now *requires* new licensees seeking a full-status casino to build a minimum number of hotel rooms.

METAMORPHOSIS OF THE CASINO INDUSTRY

Casino operations vary in size, operational strategies, and game offerings. Today's casino operators also take exception to linking the term "gambling" with their business. Preferred and more commonly accepted phrases include: casino entertainment, gaming recreation, gaming, or gaming tourism. The term "gambling" conjures up visions of cigar-smoking pit bosses glaring at hardcore dice and card players through a veil of smoke in a crowded, dingy casino. The casino industry has gone through a major metamorphosis and has truly become an entertainment experience offering "something for everyone." Las Vegas serves as an excellent example of this transition. When casino-style gambling was legalized in Nevada in 1931, the town of Las Vegas focused on table and card games to attract business, with slots viewed as a secondary source of income. During the next two to three decades, big-name entertainers, stage productions with showgirls, and lounge acts were added to lure the high-rollers. Domestic and international junkets (i.e., flights chartered by the casinos for high-rollers) were a frequent form of marketing, and individuals with high credit limits were wined and dined by the casinos. Certain cities or markets were viewed as financially lucrative, and casino hosts or junket representatives were added to the hotel/casino staffs to seek out players in the Middle East, Mexico, and the Asian Rim countries. As airline charter costs increased and foreign markets either became politically unsettled or witnessed major economic downturns, casino operators turned their attention to other markets, specifically, the convention business. Conventions, trade shows, and tour and incentive travel groups represented the next transitional phase for Las Vegas. Casino/hotel room taxes were funneled to the Las Vegas Convention and Visitors Authority to help attract citywide conventions which bring in excess of 100,000 people to Las Vegas. The convention business witnessed the increased visitation of females and nontraditional table game players, and slots took on a more significant role in the traditional gaming menu. Casinos quickly expanded their slot operations, eventually sacrificing table game pit space—once the sacred cow of the industry—and marketed slot tournaments and slot clubs to entice and retain slot players. The traditional five-cent and ten-cent slot machines now shared space with an increased number of quarter, fifty-cent, dollar, or higher-denomination machines. The electro-mechanical slot soon was displaced by the computerized slot, and a myriad of game offerings surfaced to include multiple versions of video poker machines. Two of the greatest revenue enhancers were eventually introduced: slot currency acceptors and automated teller machines (ATMs). Slot technology and ergonomics became the final customer attraction as multigame, touch-screen, slant-top, cashless, and coinless systems increased customer interaction and satisfaction levels. Concurrent with the shift toward slots, the casinos found another marketing ploy: special events. Heavyweight boxing championships, one-of-a-kind musical concerts featuring the likes of Barbra Streisand or Neil Diamond, PGA golf tournaments, Evil Kneivel jumping the fountains at Caesars Palace, and the National Rodeo Finals attracted thousands of tourists, enhancing Vegas's image as *the* Entertainment Capital of the World.

In the midst of the change, casino operators still looking for an increased market share took notice of the success of Circus Circus Enterprises and its ability to market to the family. Once again, Las Vegas shifted gears, and two

Excalibur Hotel/Casino, Las Vegas, Nevada, a Circus Circus Enterprise

Luxor Hotel/Casino, Las Vegas, Nevada *(Courtesy of Luxor Las Vegas)*

new attractions rose out of the Nevada desert: the megaresort, a must-see attraction, and the family themed property. The Mirage Hotel/Casino, although not purposely targeting the family market, created an enormous crowd-pleaser with its erupting volcano viewable from the Las Vegas Strip, a massive aquarium behind its front desk, and white tigers and dolphins on display. The Treasure Island Hotel/Casino featured a pirate ship and a British frigate engaged in a battle on the high seas. The MGM Grand Hotel/Casino and Theme Park opened as the largest hotel in the world with a decor themed on the movie "The Wizard of Oz," featuring robotic replicas of Dorothy, the Tin Man, the Cowardly Lion, and the Scarecrow. This property offered the consummate family draw with its 33-acre amusement park and kids' arcade. Circus Circus added the Excalibur Hotel/Casino, a 4,000+-room property, designed in a castle motif; the Luxor Hotel/Casino, a replica of the pyramids of Egypt, and Grand Slam Canyon, a massive amusement park with state-of-the-art rides and carnival-style attractions. Downtown Las Vegas joined the parade with its Fremont Street Experience, a $66 million computerized light show designed to draw visitors from the Strip to this must-see phenomenon. Eventually, the New York–New York Hotel/Casino was built duplicating down-

Circus Circus Enterprises, Inc., Reno, Nevada

town New York City, and the Bellagio Resort invited guests to yet another sight—a hotel/casino built around a massive man-made lake. Thus, the Las Vegas model illustrates how a mecca changed and expanded with the times, became legitimate, and took the gambling business from the "mean streets" to Wall Street.

Is the Casino Business Successful?

Make no mistake; casino entertainment is *big* business. Of the $394.3 billion gambled in the United States in 1993, three-quarters of the handle (i.e., the total amount wagered) was done at casino table games and slot machines, with 46 percent of the handle or $182.2 billion being bet in Nevada resorts and 19 percent or $76.5 billion being taken in by New Jersey hotel/casinos.[5] Mississippi riverboat gross gaming revenues went from $10.6 million in August 1992 to over $122 million by April 1994.[6] Approximately 70 percent of the United States population now lives within 300 miles of a casino, and it is estimated this figure will rise to 95 percent by the year 2000.[7] With the spread of Native American tribal casinos, there are now more casinos in Minnesota than in New Jersey, and the highest-grossing casino in the world is a Native American tribal casino in Ledyard, Connecticut—Foxwoods, with annual revenues of $800 million! Thus, the business is not only growing at an incredible rate, it is experiencing unparalleled success.

Riverboat, Dockside, and Native American Tribal Casinos

Recently, the casino industry has witnessed a number of nontraditional or expansion concepts that have impacted and changed the Las Vegas/Atlantic City approach to casino operations. Figure 1.2 illustrates the newest entrants to the casino industry: riverboat and dockside casinos.

Riverboat and Dockside Casinos

When the fictional Bret Maverick sailed up and down the Mississippi River years ago engaging in high-stakes poker games, little did he know how prophetic this approach to casino-style gaming would be. Taking a page from a Mark Twain novel, existing casino operators in Nevada and Atlantic City as well as new gaming entrepreneurs developed the latest wrinkle to casino operations: riverboat and dockside casinos.

Riverboat casinos, as distinguished from dockside boats, actually cruise on rivers or in harbors offering table and card games as well as slot operations. Dockside operations are better classified as barges moored to a dock, and, although seaworthy, they do not sail. Riverboats and docksides, much

Illinois

Alton Belle, Alton
Casino Queen, East St. Louis
City of Lights I, Aurora
City of Lights II, Aurora
Empress River Casino I, Joliet
Empress River Casino II, Joliet
Grand Victoria, Elgin
Harrah's Joliet/Northern Star, Joliet
Harrah's Joliet/Southern Star, Joliet
Jumers Casino Rock Island, Rock Island
Par-A-Dice, East Peoria
Players River Casino, Metropolis
Silver Eagle, East Dubuque

Iowa

Dubuque Diamond Jo, Dubuque
Lady Luck–Bettendorf, Bettendorf
Mississippi Belle II, Clinton
The President Riverboat Casino,
  Davenport
Sioux City Sue, Sioux City

Louisiana

Boomtown Belle Casino, Harvey
Flamingo Casino New Orleans, New
  Orleans
Grand Casinos–Avoyelles, Marksville
Grand Casinos–Kinder, Kinder
Harrah's Casino New Orleans, New Orleans
Harrah's Casino Shreveport, Shreveport
Horseshoe's Riverboat Casino, Bossier City
Isle of Capri–Bossier City, Bossier City
Players Casino, Lake Charles
Showboat Star Casino, New Orleans

Missouri

Argosy Riverside Casino, Riverside
Casino St. Charles, St. Charles
Harrah's Casino North Kansas City, North
  Kansas City
Harrah's Casino St. Louis Riverport,
  Maryland Heights
Lady Luck–Kimmswick, Jefferson County
President Casino On The Admiral, St. Louis
St. Joseph Frontier Casino, St. Joseph

Figure 1.2
Riverboat/Dockside Casinos

like all other casinos, offer a full range of casino games, slots, and food and beverage amenities. It should be noted that the variety and number of permissible games vary according to the size of the barge or boat, by state gaming regulations. Many charge an admission fee, and riverboats cruise for a predetermined number of hours (e.g., three hours per gambling cruise).

Riverboat gaming was first legalized in Iowa in 1989, and this state's first boats, the President and Casino Belle, both set sail in 1991. Three additional riverboats set sail in Iowa shortly thereafter, and during the first six months of operation, riverboat gaming in Iowa generated roughly $50 million in revenue and one and a half million visitors. Iowa's success created a domino effect, and riverboat gaming quickly spread to other states in the United States. States that had traditionally opposed gaming witnessed the tax revenues being generated in Iowa, as well as Nevada and New Jersey, and finally acquiesced to financial exigencies. This form of casino gaming quickly won legislative approval in numerous states. Mississippi and Illinois legalized riverboat gaming in 1990; Louisiana and Missouri joined the club in 1991 and 1992, respectively. In 1993, Indiana entered the riverboat race. Riverboat and dockside gaming revenues grew 250 percent in 1993 to $1.4 billion, and many analysts predict a 100 to 150 percent annual increase over the next half decade.[8] Mississippi took an aggressive posture, allowing unlimited licenses for dockside casinos, targeting specific geographic areas that were in need of an economic resurgence or traditional tourist destinations (Biloxi, Gulfport, Bay St. Louis, Tunica, etc.). When the Casino Magic Riverboat opened in Bay St. Louis, it set a record for monthly gaming revenue—$12 million. By the end of 1994, the nine riverboats operating in Louisiana were pooling gaming revenues in excess of $70 million.[9] During the first seven months of operation, the Empress Riverboat in Joliet, Illinois, grossed nearly $80 million in casino revenues. Thus, riverboats and dockside casino ventures proved to be a lucrative alternative style to traditional land-based casinos. Today, they represent nearly 4 percent of the casino market, with annual gaming win exceeding $3.2 billion.

As might be expected, riverboat and dockside casinos face several logistical challenges not encountered by a land-based operation. Riverboats are generally smaller in size and thus must maximize floorspace utilization. Since floorspace is limited, table games or slot machines that do not fare well are quickly removed in favor of more viable gaming offerings. Space limitations on smaller boats can lead to crowded conditions for guests and poor air quality. Riverboats sailing off the coast of the United States are subject not only to various state gaming regulations but also maritime regulations enforced by

Casino Magic! Corp. Riverboat, Bay St. Louis, Missouri

Harrah's Shreveport Casino, Shreveport, Louisiana

the U.S. Coast Guard. Energy requirements for casino equipment may be met through standard utility company hookups or independent generators or other power source stations. ATMs on cruising riverboats operate via telecommunication linkups. Inclement weather presents one additional problem not faced by land-based operations: passenger seasickness. Finally, the state of Iowa learned a tough lesson relative to riverboat operations. As competition and/or more lucrative markets opened in other states for gaming operators, Iowa saw several of its riverboats weigh anchor and sail into other jurisdictions. Iowa finally lifted its caps on wagers and betting losses as a competitive move, but a message was sent to legislators contemplating legalization of riverboat gaming: Unless legislated to the contrary, riverboats could easily leave a gaming site for more favorable tax advantages or markets.

Although some industry analysts speculate that riverboats will eventually be phased out in favor of land-based casinos, their popularity is at a zenith and the immediate future of riverboat and dockside casinos looks bright.

Native American Tribal Casinos

Native American tribal casino gaming (aka Indian gaming) has witnessed a seventeen-fold increase in revenue since 1990.[10] Figure 1.3 lists tribal casinos currently found in the United States (circa 1994–1995).

Arizona

The Arizona Club, Tucson
Cocapah Bingo & Casino, Somerton
Fort Mcdowell Gaming Center, Scottsdale
Mazatzal Casino, Peyson
Papago Bingo, Tucson
Yavapai Bingo, Prescott

California

Barona Bingo, Lakeside
Cache Creek Indian Bingo, Brooks
Casino Morongo, Cabazon
Cher-Ae-Heights Bingo, Trinidad
Chicken Ranch Bingo, Jamestown
Colusa Indian Bingo, Colusa
Gold Feather Casino, Oroville

Indio Bingo Palace & Casino, Indio
Jackson Indian Bingo/Casino, Jackson
Palace Bingo, Lemoore
San Manuel Indian Bingo, Highland
Sycuan Gaming Center, El Cajon
Table Mountain Casino & Bingo, Friant

Colorado

Sky Ute Bingo, Ignacio

Connecticut

Foxwoods Casino, Ledyard

Idaho

Shoshone-Bannock Gaming Ent., Fort Hall

Figure 1.3
Native American Tribal Casinos

Iowa

Casino Omaha, Onawa
Mesquaki Bingo, Tama
Winnavegas, Sloan

Michigan

Bay Mills Indian Bingo, Brimley
Chip-In Casino, Harris
Clarion Kewadin Hotel & Casino, Sault
Ste. Marie
Kewadin Shores Casino, St. Ignace
Lac Vieux Desert Casino, Watersmeet
Leelanau Sands Casino, Suttons Bay
Mt. Pleasant Indian Bingo, Mt. Pleasant
Ojibwa Casino–Big Bucks Bingo, Baraga
Saginaw Chips Cardroom/Casino, Mt.
Pleasant

Minnesota

Black Bear Casino, Cloquet
Fire Fly Creek Casino, Granite Falls
Fond Du Luth Casino, Duluth
Fortune Bay Casino, Tower
Golden Eagle Bingo Lodge, Mahnomen
Grand Casino Hinckley, Hinckley
Grand Casino Mille Lacs, Onamia
Grand Portage Lodge & Casino, Grand
Portage
Jackpot Junction Bingo & Casino, Morton
Lake of the Woods Casino, Warroad
Mystic Lake Casino, Prior Lake
North American Indian Fellowship Center,
International Falls
Northern Lights Casino, Walker
Palace Bingo & Casino, Cass Lake
Red Lake Tribal Bingo Hall, Red Lake
River Road Casino, Thief River Falls
Shooting Star Casino, Mahnomen
Treasure Island Casino, Red Wing

Montana

Fort Belknap Bingo, Harlem
Wpco Casino, Wolf Point

New Mexico

Bingo of Mescalero, Mescalero
Inn of the Mountain Gods, Mescalero
Isleta Gaming Palace, Albuquerque
Jicarilla Inn Bingo, Dulce
Pojoaque Casino, Pojoaque
Sandia Indian Bingo, Albuquerque
Tesuque Pueblo Bingo, Santa Fe

New York

Mohawk Bingo Palace, Hogansburg
Oneida Indian Nation Bingo, Oneida
Seneca Bingo, Salamanca
Tony's Vegas International, Hogansburg

North Dakota

Dakotah Bingo Palace, St. Michaels
Dakotah Sioux, Ft. Totten
Four Bears Casino & Lodge, New Town
Turtle Mountain Chippawas, Belcourt

Oklahoma

Ada Gaming Center, Ada
Bristow Indian Bingo, Bristow
Cheyenne Arapahoe Bingo, Concho
Choctaw Indian Bingo, Durant
Cimarron Bingo Casino, Perkins
Comanche Nation Games, Lawton
Creek Nation's Okmulgee Bingo,
Okmulgee
Creek Nation's Tulsa Bingo, Tulsa
Firelak Entertainment Center, Shawnee
Goldsby Gaming Center, Norman
Grove Bingo, Grove

Continues

Figure 1.3
(Continued)

Kaw Bingo Enterprises, Newkirk
Roland Bingo Outpost, Roland
Sulphur Gaming Center, Sulphur
Thlopthloco Bingo, Okemah
Thunderbird Entertainment Center,
Norman
Touso Ishto Gaming Center, Thackerville
United Keetoowah Bingo, Tahlequah

Oregon

Cow Creek Indian Bingo, Canyonville
Mission Bingo, Pendleton

South Dakota

Agency Bingo & Casino, Agency Village
Bear Soldier Jackpot Bingo, Mclaughlin
Dakota Sioux Casino, Watertown
Fort Randall Casino, Wagner
Golden Buffalo Casino, Lower Brule
Lodestar Casino, Fort Thompson
Royal River Casino, Flandreau

Washington

B.J.'s Bingo, Tacoma
Lummi N.W. Casino, Bellingham

Microdome Bingo, Milton
Muckleshoot Indian Bingo, Auburn
Puyallup Tribal Bingo Palace, Tacoma
Spokane Indian Bingo, Chewelah
Swinomish Indian Bingo, Anacortes
Tribal Bingo Palace, Tacoma
Tulalip Bingo & Casino, Marysville

Wisconsin

Bad River Casino, Odanah
Grand Royal Casino, Crandon
Ho-Chunk Bingo, Baraboo
Isle Vista Casino, Bayfield
Lac Courte Oreilles Casino, Hayward
Lac Du Flambeau Tribal Bingo, Lac Du
Flambeau
Lco Casino, Hayward
Majestic Pines Casino, Blackriver Falls
Menominee Nation Casino, Keshena
Mohican North Star Casino/Bingo, Bowler
Oneida Bingo & Casino, Oneida
Potawatomi Bingo, Milwaukee
Potawatomi Northern Lights, Wabeno
Rainbow Bingo & Casino, Nekoosa
St. Croix Bingo, Turtle Lake

Figure 1.3
(Continued)

Native American gaming truly arose out of economic need and unique legal circumstances. Historically, tribes were regarded or regarded themselves as sovereign nations living on reservations arranged through treaties with the United States government. Two court decisions in the 1980s (Seminole Tribe v. Butterworth and the State of California v. Cabazon) set the legal foundation for Native American casino-style gaming, since these decisions asserted that if a state currently regulates a form of gambling, then tribes living within that state can engage in gambling without state control.[11] Shortly thereafter, a number of tribes entered into legal contracts known as compacts with various states, designed to offer a form of regulation on tribal casinos and to establish a basis for collecting taxes on gaming revenues. It should be noted that compacts were not always easily achieved, and, in fact, differences over tribes'

Grand Casino Mille Lacs, Minnesota (Tribal Casino) *(Courtesy of Grand Casino Mille Lacs Hinckley, Minnesota)*

legal rights frequently spilled over into the courts. In an attempt to federally regulate Native American gaming, Congress passed the Indian Gaming Regulatory Act in 1988 (IGRA). This law had the following goals in mind:

1. Provide a legal and statutory foundation for sovereign tribes to be involved in gaming.
2. Ensure that the tribes would be the beneficiaries of gaming revenues and ensure their right to sole ownership of gaming operations. Economically, the law was hoping to provide a financial means of reducing the 85 percent unemployment rates among Native Americans residing on reservations.[12]
3. Provide a framework to prevent organized crime's potential infiltration into tribal gaming.
4. Establish a framework for state-negotiated compacts which define the types of games played, payoff percentages, internal control procedures, and other enforcement concerns.
5. Establish regulatory tiers based on the type of gaming being offered:
   a. Class I licensees encompass the traditional forms of Native American gaming, such as "social games solely for prizes of minimal value."[13] These types of operations were assessed virtually no or minimal regulatory requirements. It was specified that Class I gaming did not include pari-mutuel betting on sporting events such as horse racing.

b. Class II licensees make up the most frequent type of Native American gaming. Class II operations include bingo, pull tabs, and card games that have been authorized by the various states. Not included under the heading of card games are baccarat, chemin de fer, blackjack, and electronically simulated games of chance or slots.

c. Class III licensees incorporate all other forms of gaming, including casino games, lotteries, pari-mutuel betting, sports betting, and slots. Basically, this tier covers any gaming not viewed as Class I or Class II style gaming.

6. Ensure that tribal gaming is fair and reasonable for both the tribes and the customers.

In conjunction with IGRA, the National Indian Gaming Commission was established to monitor tribal casino activities in the United States.

Under the provisions of IGRA, a tribe would advise a state of its intent to enter into a gaming compact, and the state would then negotiate the terms and conditions of the contract. Some states have resisted the concept of gaming, and these cases have been litigated in U.S. District Court and/or submitted to the secretary of the interior for resolution. It should be noted that in 1996 the U.S. Supreme Court rendered a landmark decision which could significantly impact a state's obligation to enter into a Tribal Compact and/or will significantly impact the parameters of existing compacts.

Has Native American Gaming Been Successful?

Tribal casinos now represent 3 percent of the casino market, with one-third of the nation's 545 federally recognized tribes sponsoring some type of gambling.[14] With total gaming revenues of approximately $5 billion, many Native American casinos are experiencing strong economic growth and creating impressive employment profiles. Wisconsin's 15 tribal casinos run payrolls of $68 million, employing 4,500 people, half of whom were previously unemployed and 20 percent of whom were on welfare.[15] Prior to the opening of the Grand Casino Mille Lacs, the Minnesota Mille Lacs band of Ojibwe Indians had a reservation unemployment rate of 45 percent; unemployment was virtually eliminated within four months of the opening.[16] Foxwoods Casino in Connecticut, the most financially successful casino in the United States, has a 37 percent win-to-wager return factor, compared to the industry norm of approximately 10 percent. The Oneida tribe, located in northeast Wisconsin, is one of the state's major employers.

Like all gaming ventures, tribal casinos are not without problems and have not proven a cure-all solution for all community and tribal concerns. But certainly their economic impact is significant, and many industry analysts believe tribal casinos will expand by 200 to 300 percent in the immediate future.

In summation, land-based, dockside, riverboat and tribal casinos represent an extraordinary story in growth and success with no imminent signs of stagnation or reduction. All indicators point to continued expansion and record-breaking revenues.

WILL ALL CASINO OPERATIONS BE SUCCESSFUL?

As with any business, the astute operators thrive while those who do not apply cutting-edge management principles merely survive or fail. As more competition enters the casino arena, the key to success will be well-trained, well-educated management who make decisions based on sound business principles and not superstitions or archaic ways of thinking. Casinos are really based on numbers and statistics, whether they are gaming odds, hold percentages, or accounting figures. Contemporary casino executives *must* comprehend the real mathematics of the games and be able to interpret the financial data and statistics generated in the casino.

WHY DO PEOPLE VISIT CASINOS?

In attempting to answer the question "Why do people visit casinos," a number of socioeconomic and psychological factors must be considered.

 1. The Lure of Gambling. Let's face it, many people just like to gamble, wager, enter games of chance or skill. For some it equates to a chance to strike it rich or win some extra pocket money. The thrill and excitement of winning entices people, and casinos embellish this experience by using ambiance, color, "live" games with dealers excitedly calling out "winner" at the craps and baccarat tables, and ringing bells from slot machines announcing a big winner. Others look at a chance to "break the bank" or test their skills with their "gambling system" pitted against the casino. Unfortunately, gambling brings two negatives into the industry: problem gambling and cheating. Addiction to gambling affects approximately 3 to 6 percent of the total gaming population. Many casinos and gaming regulatory bodies are taking a more positive and aggressive attitude in assisting customers *and employees* who develop problem gambling tendencies. Several gaming regulatory agencies mandate that casinos contribute to institutions that address problem gambling, or develop programs to assist individuals with an addiction problem. Many casinos have incorporated referral services through their employee assistance programs to therapy or rehabilitation centers.

 2. Recreation/Entertainment. Individuals with discretionary income are looking for new and different ways to enjoy their money, and casinos offer an attractive alternative. The casino environment is an exciting, out-of-living-room form of entertainment and, for many, a mental escape from the mundane or stressful pressures of work. Casino entertainment comes in multiple varieties, including the various types of gambling as well as live entertainment in the showroom and lounges. Normally, there are numerous eateries, often including national chain restaurants, which appeal to the culinary and epicurean palates of customers. Other forms of entertainment include bowling, movie theaters, karioke sing-alongs, and shopping in the casino's retail outlets. Visitors to casinos in Lake Tahoe and Laughlin, Nevada, and Atlantic City incorporate water activities as part of their entertainment package. Lake Tahoe casinos have the added luxury of snow skiing as a recreational draw. Gaming club operations in Australia arrange trips for members and organize various types of recreational clubs (e.g., photography) for their customers. Pachinko parlors in Japan play loud music and use flashing neon lights to add excitement to the atmosphere. Casinos in America have capitalized on the interest in country-and-western music, featuring line-dancing lessons in a saloon-style decor. Add musical concerts, boxing matches, and golf into the equation, and it is easy to understand the recreational and entertainment appeal of casinos.

3. Social. Senior citizens and retirees more than any group are drawn to casinos for the social interaction that occurs with other customers and the casinos' employees. This is especially true in casinos that cater to a local clientele. Employees know these frequent guests and really become part of the regulars' extended family. Additionally, many civic organizations, clubs, and associations utilize casino meeting rooms for social gatherings.

4. Economic. Since gaming represents the main source of revenues for hotel/casinos, they are able to offer some of the best room rates in the United States and restaurants featuring value-priced buffets that appeal not only to the gambler but also to business travelers and convention goers seeking to maximize their budgets. Frankly, some casinos operate their rooms division at breakeven or offer low room rates as a loss-leader to attract gamblers. However, recent industry trends indicate a move toward increased profitability among noncasino revenue centers. Las Vegas has added an assortment of affordable family attractions that make this city a viable family vacation destination.

5. Curiosity/Must-See Attractions. Today's megaresorts cause curiosity seekers to visit these must-see attractions. Since casino gaming has progressed from being merely legal to legitimate, more people are now willing to visit gaming operations.

6. Amenity Offerings. Today's hotel/casinos draw people to their health spas, hair salons, beauty parlors, barber shops, amusement centers, or theme parks. Casinos operating 24 hours a day serve as quasi-banking facilities, cashing payroll and personal checks. Suites and public spaces serve as ideal locations for weddings and parties, and casinos offer their showrooms or ballrooms to high schools for proms and graduation ceremonies.

7. Prestige/Self-Gratification/Bragging Rights. One of the ways casinos attract gamblers is by providing complimentary rooms, entertainment, food, beverages, gifts, and even airfare. Many people look forward to this V.I.P. status and treatment. Upon return to their hometown, recipients of the complimentaries love to brag about the "comp" suite or "free" gourmet meals provided by the casino.

These are just some of the reasons for the popularity of casinos. As can be seen, there is a strong magnetism, and for many years, gaming operators were afforded the luxury of merely opening their doors and being successful. Competition has changed this approach. Contemporary operations must have a strong business plan; Chapter 2 will provide the foundation for an effective organizational plan.

 ## SUMMARY

Gambling is perhaps as old as mankind, and its origin can be traced to the ancient Egyptians, then to the Greek and Roman Empires, on through the Middle Ages and to modern times. From its legalization by the State of Nevada in 1931, its growth has become a business phenomenon, primarily in the form of casino-style gaming. Today, 48 states, plus Puerto Rico and the District of Columbia, have some form of legalized gaming. It is an industry that directly or indirectly employs more than one million people, generating in excess of $7 billion in payroll while contributing over $1 billion in state and local revenues.

With its unprecedented growth as an entertainment alternative, legalized gaming has not been without opponents morally and socially opposed to its existence. The year 1995 witnessed the introduction of a federal bill to establish the National Gambling Impact and Policy Commission to investigate gambling's economic and social effects. Native American tribal casino gaming also fell under scrutiny of the federal government with the introduction of a bill which for the first time would levy corporate taxes on Indian reservation gambling.

Critics of all forms of gaming entertainment, intrusion of the federal government to legislate the industry in opposition to the rights of states, questions of economic benefits, problem gamblers, and increased competition are challenges faced by the gaming industry as it prepares to enter the twenty-first century.

 ## DISCUSSION QUESTIONS

1. Cite reasons why gaming entertainment represents the single largest growth industry of the decade of the nineties.
2. Other than casinos, what other segments are included in the gaming industry?
3. List types of gaming typically offered by a full-fledged casino.
4. Why do casino operators take exception to linking the term "gambling" with their business?

5. What effect did the launching of Iowa's first riverboat casino have on the gaming industry?

6. What impact did the court decisions of the 1980s (Seminole Tribe v. Butterworth and State of California v. Cabazon) have on legalized gaming?

7. What were the goals of the Indian Gaming Regulatory Act of 1988?

8. Cite reasons why people visit casinos.

ENDNOTES

1. *The Kiplinger Washington Letter* (Jan. 14, 1994), p. 1.

2. *National Gaming Review,* Smith Barney Shearson (December 1993), p. 2.

3. *Gaming Industry Update, Annual Industry Review,* Wertheim Schroder & Co. (Mar. 11, 1994), p. 8.

4. *Funk & Wagnalls New Encyclopedia,* 1986 Ed., Vol. 13, p. 220.

5. "Nevada Casinos on a Roll—National Betting Up," *Las Vegas Review-Journal* (Aug. 14, 1994), p. 18E.

6. *Hemisphere* (United Airlines Magazine), Pace Publications (October 1994), p. 80.

7. *Monthly Casino Review,* Prudential Securities (March–May 1994), p. 13.

8. *Gaming Industry Update, Annual Industry Review*, p. 5.

9. *Las Vegas Review-Journal* (Oct. 6, 1994), p. 11D.

10. *Gaming Industry Update, Annual Industry Review,* p. 4.

11. *The History Leading to Tribal Government Gaming,* Tribal Government Gaming Issues, Little Six, Inc.

12. "Indian Gaming Skyrocketing," *Las Vegas Review-Journal/Sun* (Nov. 13, 1994), p. 6F.

13. *Reservation-Based Gaming,* National Indian Policy Center, George Washington University, p. 25.

14. "Indian Gaming Skyrocketing."

15. Ibid.

16. "Gaming, Indian Reservations and Economic Development," *Grand Casino Gazette,* Grand Casino Mille Lacs Community Publications (Fall 1991), p. 1.

2

DEVELOPING A
STRATEGIC PLAN
FOR SUCCESS

 ## LEARNING OBJECTIVES

This chapter will enable the reader to:

- Understand the importance of preplanning by management involved in casino operations.
- Realize the importance of an effective mission statement.
- Determine how and why business plans for casinos are written.
- Comprehend the significance of internal controls and the contribution that controls make to a successful casino operation.
- Focus on the overall need for advanced and continued strategic planning.

INTRODUCTION

Have you ever wondered why some casinos or businesses are enormously successful while others flounder or fail miserably? For those contemplating entry into the casino entertainment field, is there a success formula, a paradigm that can be studied? The answer to this question is . . . yes! The difference between a successful and a marginal or failing operation is the preplanning done by management. Before a casino purchases one slot machine or hires its first employee, management must devise a business plan for the operation. In so doing, key concerns and concepts must be interwoven into the plan to ensure not only the immediate success but also the long-range stability of the business.

Steve Wynn, owner/operator of Mirage Resorts, during a recent interview detailed in *Casino Journal* magazine, talked about the "central ingredients" that go into the design and business plan for any/all of his casinos, which are some of the most successful casinos in the world. This key industry leader realizes that a business does not begin operations when the doors are first opened; rather, the process must begin with a clear vision and goal setting.

Over the years, a number of sports franchises have been consistently successful, and a sports pundit would likely ask the question, "What is it that these sports teams know that others don't?" Quite simply, they have taken the time to develop a profile of what types of team players will work best for their organization, what plays or strategies will most likely result in a winning effort. Part of their plan involves a drafting strategy based on their predetermined benchmarks for excellence at every playing position. Therefore, their selection process involves a careful review of all the traits of players in the annual college draft and choosing those individuals who best meet their plan, and not necessarily the number one or two ranked college athletes. This same scenario plays well in the business world; each organization must have a concise and vivid picture of its goals and develop a plan to achieve the results. In the casino industry, this plan is anchored to the following triad:

1. A mission/vision statement
2. A business plan
3. A system of internal controls

With this in mind, let us now examine the application of these concepts.

In today's competitive casino industry, businesses will succeed or fail based on their ability to develop a strategic plan, which must encompass a clear philosophical mission statement, a business plan or action plan, and a strong system of internal controls. This chapter examines the steps to be followed to implement these concepts.

MISSION STATEMENTS AND BUSINESS PLANS

Ensuring the financial success of a casino is predicated on a great number of factors. New developments require a detailed business plan which must include adequate project financing, site suitability studies, architectural designs, selection of a construction firm, identification of the management team, and a well-conceived critical path that chronologically enumerates the steps needed prior to the property's opening. Further strategic planning encompasses training requirements for all levels of employees and supervisors, facility promotion, development of a marketing plan based on projected customer demographics and desired market segmentation, identification of revenue and support centers, and establishing operational policies and procedures. In addition to the business plan, completion of market and economic feasibility studies will provide valuable data in calculating the facility's financial viability as well as its impact on the local community economy.

As important as the business plan and feasibility studies are as predictors of the casino's financial success, consideration must also be given to three fundamental "building blocks" in seeking to develop sound operational strategy:

1. Developing the casino's mission/vision statement
2. Implementing a plan of organization
3. Creating a system of internal controls

THE MISSION STATEMENT

An initial management task is to prepare the casino's mission statement. This statement serves as an operating philosophy reflecting the casino's sense of values, business ethics, and integrity. It addresses the interests of the casino's owners, management, customers, and employees. Simply stated, it is the common goal shared by all parties involved in the operation of the business and where the business is ideally heading (the vision).

Owners

The owners have a vested interest in the success of the business, and a part of the mission statement needs to speak to the investors' goals. However, many mission statements *only* address the needs of the owners or stockholders and fail to respond to the expectations of their management team, employees, and customers. Therefore, a meaningful statement will not only speak to the needs of the investors but also will incorporate a plan of success for management, customers, and employees.

Management

Obviously, a key management function is to ensure sufficient operating revenues to cover all fixed and variable costs and to generate a net income to justify the major investment in the facility. The mission statement will reflect management's pride in the operation of a viable economic entity that provides its investors with a fair financial return, provides employment opportunities for hundreds and even thousands of individuals, and is an employer that has set high standards of excellent performance.

Customers

A casino will expend hundreds of thousands of dollars in publicizing, advertising, promoting, and marketing its facility. The objective is threefold: (1) get customers to walk through the door; (2) while in the casino, get them to play, to visit the restaurants, to enjoy the entertainment provided, to stay as guests of the hotel, and so on; and (3) finally—and most importantly—to get them to return. As the gaming industry proliferates, competition will become more intense in attracting and maintaining customer discretionary dollars. The casino's mission statement will necessarily reflect the importance of customer relations by stressing that the casino's business strategy is built on customer satisfaction; service standards are established to make every guest feel welcome and important and that his or her needs will be met with efficiency, care, and courtesy. The underlying message conveyed is "Without the customer, our casino will not survive."

Employees

In the final analysis, the casino's profitability and customer relations rest with its employees who, after all, must be empowered and entrusted to carry out the mission statement and serve as the casino's representatives to its guests. Once again, the mission statement serves as an excellent vehicle to convey management's positive attitude toward employees, their most valuable asset and resource. This attitude may be expressed in a number of ways: management's intent to foster respect for the individual as a means of maintaining integrity in internal as well as external relationships; promoting a climate of enthusiasm, teamwork, and human dignity; motivating, training, and promoting superior personnel; rewarding superior performance through gainsharing; empowering employees as a commitment to the delivery of excellent service to every customer. Later in this book, the concept of a human resources mission statement will be developed.

The Effective Mission Statement

Regardless of how well conceived and written, the mission statement, in order to be effective, must be communicated *and* accepted by employees, supervisors, and management. The ultimate goal is to develop an organizational team spirit, which will only occur when employees understand how, where, and why they fit into the team picture. Achievement of this objective may be realized by adherence to the following suggestions.

1. Develop and conduct an effective new employee orientation program. An integral part of the program is the issuance and review of the employee handbook. Included in the handbook will be the Casino Mission Statement which should be read verbatim to the participants. Since a major purpose of the orientation is to excite and motivate employees, the Mission Statement will stress excellence, customer service, and company values that hopefully will be shared by the work force. Conveyed at this time is the concept that, as an employee, "You are the best, working for the best." The successful delivery of the Mission Statement during an orientation session should result in a sense of self-pride for employees and pride in the company.

2. Post the Mission Statement in the casino public areas. Large placards duplicating the Mission Statement can be strategically mounted throughout the casino, thus resulting in positive customer reaction. The posted Mission Statement also serves as a frequent and constant reminder to employees.

3. Continue building employee morale and motivation. Although the Mission Statement was stressed during orientation, employees require continued reminders of management's sincerity. A posted Mission Statement lacking managerial commitment equates to mere lipservice, and this will quickly be discerned by employees. Managers and supervisors must play key roles in this endeavor by actively building team unity. Effective strategies include:

- Recognition of employee achievement and publishing this information to all other employees (e.g., a story of the Employee of the Month in the casino's employee newsletter).
- Sound promotion policies and cross-training opportunities.
- Allowing employees to attend educational seminars and conventions, and supporting employee desires to take classes at universities and community colleges.
- Offering monetary and nonmonetary incentives, prizes, or awards for exceptional job performance, especially when it relates to customer service or team effort.

The intended message is that management is paying attention to its employees and offers positive recognition of the important contribution employees make to successful customer service. Figures 2.1 depicts mission statements from two casinos.

THE BUSINESS PLAN

An effective business plan incorporates a road map or plan for the entire organization. The term *organization* lends itself to a number of definitions, including the manner in which individuals are systematically united to accomplish goals and work assignments. One may conclude that the essence of an organization is a group of people working together toward the attainment of a common goal. Management's function, then, is to design a business plan that provides:

1. Appropriate segregation of functional responsibilities.

2. The framework to allow for a system of authorization and record procedures adequate to provide reasonable accounting controls over assets, liabilities, revenues, and expenses.

3. Sound practices to be followed in performance of duties and functions of each of the organizational departments.

4. A procedure for selecting quality personnel commensurate with responsibilities.

The casino's completed business plan will include an organizational chart indicating all gaming and related departments as well as written job descriptions for each position on the organizational chart.

The Organization Chart

The organization chart graphically depicts lines of reporting responsibilities and authority. As such, it serves as a valuable tool in establishing lines of communication and developing staffing requirements and provides a blueprint for

---

Imperial Palace

We recognize that the greatest assets of our business are our employees. Development of our people is not only of material benefit to the hotel, but also fulfills a moral obligation to each person on our staff. It is our purpose to deal with each employee as a respected individual. Our success may well be measured by the extent of our efforts which give meaning and dignity to each employee's life as reflected by his or her attitude toward their work and the customers we serve.

Mirage

We are proud to have you as a member of our team. You were selected to join the Mirage because of your desire to meet our high standards of excellence. Although we have spent a great deal of money creating the Mirage, our business strategy is built around people.
Our service standards are quite simple. Make every guest feel welcome and important; respond to their needs efficiently, with the utmost care and courtesy; and project a polished image. You will have made a valuable contribution to the future success and progress of the Mirage when you fulfill these expectations.

Figure 2.1
Mission Statements (Courtesy of Imperial Palace, Las Vegas, and The Mirage Casino Hotel, Las Vegas)

preparing written job descriptions. A key consideration in developing the organization chart is identification of the casino's revenue and support centers, as typified by the following departments:

Revenue Centers

- Live table games (e.g., blackjack, craps, roulette, the money wheel/Big 6, baccarat, Caribbean stud poker, pai-gow, and pai-gow poker)
- Card games (e.g., poker and card rooms)
- Keno
- Bingo
- Slots
- Race and sports book
- Hotel/rooms division
- Restaurants division

Support Centers

- Accounting/auditing
- Security
- Surveillance/eye-in-the-sky
- Human resources
- Marketing
- Casino cage
- Engineering/maintenance

Ensuing chapters will examine the function, role, and organizational structure of the various casino revenue and support centers. The illustrations provided in this chapter are not intended as the definitive casino model; rather, they should be viewed as a guide in the development of organizational charts.

Position Descriptions

With the organization chart completed, attention is focused on preparing written job descriptions for each position identified on the organization chart. Indicated on each job description is position title, direct supervisor, job summary, list of essential functions, and list of job specifications or qualifications. Indicating those job functions that are essential is especially important for casinos covered by the Americans with Disabilities Act. The job description should indicate whether or not the position has access to sensitive areas such as the casino cage, table drop boxes, soft- and/or hard-count audit rooms; and

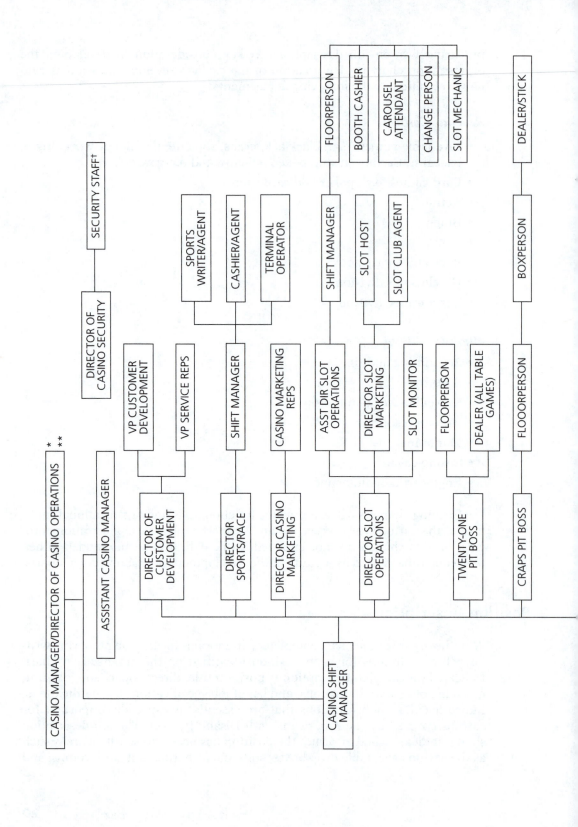

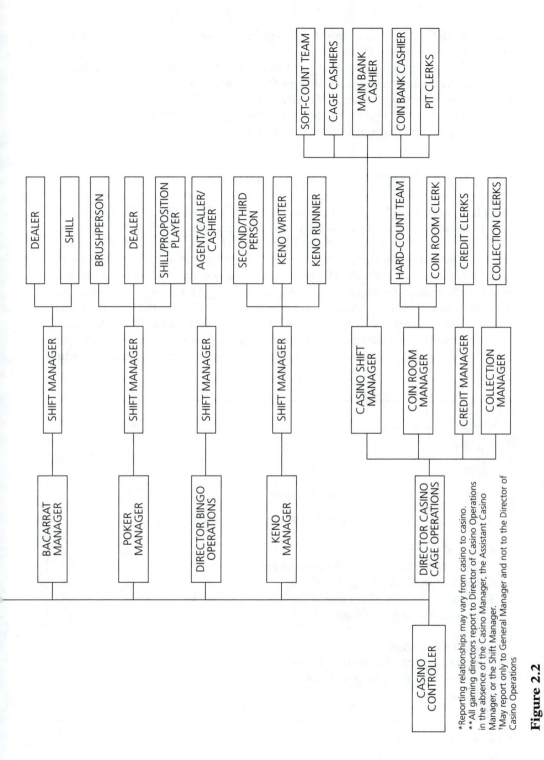

Figure 2.2
Typical Organization Chart for a Full-Size Casino

*Reporting relationships may vary from casino to casino.
**All gaming directors report to Director of Casino Operations in the absence of the Casino Manager, the Assistant Casino Manager, or the Shift Manager.
†May report only to General Manager and not to the Director of Casino Operations

signatory ability. Job descriptions should be written to conform with a brief standardized format as illustrated in Figure 2.3.

It should be noted that job descriptions will be extremely useful during the employee selection process as well as for the orientation program, training, and performance evaluations. Finally, job descriptions should be dated or marked with a revision date to ensure that they are current and in compliance with newly passed state or federal employment laws.

THE SYSTEM OF INTERNAL CONTROLS

With the passage of the Gambling Act in 1931, the State of Nevada became the first to legalize casino-style gaming, and it was to retain this unique position for nearly fifty years. It was not until 1946 that the state levied its first gaming tax on casino revenues, which generated slightly under $25 million to the state's treasury (by the mid-1990s, gaming tax revenue exceeded $3 billion, making up nearly 40–50 percent of the state's budget). From its inception and especially during the rapid development of casinos during the 1950s, Nevada gaming faced open hostility from the federal government. Pervasive social attitudes throughout the country perceived gaming as a vice, and to many, Las Vegas was "Sin City." Recognizing the threat to what was now a major indus-

---

Date_____

Job Title	Bingo Manager
Department	Casino-Bingo
Reports to	Casino Manager
Job Summary	Operation of all bingo games

Essential Functions
1. Responsible for running all bingo games.
2. Establishes bingo jackpots.
3. Responsible for staffing and all personnel paperwork.
4. Creates bingo promotions to solicit customers.

Job Specifications
1. Knowledge of all aspects of Casino Bingo.
2. Must know all gaming regs (6 & 6A).
3. Marketing Skills.

Figure 2.3
Casino Job Description

try, the state legislature in 1954 began exerting strong efforts for state control over licensing requirements, licensing investigations, and gaming control procedures. The end of the decade of the 1950s saw the creation of a full-time state Gaming Control Commission and Gaming Control Board. The creation of these governmental entities sent the message that Nevada could and would regulate its gaming industry and ensure the operational integrity of its casinos. The role of the state in gaming regulatory controls and enforcement was firmly established . . . protection of the gaming industry and the state's economic interests. Through strong regulatory controls, the state could not only assure itself but also the general public, gaming investors, and gaming patrons that the industry was free from criminal elements and was honestly operated. Thus, from the underlying premise that the state must keep criminals out, an entire system of regulatory controls evolved. Today, the Nevada gaming industry is one of the most stringently regulated businesses in the United States. Nevada's success has been replicated by other emerging gaming jurisdictions or even intensified, as in the case of New Jersey's gaming control laws. In summation, the key to a flourishing and stable casino industry is strong and effective gaming control based on gaming regulations that do not strangle potential investors yet send a message that illegal and criminal activities will be dealt with in a forceful manner.

Gaming Regulations

Various state gaming regulatory agencies, including those in Nevada and New Jersey, require an applicant for a gaming license to submit a written system of internal controls to a designated state gaming control board or commission. In preparing the system, the applicant models its presentation after the state's Minimum Internal Control Standards (M.I.C.S.). The submitted system may exceed those established by the M.I.C.S. but must not fall short of the requirements. Once submitted and approved, the system effectively becomes the operating regulations for that particular casino. The licensee understands that all operating procedures are henceforth subject to review by the state's audit division to ensure compliance.

The system of internal controls, relative to gaming operations, requires a plan of organization and a description of the procedures and records designed to provide reasonable assurances that the following objectives will be attained:

1. The safeguarding of assets.
2. Reliability of financial records.
3. That transactions are executed in accordance with management's general or specific authorization.
4. That transactions are recorded as necessary to permit accurate accounting of gaming revenues and to maintain accountability for assets.
5. That access to assets is permitted only in accordance with management's authorization.

6. That the accountability for assets is compared with existing assets at reasonable intervals and appropriate action taken with respect to any differences.

To achieve the above-stated objectives, the licensee structures its internal control procedures to ensure accountability of daily operations. Thus, the system intrinsically results in the creation of forms and documents to effectively provide a transactional audit trail while establishing performance requirements and responsibilities of casino departments.

Developing a System of Internal Controls

The following narrative is not intended as a definitive model for structuring a system of internal controls but rather to offer insight into the various contents which may comprise an acceptable system.

General and Administrative Procedures

A system's first section usually opens with an organizational structure, gives general and administrative procedures, and concludes with a specified method of internal audit support and procedures.

Since a key characteristic of a satisfactory system of internal controls is a plan of organization, as previously discussed, it necessarily follows that the licensee will include the organization chart. Topics covered under General and Administrative Procedures vary but often include:

1. The purpose of designing the submitted system of internal controls.
2. Identification, by position title, of primary management officials to be on premises at all times when wagering is conducted.
3. A stipulation that all gaming employees must be holders of valid gaming licenses or work permits as required by the state's gaming regulations.
4. The location of gaming records, reports, and supplemental information and the stipulation that these records will be retained for the required statutory period.
5. The requirement that all casino financial records are to be audited annually by an independent certified accounting firm.
6. A stipulation that all loans and leases are to be reported to the appropriate gaming authorities.
7. A stipulation of the utilization of a double-entry accounting system and the maintenance of detailed records for each operating department identifying revenues and expenses.
8. Identification of company records retained for inspection by gaming regulators.

9. A policy statement that fill or credit slips will accompany gaming chips and coins when delivered to or removed from gaming tables.
10. Policy and procedure regarding sorting, accounting, and disposition of foreign gaming chips and tokens (i.e., chips or tokens from another casino establishment).
11. The procedure to be followed before adding or eliminating table games, mechanized gaming devices (slots), or computerized equipment.
12. Identification, by denominational value and color, of gaming chips to be utilized, by gaming purposes.

Topics covered under Nevada's Internal Audit Support section include identification of internal auditing staff; to whom internal auditing personnel report; location of audit reports; and findings for review.

Minimum standards established for internal audit procedures include identification of documentation evidencing performance of audit work; report requirements of internal audit results; and the schedule of games and departments to be reviewed quarterly, semi-annually, and annually.

Employee Duties and Responsibilities

The next major section of a system of internal controls consists of employee duties and responsibilities. This section can be prefaced with an index of job positions subdivided into two major categories: managers/supervisory personnel and non-supervisory personnel. Following the index, the submittal should include written duties and responsibilities of each position identified on the organization chart.

Forms Description and Usage

An effective system of internal controls is predicated on the utilization of forms that not only provide documentation of transactions but also serve as source documents for accounting entries. Consequently, the next section of the system should provide an index of all forms utilized in the operation, followed by a description of each form and controls over their usage. By way of example, the following is a partial list of forms included in such an index:

Order for Fill
Order for Credit
Fill Slip
Credit Slip
Key Control Log
Table Card
Closing/Opening Chip Tray Inventory

1. The Key Control Log form is used by designated individuals who have access to such sensitive areas as table drop boxes, soft- and hard-count rooms, time/date stamp machines, drop box storage racks, coin scales, etc.
2. The Key Control Log form is updated by the designated individual whenever keys are issued.
3. The Key Control Log form contains the following minimum information:
   a. Description of key
   b. Date issued/returned
   c. Time key was issued
   d. Time key was returned
   e. Authorized signature of individual issuing the key
   f. Reason key was issued
   g. Initial of individual to acknowledge return of the key

Figure 2.4
Key Control Log

Master Games Summary

Authorized Signature Listing

Inventory Control Log

Slot Count Sheet

Credit Card Application

Slot Revenue Report

Slot Jackpot/Paid Out/Fill

Casino Cash Bankroll Control

Main Cashier Bank Reconciliation

Daily Cashier Report

Coin Transfers

Cash Expenditure

Slot Maintenance Record

Department Cashier Report

Figure 2.4 serves as an illustration for writing a description of a form; in this case, a "Key Control Log."

Equipment and Sensitive Areas of Control

By its very nature, a casino utilizes a wide variety of equipment as well as designated areas identified as "sensitive." The fourth major section of the system needs to provide an index of equipment and sensitive areas of control, to include:

> Fill/credit slip dispensing areas
> Time/date stamp machine
> Drop boxes
> Unused playing cards and dice
> Coin scales
> Count rooms
> Slot hopper loads
> Slot booths
> Bingo/keno ball mixers
> Key cabinets
> Duplicate gaming keys
> Video surveillance

This section will continue with a description of control procedures utilized for each area and gaming support equipment identified in the index.

Customer Credit and Collection Procedures

Credit play is the process of allowing patrons to gamble without upfront cash through the issuance of instruments known as gaming markers. The gaming industry has historically considered the extension of gaming credit and customer check cashing as a customer privilege. For those casinos desiring to be involved in casino credit and where permitted by state gaming laws, stringent policies and procedures are required. Additionally, the system must include a section detailing credit issuance guidelines. Consideration of the following questions serves as a basis for this section of the system:

Customer Credit Extension

- Will a separate credit department be maintained? If not, what department will have jurisdiction over the credit function?
- What procedures will be utilized to extend pit credit?
- How will the casino ensure that gaming credit issued to patrons is wagered?
- Will customer check cashing be allowed to include personal checks, payroll checks, travelers checks, money orders, and cashier's checks? If so, what procedures are to be followed, and how will credit authorization thresholds be established?

- Will the casino utilize customer credit application forms, and, if so, what information will be required?
- What procedure is to be followed should a customer request an increase in credit?
- Will the credit system be computerized?

Collection Procedures

- What department will be responsible for collecting unpaid customer obligations and returned checks?
- Will a reasonable effort be made requesting players to apply chips against payment of outstanding markers when presented at the casino cage for redemption?
- What is the policy for transferring unpaid markers to the casino cage?
- What is the policy on mailing collection letters, and where will they be maintained?
- How will marker payments—either in person by the patron or by mail—be handled?

Returned Customer Check Procedures

- How will customer returned checks be accounted for and controlled?
- What is the casino policy for collecting returned checks?

Bad Debt Write-Offs

- How will the decision be made to write off markers and returned checks as uncollectible?
- What forms will be utilized for the write-off process, as well as signatory requirements?
- What procedure is to be followed for credit instrument write-offs?
- Where will written-off credit instruments be stored?
- What procedure is to be followed should a written-off instrument subsequently be paid?

Casinos have been victimized through marker scams issued to agents working with casino personnel; hence, rigid control over marker issuance is absolutely mandatory.

Table Games Procedures

Succeeding chapters will detail specific procedures involved in the operation of casino table games. However, the system of internal controls must include a section on table games procedures, with specific coverage of the following topics:

1. Credit Play. Assuming that a casino utilizes a computerized pit credit system, the system will describe the type of information available and the procedure to be followed in the event of a system failure. Whether credit play is computerized or manual, the narrative will detail procedures required when a player requests credit at a table game; utilization and disposition of all parts of the marker instrument evidencing extension of credit; the method for handling customer payment of markers in the pit—either in full or partial payments; and the procedure followed in transferring unpaid markers from the casino pit to the casino cage.

2. Table Chip Fills. A "fill" is the process of furnishing gaming chips or tokens to a gaming table. The process involves a pit supervisor, a table dealer, a casino cage cashier, and a chip runner who usually is a security officer. As with credit play, the tracking paperwork may be recorded via a computerized system or the procedure may be recorded manually. Whatever the method, the system will describe each step performed in the fill process including support documentation, disposition of all parts of the forms utilized in the process, and signatory requirements of individuals involved in the process.

3. Table Chip Credits. A table chip credit is the process of removing an amount of chips or tokens from a gaming table and returning these to the custodianship of the casino cage. As with table chip fills, the system should describe the procedure to be followed including necessary personnel, forms utilized, signatory requirements of all personnel engaged in the process, and disposition of all documentation utilized.

4. Table Game Drop. Gaming tables are equipped with metal drop boxes which are attached to the bottom of the gaming table. Dealers slip currency through a slit in the top of the table and the money "drops" into the box. Copies of table fills and credits are dropped the same way.

Described by the system is the procedure of removing gaming table drop boxes at the end of a working shift, affixing table drop boxes for the succeeding shift, and transporting the drop boxes to a designated secure area for storage. The narrative will identify department personnel involved in the process and steps to be followed to access empty drop boxes for transportation to designated tables, as well as responsibilities of pit supervisors for recording to the "Closing/Opening Chip Tray Inventory form."

5. Game Count. The game count (i.e., the soft-count audit) is the process of opening table drop boxes and removing, sorting, counting, and verifying table drop box contents. The system's narrative will specify a minimum number of employees involved in the game count, which department employees should and should not be involved in the count, and a method of rotating employees involved in the count; accessing sensitive keys required to conduct the count; the procedure used to record the cash count to a Master Games

Summary form; and signatory requirements of count team members attesting to the accuracy of the games drop count and to document their participation.

Slot Procedures

Since a casino's slot department is typically the single largest revenue generator, gaming operators will want to prescribe very exact control procedures for this department. A system of internal controls would address:

1. Functions of any computerized slot tracking system. Details would include location of the main processor and computer terminals as well as computer security; the method by which customers may apply for a slot card to be used with the computer; and how the value of customer points earned by playing the slots is derived.

2. Procedures involved when a customer hits a slot jackpot requiring a hand payout. A hand payout occurs when the amount exceeds the slot hopper capacity, such as a $1,000 jackpot for a Royal Flush on a 25-cent video poker machine with a hopper capacity of only 1,000 quarters. The narrative will include documentation utilized for verification and authorization of payment of the jackpot to the player.

3. The process by which slot hopper fills are made, including access to required keys, individuals involved, use of documentation, routing of documentation, and signatory requirements. Many times the slot payout or jackpot exceeds the coin capacity of the hopper which contains coins needed for payouts and jackpots. A fill requires more coins being placed in the hopper.

4. Slot machine maintenance, including machine servicing requirements; how machines will be placed, moved, and removed from the casino floor, along with documentation for this procedure; and the policy to be followed before new slot machines are placed on the floor or put into operation.

5. Procedures involved in slot drop, the process of removing coins from the drop buckets found in the lower portion of the slot stand and transporting the "dropped" coinage to a designated area as a prelude to a slot weigh and drop (aka hard count). The slot drop is conducted by a hard-count team, and the method of securing sensitive keys and procedures to be followed for this drop must be addressed by the system.

6. Slot weigh/wrap policies, detailing the number and duties of personnel involved in the procedure, validating accuracy of the weigh/count, and documentation utilized attesting to the accuracy of the revenue generated. The word "wrap" refers to the wrapping of coins in paper as done automatically via the coin-counting apparatus.

7. Slot booths, located on the casino floor, responsible for customer transactions, as well as activities of change personnel regularly requiring cash transfers involving the casino cage. The system will describe required procedures for cash transfers, documentation utilized, and verification of slot booth and change persons' banks at the end of each shift.

Keno Procedures

Typical contents of this segment of a casino's system of internal controls address the "writing area" (i.e., where keno tickets are written) and the verification area of the keno department, as well as surveillance monitoring of each keno game played. Use of a computer system requires details regarding how tickets will be printed and recorded. Further descriptions include computer capability allowing limited access to such vulnerable areas as winning ticket payouts, ticket replays, ticket voids, and terminal access. Cash control, calling procedures, verification and payment of winning tickets, shift-ending checkout procedures, as well as keno audit procedures are all topics requiring system narratives.

Bingo Procedures

The system of internal controls would include the following:

1. A method of conducting an inventory of bingo paper packs or cards prior to and at the conclusion of each bingo session.
2. How proceeds from bingo sales are counted, verified, and transferred to a main casino bank.
3. Duties and responsibilities of bingo agents during each bingo session. The method of ball calling from a blower-type machine and visual display of the called ball is also described. Payout procedures to winning patrons as well as session and shift closing procedures must be adequately addressed, as well as responsibilities for performing the bingo audit.

Card Room (Poker) Procedures

Operation of a card/poker room by a casino includes the following coverage in a system of internal controls:

1. Location of the table drop boxes underneath each card table, bearing that table's number.
2. Stipulation that each table has a predetermined spot where the dealer temporarily places the "rake" before its insertion into the table drop box. A rake is the casino's commission or "vig" automatically withdrawn from all poker pots.
3. Acknowledgment that house rules pertaining to conduct of games are clearly posted and legible.

4. Procedures for receiving cash or chips from patrons prior to participating in the game.

5. Shift end accountability of table banks required of dealers and a designated shift supervisor.

6. Shift-ending card room bank reconciliation required of the oncoming and off-going shift managers.

7. Procedures for conducting the card room drop and count.

Surveillance Department

Gaming regulations typically require casinos to install, maintain, and operate a surveillance system to ensure adequate coverage of daily gaming operations. The system should address use of cameras, monitors, video tape recorders, video printers, and the security and privacy of the casino's surveillance room. The written system of internal controls for this department stresses:

1. An overview of the surveillance system, including equipment, security of the system to prevent tampering, and an auxiliary power source in the event of power loss.

2. Stipulation of the capability to monitor and record clear and unobstructed views of:

   a. The hard-count room, the soft-count room, and the casino cage.

   b. All table games and card room areas with sufficient clarity to permit identification of all dealers, patrons, spectators, and pit personnel; table game and card table surfaces, including table bank trays; all drop box and table numbers; and card room podium banks.

   c. All keno/bingo desks and satellite stations, including counters, windows, cash drawers, and transaction areas, as well as ball drawing devices.

   d. Slot change booths, including cash drawers, countertops, counting machines, and customer and employee windows.

   e. All areas of any security office where persons may be detained, questioned, interviewed, or interrogated.

3. Stipulation that the casino must maintain a written log of any surveillance system equipment malfunctions, as well as repair reporting procedures.

Rules of Play

A wide variety of gaming is offered by casinos subject to limitations imposed by state law or, in the case of Native American gaming, by tribal-state enacted compacts (see Chapter 1). Table and card games may include craps, roulette, blackjack, the money wheel/Big 6, baccarat, mini-baccarat, pai-gow, pai-gow poker, Caribbean stud poker, let it ride, and red dog. Although individual game manuals are written by casinos to structure dealing training and game procedures, the system of internal controls will need to include rules of play for these games. In addition to providing definitions of gaming terminology, the system can stipulate methods of accepting wagers, minimum and maximum game betting limits, a display of payoff schedules and/or awards, and how payments will be made for customer winnings and/or noncash prizes. Descriptions of gaming equipment identifying the physical characteristics of dice, playing cards, dealing shoes, and roulette balls are recommended inclusions in the written narrative section.

SUMMARY

As can be seen, a strategic plan, a mission statement, a business plan, and a strong system of internal controls are critical to the successful operation of any casino. The process starts at the top of the organizational structure and must be followed at every level by all employees. Failure to adhere to a strategic plan will lead not only to significant economic problems but also to legal and governmental regulatory intervention.

DISCUSSION QUESTIONS

1. What is a mission statement? Who should participate in writing the mission statement?

2. How often should casino organizations revisit their mission statement to determine whether it is being realized or possibly to revamp the intent?

3. What is a business plan? How should a casino hold its personnel accountable for compliance with the business plan?

4. Discuss an effective strategy for writing and developing a system of internal control procedures.

5. How do you measure the effectiveness of strategic planning?

3

TABLE GAMES: BLACKJACK/TWENTY-ONE AND CRAPS

 ## LEARNING OBJECTIVES

This chapter will enable the reader to:

- Understand the rules and procedures of the casino table game of blackjack/twenty-one.
- Review the organizational structure of a blackjack/twenty-one pit and the responsibilities of the pit manager.
- Discuss the role and duties of a blackjack/twenty-one floorperson as a front-line game supervisor.
- Identify the skills, proficiency, and responsibilities required of the professional blackjack/twenty-one dealer.
- Understand the rules and procedures of the casino table game of craps.
- Review the organizational structure of a craps pit and the responsibilities of the craps supervisor, especially the role of the boxperson.
- Identify methods by which the game of craps might be cheated.
- Discuss the duties and responsibilities of dealers assigned to the game of craps.

INTRODUCTION

The game of blackjack, also known as twenty-one, or *vingt-et-un* in European casinos, has been a mainstay of casinos for years. Its ease of play and chal-

45

Figure 3.1
Twenty-One Dealer Shoe. The shoe, as located under the dealer's left hand, holds multiple decks of cards. (Courtesy of Trump's Castle Casino Resort, Atlantic City)

lenge to beat the dealer makes it one of the favorite games of skill in the industry. This chapter will examine the rules of the game, employees involved in the game, and some of the game's nuances.

THE GAME OF TWENTY-ONE

Rules and Procedures of Twenty-One

The game of twenty-one can be played with a standard 52-card deck held in-hand by the dealer or with multiple decks (i.e., two decks, eight decks) dealt by the dealer from a shoe (see Figure 3.1). The player's object in the game is to beat the dealer by getting 21 or closer to 21 than the dealer without going over, based on the point value of the dealt cards. The game begins with the players placing their wagers in the appropriate betting circles on the table layout. Assuming this is a hand-held deck(s), the dealer then deals one card to each player at the blackjack (BJ) table; normally there are six or seven seats or "spots" at each table. The player at the far left of the dealer (also known as "first base") receives one card, and the dealer begins to pitch cards to all other players, proceeding from left to the last player to the dealer's right (aka third base). The dealer then deals one card face up to herself.

Once this is done, the dealer pitches the second card to all players first, repeating the same clockwise distribution procedure. *All* players' cards are dealt face down, and although the dealer's first card is dealt face up, the second card is dealt face down and not visible to the players. (Quite frankly, some casinos deviate from this procedure as a marketing ploy or when using a shoe). Placing the second card directly under the first card or "up card" (also known as "the hole card"), the dealer goes around the table in a clockwise sequence determining if any players want an additional card or a "hit"; players do not ask for extra cards but rather scratch their cards on the layout a couple of times making a snappy, raking motion toward themselves or use hand signals. Face cards (kings, queens, and jacks) count as ten points, and the other cards count at face value (e.g., a four of hearts is four points), with one exception: Aces count as either one or eleven. Unlike poker, the suits of the cards have no effect on the outcome of the game.

Players do not have to take a hit if they are satisfied with their point total. After all players have indicated their desires, the dealer turns over the hole card and, based on the point total, will either "stand" or take a hit(s). If the point total is 17 or over, the dealer must stand, by house rules, unless the 17 is a "soft 17." A soft 17 occurs when an ace appears in any combination with the other cards for a total of 7 or 17 (e.g., the dealer has a 6 and an ace, which equals a soft 17). In reality, this hand is viewed as 7, and most casinos require the dealer to hit this hand.

If the point total is 16 or less, the dealer must draw cards until the point total either is between 17 and 21 or the dealer "busts"—goes over the total of 21, in which case all players with point totals 21 and under automatically win. It should be noted that the dealer does not reveal her full hand or hit her hand until *all* players have played their hands, or taken all their "hits," giving the casino a significant advantage, since many players bust their hands prior to the dealer completing her hand.

When the dealer's first two cards are dealt, if the dealer's "up" card is a ten, a face card, or an ace, the dealer, before hitting the players, checks the hole/bottom card to determine if there is a blackjack. A blackjack is defined as one ace and one ten-value card (a face card or a ten), and should not be confused with several cards totaling 21 points. Thus, a blackjack only occurs based on the two originally dealt cards. If the dealer has a blackjack, or "snapper," the casino automatically wins. Players who also have blackjacks under these circumstances realize a "push"; they neither win nor lose their original bet, and their bet is returned or they can let it ride to the next hand. If the dealer's up card is an ace, the dealer will first ask the players if they want "insurance." Insurance is a voluntary hedge bet, with players wagering that the dealer *does* have a blackjack. If the dealer does have a blackjack, the insurance wagers are paid two to one but the players then lose their original bet—unless they also have a blackjack, which would then result in a push. Conversely, if the dealer does not have a blackjack, players forfeit their insurance bets.

Some casinos have an additional rule called "surrender," which allows players to surrender one-half of their bet after the first two cards are dealt if they feel their hand is going to lose based on the dealer's up card. Players with significant wagers and card counters are most likely to utilize this option since they can cut their potential losses.

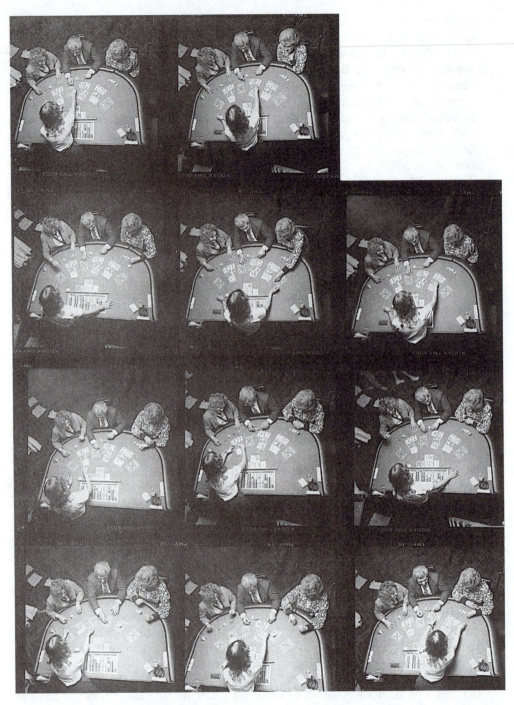

Blackjack Tables *(Courtesy of Harvey's Resort Hotel/Casino, Lake Tahoe, Nevada)*

Other playing options featured in the game of blackjack include doubling down and splitting pairs:

1. Doubling down. Once the first two cards have been dealt, players may opt to double their bet but then are only entitled to one and only one extra card. Strategy players double down when their two cards total ten or eleven or if they think the dealer's up card puts the dealer at a disadvantage. Some casinos have additional restrictions on doubling down options.

2. Splitting pairs. If the first two dealt cards are the same (e.g., two fours are a pair) or are any two ten-valued cards, players can split these pairs or two cards and play two hands. Players must place an additional wager on this hand of equal value to that of the first hand, and can receive as many cards as they wish with the exception of aces.

Let's assume that all hands have been dealt and the dealer does not have a blackjack. All players, starting with first base, would then exercise their option to stand (i.e., not take any more cards) or be hit. Players can take as many cards as desired provided they have not busted their hands. (As a sidenote, a hand with five cards that totals 21 is referred to as a "five-card charley.") The dealer then turns up the hole card and will hit or stand based on the previously discussed house rules. Players beating the dealer win the same amount as wagered, also referred to as even money or one-to-one. Casinos place placards on twenty-one tables that indicate table limits (e.g., $5 to $1,000) and offer multiple table-limit variations.

In a basic, single-deck game of twenty-one, the casino has a house advantage over the players. Therefore, casino operators are extremely concerned about the number of hands dealt by dealers, knowing that more hands dealt equates to more winnings. Many casinos have introduced automatic shufflers, which reportedly have increased hand productivity by as much as 20 percent. Some operators feel that a potential danger in hand maximization is the potential for increased dealer mistakes and dealer burnout.

Players seeking an advantage over the casino have resorted to a number of tactics:

1. Card counting, which is really keeping track of ten-value cards that have been dealt and then increasing wager amounts when the card probability is to the player's advantage.

2. Basic money management and card strategy.

3. Cheating. This can be done individually, with other players or a team of cheaters, or with a casino worker. This topic will be discussed in greater detail later.

The game of twenty-one, although based on math and strategy, can be a fun and exciting entertainment experience for players. At one time, dealers were told to "dummy-up and deal" and casino workers were discouraged from

Blackjack Table *(Courtesy of the Excalibur Hotel/Casino, Las Vegas, Nevada, a Circus Circus Enterprise)*

interacting or communicating with players. Today's casino workers are now focusing on customer service and entertainment value. Let's take a look at the employees involved in the twenty-one pit.

Twenty-One Organization Chart

Figure 3.2 illustrates the organizational structure for a twenty-one/blackjack pit. The *pit* is the term used to identify the physical area where the twenty-one tables and pit clerk station are found on the casino floor. Large casinos have multiple twenty-one and dice pits.

The Twenty-One Pit Boss/Manager

As noted in Figure 2.2 in Chapter 2, the twenty-one pit boss reports to the shift manager, who reports to the assistant casino manager or casino manager. Pit bosses (aka pit supervisors or pit managers) oversee the efficient operation of their respective pits, with one pit boss assigned to one pit. Some pit boss responsibilities are:

1. Maintaining the integrity of the game, making sure the conduct of floor-persons and dealers are in accordance with rules of the game, internal control procedures, and customer service standards.

2. Ensuring that the activities of the players and customers are in accordance with the rules of the game and that no collusion is occurring between the customers and casino employees.

3. Referring initial or additional requests for lines of credit to the credit manager with the exception of preapproved rim credit.

4. Resolving customer disputes relating to rules of the game, wagering, or employee problems.

5. Signing pit transaction forms.

6. Assigning floorpersons to their respective games.

7. Issuing new decks of cards to the pit and ensuring that they are properly secured.

8. Initiating investigations into suspected game cheating.

9. Exercising disciplinary authority with pit personnel.

10. Maintaining procedures for monitoring currency transactions as required by the Bank Secrecy Act.

11. Maintaining proper staffing levels with pit personnel.

12. Implementing customer service standards. Pit bosses especially follow the wagering of high-rollers, big winners and losers, and will keep a log of pit activity to include large bill transactions. As casinos become more sensitive and responsive to compulsive and problem gamblers, pit bosses as well as all personnel need to take a more proactive role in dealing with this problem.

13. Auditioning new or prospective dealers. Applicants for dealers' jobs are required to demonstrate a high level of dealing proficiency, while the pit

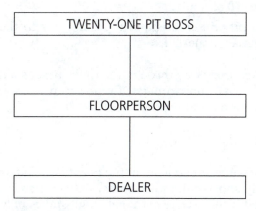

Figure 3.2
Twenty-One Organization Chart

Grand Casino Mille Lacs has 48 Blackjack tables, including two instructional tables for novice players. *(Courtesy of Grand Casino, Mille Lacs, Minnesota)*

boss or another pit supervisor rates their performance. Proficiency includes ability to shuffle the deck or multiple decks, pitch the cards to player spots on the table, make correct payoffs, and do so with speed and accuracy. A casino may set a standard of shuffling a single deck and dealing a hand (e.g., every 60 to 70 seconds).

14. Keeping track of the total pit win or loss and reporting this to the shift manager or casino manager as requested.

Most pit bosses have worked their way through the ranks first as a dealer, then floorperson, and normally have approximately five to seven years' experience prior to assuming the position of pit boss.

The Twenty-One Floorperson

Floorpersons are *the* front-line game supervisors in the twenty-one pit and are usually responsible for directly supervising four twenty-one games or tables. This number would be reduced if there were extremely high-stakes players at one or two of these tables. Visibly noticeable in the pit due to their business attire as opposed to the dealers who wear uniforms, floorpersons constantly

Note the reference to gambling problems in this ad. *(Courtesy of Trump's Castle Casino Resort, Atlantic City)*

move from one game to the next carefully watching each dealer, ensuring that cards are being handled correctly and that proper betting payoffs are being made. Added responsibilities include:

1. Accounting for table fills. A table fill occurs when there is a need for additional casino chips or cheques at a particular twenty-one table. Fills frequently are needed, especially if a player wins a large amount from the casino or the table bank is increased to accommodate a high-stakes player. Finally, any new games added to the floor will require a chip fill or "opener." A casino security guard brings chips to the table from the casino cage, and the table dealer breaks down the amount while the floorperson verifies the count. All

Blackjack Tables *(Courtesy of Luxor Las Vegas)*

three employees then sign the fill slip (see Figure 3.3). A copy of the slip is returned to the cage for accounting purposes, one copy is maintained in the pit, and a third copy is dropped in the table drop box via the slit in the top of the twenty-one table.

2. Accounting for table credits. Many times casinos win a large number of cheques from players and it becomes necessary to remove the extra chips from the twenty-one table. The dealer and floorperson, once again, verify the amount in the presence of a casino security guard and all three sign a credit slip (see Figure 3.4). The security guard transports the credit chips to the casino cage.

3. Rating player gaming action. One of the idiosyncrasies of the casino industry is "comping" or extending complimentary items to good players. How do casinos determine who the good players are and the amount or value of extended comps? At table games, the floorperson is responsible for rating players. This is typically done using a four-part plus-or-minus rating system based on:

a. Initial buy-in amount

b. Average wager

c. Duration of play

d. Largest bet

☐ **FILL**			**CREDIT** ☐

DATE		TIME	

SHIFT	GYD	DAY	SWING

GAME	NUMBER	Denomination	AMOUNT
Craps			
21			
Roulette			
Keno			
TOTAL			
MEMO			

RUNNER	FLOOR SUPERVISOR
CASHIER	DEALER

Figure 3.3
Fill Slip Form

This information is then calculated or put into a computer, and the computer determines the value of play. Based on the rating, players receive complimentary dinners, shows, beverages, or even airfare, or a dollar value is assigned and the player can spend the money on hotel services up to the assigned amount.

Some casinos review surveillance tapes to determine the accuracy and validity of floorperson ratings, while others will hire outside observers to ascertain this information. The key to effective comping rating services is maintaining objectivity with the rating criteria. One other quasi-form of comps is rebates on losses which allow players to recoup a portion of their losses based on a percentage determined by the casino. Inaccurate control of rebates can result in financial mismanagement, and these programs require careful scrutiny.

☐ **FILL**   **CREDIT** ☐

DATE		TIME	

SHIFT	GYD	DAY	SWING
GAME	NUMBER	Denomination	AMOUNT
Craps			
21			
Roulette			
Keno			
TOTAL			
MEMO			

RUNNER	FLOOR SUPERVISOR
CASHIER	DEALER

Figure 3.4
Credit Slip Form

4. Settling customer disputes. Occasionally, a player may have a dispute regarding a wager payoff, the conduct of a dealer, or some similar type of problem. Floorpersons must be able to effectively manage the situation by listening to the customer and making a sincere effort to resolve the matter. Resolution may involve making a determination as to whether game rules were violated unintentionally by the dealer or, worse, cheating was involved. All decisions must be made in accordance with established company rules, applicable gaming regulations, and internal control procedures. Thus, today's floorperson must be extremely knowledgable in game rules, game protection, gaming regulations, and effective customer relations skills. Unresolved disputes are referred to the pit boss who will either resolve the situation or refer it to the shift manager. In Nevada, customers have the right to contact the Nevada Gaming Control Board, and an enforcement division agent will be dispatched to mediate a customer-casino dispute. If it is determined that the casino erred, the agent decides in favor of the player. However, if it is determined that the player has cheated the casino, the player is arrested and charged with a felony. (Many people think that card counting is illegal in all U.S. casinos, which is not the case. Detected card counters in Las Vegas casinos are asked to leave since Las Vegas casinos reserve the right to refuse service to any patron.)

5. Developing and maintaining team work. A critically important attribute for floorpersons is their human resources management and human relations skills. Floor supervisors must encourage, coach, and mentor dealers and use constructive, positive discipline in correcting work-related deficiencies. For years, many floorpersons viewed their jobs as task-masters responsible for the strict enforcement of casino rules through the use of abusive power. Astute gaming operations can no longer afford supervision based on intimidation and fear.

6. Handling customer credit requests. Some customers initiate credit or ask for credit extensions in the pit. The floorperson may refer initial requests to the credit department in the casino cage. If the casino issues a player identification card, this can be shown to the floorperson, who will ask the pit clerk to retrieve credit information on the requesting player.

Other floorperson responsibilities involve requesting cocktail service for players, requesting casino porters or maintenance services for refuse removal

ABC CASINO
Player Rating Card

Player's Name _____
Time of Observation _____
Rater's Name/Shift _____

	(+)	(−)
Initial Buy-In		
Average Wager		
Largest Wager		
Duration of Play		

Signature _____
Date _____

Figure 3.5
Rating Card

from the pit, reporting game win/loss to the pit boss, and issuing and removal of decks of cards to individual tables.

Floorpersons generally have two to five years of dealing experience prior to promotion to the floor. The ideal floor supervisor knows craps as well and can be moved to the dice pit during emergency situations. Some casinos may, in fact, use employees as combination dealer/floorperson. Floorpersons are salaried and are exempt from overtime earnings in many casinos. As exempt individuals, they do not share in dealer tips.

The Twenty-One Dealer

Although the primary function of the dealer is dealing the game of twenty-one, this must be done in strict accordance with game rules and internal control procedures to protect the security and integrity of the game. Uniform and consistent dealing procedures and motions are mandated, while other dealer physical moves are strictly prohibited. A slight deviation can skew the casino's advantage; a dealer who inadvertently shows cards to players gives them an unfair and, in some gaming jurisdictions, illegal advantage. Additionally, deviations detected by casino surveillance can lead to an investigation of cheating. Major procedural problems that violate gaming regulations can result in fines and reprimands. Therefore, casinos are adamant that employees strictly follow game procedures, and failure to do so could result in disciplinary action against the employee, including immediate termination.

Prior to the commencement of a game or at a "dead" game (with no player activity), the dealer fans or spreads the deck of cards *face down* inside the insurance line on the table layout. This gives surveillance and the players assurance that a complete deck is in use. Cards fanned face up invite an unscrupulous player or dealer to study the cards and rig hands or wagers. Even though dealers are to shuffle the deck prior to the start of a game, dealers looking to cheat will do a false shuffle which keeps a section of the deck intact.

Prior to the commencement of the game, the dealer checks the deck for flaws (e.g., marked cards, bent corners, etc.) and for the total number of cards and any deviations must immediately be reported to the floorperson.

Shuffling the Deck. When the game is opened, the dealer is required to shuffle the deck, and this too is done according to standards set by the casino. For instance, the dealer removes a number of cards from the bottom of the deck (less than half), places these on top of the deck, and then pivots the top half. The deck is then cut in half, after which a riffle shuffle is done and the deck is squared or straightened out. This process is repeated. The dealer next strip-shuffles the deck, pulling clumps of cards from the deck and reinserting them in the deck using a rapid motion. Approximately one-third of the deck is again removed from the bottom and placed on top of the deck. Finally, the dealer riffle-shuffles the deck and squares it. Casinos require four to five repetitions of the procedure before the first hand is ready for the deal or any time a shuffle is required. Many casinos require the dealer to announce "Shuffle" to the floorperson and will not let the dealer shuffle or square the deck until the floorperson visually watches the shuffle or approves the final squaring move. Recently, automatic deck shufflers have been added to twenty-one tables, which has resulted in higher game productivity.

Multideck shuffling requires a slightly different technique. The decks are broken into equal halves/portions, and each pile is then shuffled in accordance with the previously described technique.

With the shuffle completed, the dealer now offers the deck to a player to be cut. The deck is to remain flat on the layout during this procedure, and casinos specify a minimum cut (i.e., at least 10 to 15 cards) by the player. Once the cut has been made, the dealer inserts a cut card into the deck, removes the top portion of the cut and puts the bottom portion on top. A second cut card is inserted two-thirds of the way into the deck by the dealer, and finally, the top card of the deck is removed and placed into the discard holder on the twenty-one table. This is known as "burning the top card."

Dealing from a Shoe. Let's assume that the casino is using multiple decks and uses a shoe. Shoes are employed when the cards are too bulky to be hand-held, and some casinos feel it is harder to cheat dealing from a shoe. The shoe is located to the dealer's left, and the dealer pulls cards one at a time using the middle finger of the left hand. Cards are then slid to each player starting with first base; procedurally, the cards should be dealt to a spot directly behind each player's bet. Once a hand is completed, all the cards for that particular hand are scooped by the dealer and placed in a discard holder found to the dealer's right on top of the twenty-one table (see Figure 3.6).

Figure 3.6
Discard Holder (Courtesy of Andrea Waller Photos)

Single/Double-Deck Dealing. Hand-held deck dealing is subject to exact procedures. The dealer is required to hold the cards so players cannot see the bottom card or other cards that might be inadvertently exposed. An accepted procedure is holding the deck at a 45-degree angle close to the body. Cards are then dealt or pitched by the dealer, making sure each card stops behind the bettor's chips. Accurate and efficient card dealing requires extensive practice. As previously noted, job applicants must pass a card dealing audition before a pit supervisor prior to being hired. The audition measures dexterity in handling the deck, shuffling, speed of deal, card pitching, accuracy of payoffs, and customer service skills. Thus, table game employees face multiple skills testing as well as the eventual pressure of dealing to high-stakes players.

Cutting Chips/Cheques and Paying Wagers. Handling casino chips, much like dealing, requires special dexterity and an equal amount of practice. Three cheque-cutting methods most frequently used in the casino industry are:

1. Sizing. This method involves counting one stack of chips (e.g., five $5 chips), stacking them, and then sliding equal stacks of chips next to this stack. Thus, the size of the first stack creates a denomination standard that can easily be used for counting. Rather than counting each chip, the dealer "sizes" additional payouts, which really expedites counting and wager payoffs; and this allows casino surveillance to follow dealer hand movements. Customers are also provided with an easy-to-follow payoff method, and if a dispute occurs, the floorperson can quickly read the payoff made by the dealer.

2. Picking. Each twenty-one table has an imbedded rack that holds different-colored chip denominations (e.g., black chips or "blacks" = $100, green chips or "greens" = $25) (see Figure 3.7). When making payoffs, dealers reach into the rack and pick up "x" number of chips in a stack. Many times, this is

Figure 3.7
Chip Rack (Courtesy of Trump's Castle Casino Resort, Atlantic City)

done with smaller payoffs where the exact number can be counted and separated in the twenty-one rack.

3. Drop Cutting. This is a variation of sizing and is used for large payoffs or exchanging large cash amounts for chips. Once the first sized stack has been placed on the layout, the dealer secures a large stack of additional chips in one hand from the rack and then drops/places equal-size stacks next to each other. A good measure of coordination and speed is required when using this method.

Payoffs are done color-for-color as follows:

$	1	= Silver
$	5	= Red
$	25	= Green
$	100	= Black
$	500	= White
$	1,000	= Pink

Minor payoff errors can be rectified by the dealer while the payoff is being made; however, once the payoff is made, the floorperson must be summoned to adjust any remaining disputes.

Handling customers' money also requires precise procedures. Dealers are required to announce receipt of large-denomination bills (e.g., "changing a hundred"). Once the cash has been exchanged, the dealer must insert the currency into the table drop box, located directly under the table, through the table slot using a plastic or wooden paddle.

Securing Lost Wagers. For the benefit of the eye-in-the-sky and the floorperson, many casinos now require dealers to first call out the total of their hands, then secure players' lost wagers. Secured chips are placed in the table rack, and all cards are scooped by the dealer and placed in the discard holder. If there is a push, dealers will tap next to the bet, which lets the player know a push has occurred and no payoff is due. Should money be dropped to the floor, many casinos require dealers either to announce "Money down," clap their hands, show them to the customer, and then advise the floorperson who retrieves the money.

Sometimes dealers receive a tip or may win money on hands played for them by players. Receipt of these tips requires special hand gestures. Dealers tap the tip or "toke" (short for *token*) on the table so the floorperson, customer, and casino surveillance know it is a tip, and the money may then be placed in the dealer's shirt pocket.

Preventing Customer or Dealer Cheating. Dealers are not to make any unusual hand motions when dealing. Standard procedures require dealers to wear uniforms which include dealer aprons worn over the slacks pockets to prevent chips from being stolen by dealers. A scratching behind the neck, fumbling with shirt cuffs, or any similar nonapproved motion could signal casino surveillance or the floorperson to keep a close eye on the dealer. Casinos have been cheated by dealers through the use of "subs." A sub is a pocket or a catching device used to hide chips. Dealers have used subs in their shirt collars, behind neckties, and even in the issued apron, making off with thousands of dollars from casinos.

Body positioning is a critical job requirement for dealers. Dealers are trained to always face the game and players and to maintain physical as well as visual control of the game and cards at all times. Dishonest players working with an agent or in teams often use a distractor to get the dealer to turn away while a cheating scam is in progress. If there is a question or game dispute, dealers are to call for a supervisor rather than turn around.

Cheating has taken place through the use of foreign objects placed on the table by players. Therefore, dealers are trained to inspect the playing surface and only allow authorized items on the layout (e.g., an ashtray).

Some casinos require players to adhere to additional game conditions such as refraining from wearing sunglasses (decks of cards have been marked with infrared daubs or smears that can only be detected by wearing sunglasses). "Edge work" refers to markings on the edge of cards done by a player wishing to cheat or working in concert with a dealer who is in on the scam. Cards can be marked in a myriad of ways, including "nailing" or using a fingernail to mark cards. Players or dealers working with an agent have been known to "crimp" or bend certain cards (aces or face cards) as a way of marking the deck.

Other cheating scams include "cooler or cold decks" or decks that have been opened and arranged in a certain sequence prior to the start of play. Dealers working with cheating players (aka crossroaders) to rig games use a false or fake shuffle; it appears that the dealer is mixing/shuffling the cards in the deck, but in reality the shuffle is done in such a way as to leave the cooler deck intact. Even when the deck is offered to the agent (a player working with the dealer to cheat the casino), it may be "hopped" or moved, resulting in a false cut, which avoids the deck from really being cut. A "bottom deal" involves the dealer dealing cards from the bottom of the deck to an agent. Some old-timers refer to a dealer with a "dead thumb" who is involved in dealing "seconds" (i.e., not the top cards in the deck).

Dealers can also use an assortment of ways to either peek at cards in the deck or show them to their agents. For instance, a "bubble peek" is a slang term used when a dealer applies pressure to the top card on the deck, which causes the card to bubble, and thus the dealer or player can peek at the next card. If the dealer has peeked and is working with an agent, the dealer may use hand or facial signals to tip off the agent, thus giving the cheater an unfair and illegal advantage over the casino. Dealing shoes have been "gaffed" or tampered with through the use of mirrors or "shiners" that will show cards being dispensed.

"Capping off a bet" in the illegal sense occurs when a player places additional chips on a bet after observing the total of the dealer's hand, thus allowing the player to win more than originally wagered; this scam is typically pulled on new or novice dealers. A dealer falling victim to this scam was for years referred to as a "lumpy." Conversely, a player may "pinch" a losing bet or remove a portion of a bet when the dealer turns away.

Finally, many dealers have been caught "mucking" a deck or palming cards and using them later to cheat. (Note that the term "mucker" at a roulette table refers to the dealer who picks up the cheques as part of the game, and in this context, "mucking" is not a cheating term.)

These are just *some* of the ways casinos can be cheated; therefore, it is critical that dealers perform their jobs in accordance with exact procedures, and pit supervisors need to be trained to watch for any deviations from the standards. There is an old gaming saying, "Strong and rigid dealer procedures will defeat a grifter (cheater) every time."

Other Employment Conditions

As can be seen, not only does the job of a dealer require excellent technical skills, but gaming situations can also create a great deal of stress. Due to the nature of the job, dealers will only work 40 minutes, 45 minutes, or an hour at a time, with a 15-, 20-, or 30-minute break each hour. Employees at large casinos rely more on tips rather than an hourly wage for their income, since virtually every casino in the United States pays either minimum wage or only slightly more than minimum wage. It is a rarity to find a dealer being paid an hourly wage of more than $10 an hour. However, this may change in the future. For years, some dealers did not fully report their tips to the Internal Revenue Service, which prompted the government to institute a tip-compliance program known as Compliance 2000. Initiated in Las Vegas, the IRS conducted massive audits of dealers and determined that there was extensive under-reporting of gratuities. Since tips are subject not only to federal income tax but also FICA contributions from the employer and employee, the government petitioned employers for back FICA contributions on employee tips, and the potential exposure represented millions of dollars. In order to resolve the issue, the IRS agreed to forgo past employer and employee debts in exchange for employer and employee assistance with a compliance plan for tipped employees. Tip reporting scales were created for all casinos, and most employees voluntarily entered into payroll deduction programs to ensure that tips were properly reported to the government.

Although today's casino operators and workers are becoming more educated and using scientific management methods to run operations, it was not that long ago that many operational decisions were based on gaming superstitions. These beliefs are now viewed as a humorous part of our gaming past but do make for interesting reading. For instance, it was believed that a player's luck could be changed by sprinkling salt on the player's shoes, or that if you spit in your hand and slapped a player on the back, this would "cool off" a hot player. Peanuts at a gaming table were considered bad luck, as were red-headed dealers or dealers who wore eyeglasses. Some operators went so far as to remove an "unlucky" gaming table from the floor after a player had won a large amount at that table. If a player was on a winning streak, casinos would change dealers, believing that one dealer was luckier or unluckier than another. Fortunately, these misguided and unfounded concepts have given way to scientific managerial practices—although it can be stated that a little luck never hurt a casino's bottom line!

THE GAME OF CRAPS

The game of craps or dice offers players the most exciting and fast-moving interactive table game available in the casino. A score of people crowded around a dice table, cheering each roll of the dice and shouting with glee when someone's number comes up truly embodies the entertainment essence of a casino atmosphere.

Although craps is an exciting game, the wagering rules and payoffs have proven very intimidating to the general public. A whole generation of players really learned the game in the armed forces during World War II, but as newer generations emerge, many of these casino visitors do not have a thorough or even a beginning knowledge of the game, opting for the simplicity and nonintimidation of slots. Potential players who are reluctant to show their ignorance by asking questions about game rules are now being taught the game rules by casinos that offer free instructions at a "dead" game on the casino floor.

Rules and Procedures of Craps

The game of craps is based on a player (aka shooter) tossing dice onto a crap table layout and either winning or losing based on the rolled numbers. Other players at the table are given the opportunity to either bet with or against the shooter or on subsequent dice rolls by the shooter.

Coming Out

The game starts with players placing their bets before a shooter tosses the dice (comes out). There are two basic bets that can be made at this time: Pass or Don't Pass. Making a Pass bet is betting with the shooter and means that the player is putting money on the Pass Line on the crap layout (see Figure 3.8); the wager is that the shooter will throw a total of 7 or 11 on the first roll of the dice (aka a "natural"). A Pass bet automatically loses on a 2, 3, or 12. Betting the Don't Pass involves placing a wager on the Don't Pass Line on the crap layout and equates to betting against the shooter. This wager is won if the shooter "craps out" by throwing a 2 or 3 on the first roll of the dice. Obviously, most shooters bet their own luck by making a *Passline* wager, while other players can choose to bet against a particular shooter. If any other number is thrown

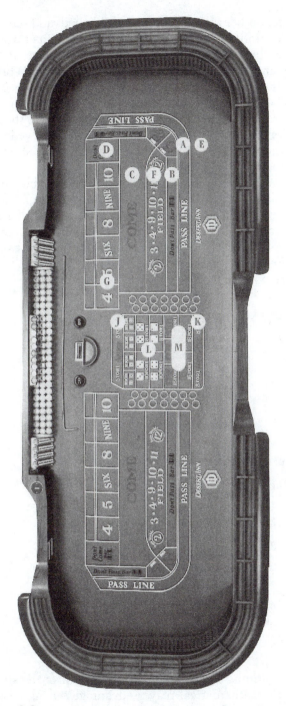

Figure 3.8
Craps Layout (From "The Sheraton Gaming Guide," courtesy of the Sheraton Desert Inn, Las Vegas, an ITT Sheraton Resort & Casino)

on the first roll, a shooter's number (aka "point") is established, and the shooter continues to roll the dice until either the point is made or a 7 is thrown. If the point is made, the shooter wins and keeps control of the dice; if a 7 is thrown, the shooter loses and forfeits the dice to the next shooter. While the shooter is trying to make the point, other players will make numerous bets in conjunction with each roll of the dice, as explained later in this section.

Prior to tossing the dice, the dealer with the croupier stick (i.e., the stickperson) will announce "Coming Out" and many shooters will then yell one of the common craps expressions such as "Yo Lev," hoping for an 11. Should the shooter toss a 7 or 11 on the first roll, the payoff is even money.

In assessing the odds on the come-out wager, there are 36 possible number combinations on a pair of dice. Comparing the combinations yielding 7 and 11 to the combinations yielding the losing crap numbers 2, 3, and 12, the totals are 12 winning and 4 losing combinations out of the 36 possible combinations. In other words, if you assess the possible numerical totals of two dice (Dice A and Dice B), the following combinations yielding 2, 3, and 12 (losing) and 7 and 11 (winning) are possible:

The Four Losing Crap Combinations

Die A	+	Die B	=	Total
1	+	1	=	2
1	+	2	=	3
2	+	1	=	3
6	+	6	=	12

The Eight Winning Crap Combinations

Die A	+	Die B	=	Total
1	+	6	=	7
6	+	1	=	7
2	+	5	=	7
5	+	2	=	7
3	+	4	=	7
4	+	3	=	7
5	+	6	=	11
6	+	5	=	11

Therefore, the odds of winning a come-out bet are in favor of the shooter, and this represents the *only* mathematical player advantage during pass line play.

Two-thirds of the 36 numerical dice combinations represent possible points.

Action at a Craps Game. Note the seated boxman and three dealers.
(Courtesy of Trump's Castle Casino Resort, Atlantic City)

Making the Point

If the shooter does not throw a 2, 3, 7, 11, or 12 on the first roll of the dice, any other thrown number becomes the player's point as previously indicated. A dice game employs three dealers per table: two dealers and one stickperson. The stickperson watches for bets made in the middle of the layout, and the other dealers control wagering at their respective ends of the table. Additionally, one boxperson sits in between the two dealers and manages the flow of money and chips in and out of the game; this person also supervises the dealers and the stickperson who controls the action of the game.

Once the point is established, the two dealers on either side of the boxperson place a point marker on the shooter's number so other players can readily know the established point. Crap layouts are identical at both ends, displaying all the possible numbers a player can make, the Pass and Don't Pass Lines, the Field Numbers, as explained later in this section, and so on. The middle of the layout depicts a series of Odds bets controlled and maintained by the stickperson. The shooter now will win if the point is made (i.e., the number is tossed with any subsequent roll of the dice) or lose if at anytime a 7 is thrown.

Let's assume that the shooter originally threw a 4 and now 4 becomes the shooter's point. There would be three combinations yielding 4 on a pair of dice:

Die A	+	Die B	=	Total
1	+	3	=	4
3	+	1	=	4
2	+	2	=	4

However, there are still six ways to make 7:

Die A	+	Die B	=	Total
1	+	6	=	7
6	+	1	=	7
2	+	5	=	7
5	+	2	=	7
3	+	4	=	7
4	+	3	=	7

Therefore, the odds are 2:1 against the shooter making the point in this instance. The two hardest points to make in a crap game are 4 and 10; therefore, the advantage afforded the shooter on the come-out toss of the dice now has shifted to the casino. Statistically, under these circumstances, the casino will maintain a 1.4 advantage over the Pass Line bettor. While trying to make the established point, all other players and the shooter can make other wagers (e.g., betting that the shooter will throw an 8 or a "hard 8" = two 4s). However, all line bets are frozen during this time period. It is interesting to note that the numbers 2, 3, 11, and 12, all of major significance on the first throw of the dice, now no longer affect the final outcome of the game and become optional wagering numbers. Remember, the shooter only loses control of the dice on a 7 roll (or "7 Out" as called by the stickperson). Once this occurs, the stickperson passes the dice to the next shooter and announces, "New shooter coming out." Dice are passed around the table in a clockwise manner, and players can either accept the dice or pass them to the next person.

Although mathematically the Don't Pass bet is the best table bet at this point on a percentage basis, the player's advantage is not significantly greater. As a general rule, for every $100 wagered on the Don't Pass Line, the casino will earn $1.402, compared to $1.414 on the Pass Line.[1]

After the point is made, there are a number of bets that can be made:

1. Come bet. This is identical to betting on the Pass Line and is bet after the point is established. As with betting the Pass Line, a wager is won if a 7 or 11 is tossed and lost on 2, 3, or 12. If none of these numbers is thrown, the wager is moved to the Come point, and, as is the case with any point, the wager is now lost if a 7 is thrown.

2. Don't Come bet. This is an opposite wager to the Come bet. After the first roll of the dice, a player can wager against the shooter and if a 2 or 3 is thrown, the bet is won. If a 12 is tossed, there is a "push" and nobody wins. If a Don't Come point is established, the Don't Come bet is lost if the shooter remakes that number and the bet is won if the shooter sevens-out.

3. Betting the Field. Many bets are drawn to that portion of the layout entitled the Field. Although all Field layouts are not the same, most will feature the following numbers in a group: 2, 3, 4, 9, 10, 11, and 12 as winners and 2 and 12 paying double. It should be noted that with some casinos, the point 12 pays triple. Betting the Field is a one-roll bet, and should any of these not be thrown, the wager is lost.

4. Big 6/Big 8. On the layout is an area denoted as Big 6 and Big 8. A player can wager on the 6 or 8 or both at any time. These are the easiest points to make, but this wager still has five chances of winning against six chances of losing:

6		8		7	
Die A	Die B	Die A	Die B	Die A	Die B
1	5	2	6	1	6
5	1	6	2	6	1
4	2	5	3	5	2
2	4	3	5	2	5
3	3	4	4	3	4
				4	3

5. Taking Odds. It would literally take an entire separate book to analyze all the odds wager possibilities in craps. However, there are other popular dice wagers not specified on the crap layout, including:

  a. Odds on the Shooter Point (aka Free-Odds on the Point). This is an even money wager. Casinos usually will allow a player to back up a wager by betting an amount equal to the original wager (aka single odds). These wagers can be removed or moved at any time during the shooter's sequence. This wager is placed behind the Pass Line wagers in front of the player.

  b. Odds on Come Points. The crap dealers handle these bets for players who indicate they want "odds" on the established point, and the dealers will place the Odds bet on top of the Come bet but a little off center so that both bets are visible. If the Pass Line point is made, on the ensuing come-out roll the dealer will announce "Odds off."

A listing of additional bets offered in the game of craps includes:

  c. Double Odds on Point Numbers

  d. Odds against the Shooter's Point

  e. Odds on Don't Come

  f. Betting the Box Numbers. A player can also buy the box numbers to win or lose by making commission bets.

Dealer at Craps Table *(Courtesy of Harvey's Resort Hotel/Casino, Lake Tahoe, Nevada)*

    g. Playing the Numbers to Win

    h. Laying the Numbers to Lose

    i. Betting the Hardway and Proposition Bets. Directly in front of the stickperson on the layout is an area that contains Hardway and Proposition bets (see Figure 3.8). This portion of the layout is virtually self-explanatory. The term "hardway" means making a point number with identical numbers appearing on each die. For instance, if the point were 10, the hardway would be a 5 on each die. A Proposition bet such as 5 for 1 on the number 7 is a one-roll bet. Other high-odds bets such as 30 for 1 on "snake eyes" (a 1 or ace on each die) or "boxcars" (a 6 on each die) and 15 for 1 on 3 or 11 are always one-roll Proposition bets. Casinos rely heavily on dealers to "talk these bets up" since they highly favor the casino and can make a significant difference to the bottom line of any crap game.

Sometimes casinos advertise "10x or 5x Odds on Craps" as a marketing ploy. This equates to allowing players to make odds wagers using the advertised odds multiplier factor times the original or flat bet. For instance, 10x odds allows players to wager $100 on an original $10 flat bet.

Craps Organizational Structure

The Pit Boss

The craps pit, like the twenty-one pit, is under the authority of a pit manager or boss (see Figure 3.9). These managers have the same responsibilities as their twenty-one counterparts, including the efficient and profitable operation of all craps tables in the pit, staffing, which can include closing games when the action is slow, and all other duties associated with the game operations.

The Floorpersons

Dice pits also employ floorpersons who are normally responsible for supervising two craps games. If there is an extreme amount of business or high-rollers on one game, then one floorperson will be assigned to watch that game. Dice floorpersons walk between their two games watching for game irregularities, greeting players, handling referred requests for credit, and assisting the pit supervisor with scheduling.

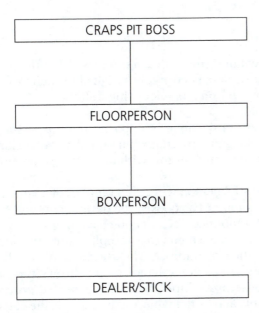

Figure 3.9
Craps Organization Chart

The Boxperson

A position unique to the game of craps is the boxperson. This is the immediate game supervisor who maintains control over the operation of the game. The boxperson is quite noticeable at the game since this is the only person not wearing a dealer's uniform and is seated on a stool in between the two dealers opposite the stickperson. Supervisors "sitting box" control the flow of currency from customers into the game and insert wagered cash into the drop box through the table slit on the layout directly in front of them. They are also responsible for the flow of chips or tokens won by the casino.

As game supervisors, boxpersons assume the lead role for game protection, which includes watching dealers and players to ensure that game rules are followed and watching for cheating activity (discussed in the next section).

Boxpersons are also responsible for table fills and credits and maintaining superior customer service. Finally, boxpersons open games, unlocking chip racks and setting up the table chip bank and verifying the opening chip inventory (aka "the opener"), and close games, filling out the closer form once the ending chip inventory has been verified. Copies of the opener and closer are inserted into the table drop box by the boxperson.

One criticism often heard about boxpersons is that they always seem to display a serious demeanor, and this is confused with either poor public relations skills or a manifestation that casino workers are not friendly. Boxpersons have an incredible responsibility and must concentrate on game action and the numerous bets being made. Therefore, game intensity should not be confused with a poor attitude.

Crap Dealers

As discussed earlier in this chapter, three dealers are used for the game of craps. Actually, a team of four dealers is normally assigned to each table, with three dealers on and one always off on a break during a shift.

The Stickperson. This dealer, found directly opposite the boxperson, controls the action and speed of the game by controlling the dice and calling the game or dice rolls. A good stickperson does this with flare and excitement and, of course, with accuracy.

Using a croupier stick, the stickperson will cuff a number of dice and slide them to the shooter. Once the shooter has chosen the desired pair and has the dice in hand, the "stick" will announce, "New shooter coming out" and will watch the dice roll. After the dice have come to a complete stop, the stickperson will "call the dice"—the thrown number. The stickperson has the first responsibility for making sure the shooter handles and throws the dice in accordance with accepted house procedures. Generally accepted procedures require the dice to roll or tumble across the table and bounce off the end of the table opposite the shooter. The inside ends of crap tables have raised, jagged foam rubber batting, which causes the tossed dice to spin off upon impact in such a manner to ensure the randomness of the dice. The stickperson will advise players to refrain from sliding the dice or tossing them short (i.e., without bouncing off the interior far end of the table). The stickperson has the authority to call a "No Dice" if the toss is considered inappropriate. Customer skills are extremely important at this time, since a novice shooter may not know accepted procedures and could be embarrassed or offended if the situation is not handled correctly. Players generally are told not to rub the dice together or move them out of the view of the stickperson.

Many times, the way the dice land or come to a stop presents some challenges. As an example, dice may land on or lean against wagered chips or stop on top of one another. These are normally considered valid rolls, with the stickperson determining the dice total. Dice that land on the crap table rail or go off the table are invalid rolls and are called "No Dice" by the stickperson.

As is the case with twenty-one, the more hands or rolls of the dice, the greater the eventual win potential for the casino; hence, maintaining the pace of the game becomes a critical function for the stick. A good pace for a craps game is: Wait until all payoffs have been made, then return the dice to the shooter. Anyone who has watched a dice game knows that it is a fairly rapid, fast-action game, so *all* table employees must do their work efficiently while maintaining a good game pace.

Calling a game of dice can sound very confusing to new players. For instance, the stickperson may say, "Six Easy, Six, The Point Is Six, Big and Red" or "Three Craps, Three, Field Roll, Three." These are simply ways of calling the tossed dice numbers: if the number was made the "hard or easy way" (8 the hard way is two 4s; 8 the easy way is 2 and 6 or 5 and 3); if a number in the field won; and so forth. It takes a while to understand the jargon of the game, much like trying to understand computer euphemisms for the first time.

The final duty of the stickperson is paying off wagers placed in the middle of the field.

The Inside Dealers. The other two dealers are referred to as inside dealers, and they are responsible for:

1. Marking the established point number. This is done by placing a puck (a plastic disc) on the rolled number. The puck has the word "On" on one side and "Off" on the other, denoting when the puck is in use and that certain bets such as odds bets are "on."

2. Securing bets and lost wagers as well as paying off winning bets. Dealers are trained to secure losing bets first, pay off winners next, and finally accept all new bets. When accepting bets, chips must be placed in exact spots on the layout in front of the wagering players or in the appropriate spot locations on the layout so everyone knows which players have made bets. Dealers will also place buttons or plastic lammers on the table to denote cash or marker transactions.

3. Promoting and explaining bets. Casinos charge a commission or "vig" on certain bets (e.g., 5 percent on a Buy bet), and a number of wagers have higher percentages favorable to the casino. Dealers can significantly increase the handle (i.e., the amount wagered) by "talking up" or explaining these bets. Other bets include a Horn bet, which simultaneously covers the 2, 3, 11, and 12; a High-Low bet, a split bet on the 2 and 12 craps; Backside bets or wagers against a number repeating before a 7 is thrown; Big Red bet or a bet on any 7. Straight-up bets are one-roll bets, and the wager is that a particular number will be the next number thrown.

3. Customer service. If gaming is truly to be viewed as an entertainment experience, then dealers must make the game not only exciting but also enjoyable. Casinos are now training employees in customer communication and service skills, realizing that quality service will enhance the gaming experience and likely result in repeat business. Craps dealers rely heavily on tips, and it is in their best interest to provide excellent service.

Cheating in Craps

As with the game of twenty-one, dice games are subject to cheating scams from employees and players. Some classic ways in which the game has been cheated include:

1. Past-posting. This is the placing of a wager by a player on a winning number *after the number has been declared a winner*. Players usually do this as a team with one person shooting the dice and one or two distractors diverting the attention of the dealers and boxperson while the other team member past-posts. Cheaters practice their timing and techniques for hours and can smoothly carry off this scam in seconds.

2. Pinching a bet. This type of cheating involves the removal of a portion of a "laid wager" on a number that did not win. Again, players will act in tandem, using a distractor to create a diversion while the scam is enacted.

3. Dice tampering. One of the primary functions of the boxperson is to watch the dice to prevent dice tampering. If the dice are tossed or bounce off the table, the boxperson must inspect the dice to make sure substitute dice are not being introduced into the game. We have all heard the expression "loaded dice," and this term originated with the game of craps. Loaded dice have lead or a weight added or inserted, causing the dice to land on a certain number. Obviously, a cheater then has an unfair advantage over the casino, and casinos regard this as a blatant form of cheating. This type of cheating is so heinous that if found guilty, the perpetrators will face a felony conviction and imprisonment in many gaming jurisdictions. "Flats" are altered dice that always land on one side. "Beveled" or "shaved" dice have had the edges rounded, which causes the dice to land on preferred numbers for the cheater, thus switching the normal house advantage to the player.

Casinos are so sensitive about dice tampering that they measure the exact dimensions of all dice to be used in a game with a micrometer prior to game use. The interior base wall of the craps table opposite the boxperson is lined with a mirror so boxpersons can increase their vantage point and observation of the dice in play. Some tables have a small magnet imbedded under the layout in front of the stickperson, and house procedures require that the dice be slid over the magnet prior to returning the dice to the shooter; the magnet will immediately detect any loads or metals that have been used to load the dice.

4. Scooting. This form of cheating is done by a shooter who tosses one dice as normal but slides or scoots the other dice across the table. The shooter will scoot a 6 up on the dice on the come-out, increasing the odds of throwing a 7 or 11.

5. Capping bets. This happens when players put more chips on their original winning wager on a particular number after the winning number has been tossed and announced by the stickperson.

In addition to the above forms of cheating, dealers have worked in concert with players or boxpersons to embezzle money from a game or have allowed players to cheat and win.

 ## SUMMARY

The game of dice is an exciting and sometimes confusing experience. Once learned, it becomes the game of choice for seasoned players. No other game can add to the ambiance and atmosphere of a casino like craps. No other game can offer the wide variety of wagering possibilities, and this game, once mastered, can offer the player a chance to earn a large bankroll. Anyone who recalls the famous "one-roll-of-the-dice" gamble taken by Sky Masterson in the movie *Guys and Dolls* will attest to the exhilarating thrill of craps.

Likewise, blackjack/twenty-one creates a venue for a full casino experience. Twenty-one still represents the largest table game revenue source for the majority of casinos and remains the game of choice for numerous players.

 ## DISCUSSION QUESTIONS

1. Define the following blackjack/twenty-one terms:

a. First base	**g.** Insurance
b. Third base	**h.** Surrender
c. Hit	**i.** Doubling down
d. Stand	**j.** Five-card charley
e. Soft 17	**k.** Card counting
f. Snapper	**l.** Shoe

2. Why have casinos introduced automatic shuffling machines to the game of twenty-one?

3. Discuss the organizational structure of a twenty-one pit.

4. List basic duties and responsibilities of a pit boss.

5. Why do twenty-one dealers often refuse promotion to a pit supervisory position?

6. What is the purpose of player rating?

7. As a twenty-one pit supervisor, how would you handle a customer claiming that the dealer did not pay a winning hand?

8. Why are casinos adamant that twenty-one dealers follow strict game procedures?

9. What procedure should a dealer follow on a "dead" game?

10. What skills must a dealer possess to professionally deal the game of twenty-one?

11. Why has the casino game of craps proven to be intimidating to the general public?

12. How many number combinations are there on a pair of dice?

13. Define the following craps terms:

   a. Pass bet   **f.** Come bet

   b. Don't Pass bet   **g.** Betting the Field

   c. A natural   **h.** Taking the Odds

   d. Coming out   **i.** Hardway bet

   e. Point marker   **j.** Proposition bet

14. Discuss the organizational structure of a craps pit.

15. What is the role of a stickperson? Boxperson?

16. Define or explain the following cheating terms:

   a. Past-posting

   b. Pinching a bet

   c. Dice tampering

   d. Scooting

   e. Capping bets

17. What are the primary duties of craps inside dealers?

ENDNOTE

1. Jim Kilby, *Casino Operations and Management*. Las Vegas: UNLV Academic Printing Services, University of Nevada/Las Vegas, January 1996.

4

OTHER CASINO
TABLE GAMES

 LEARNING OBJECTIVES

This chapter will enable the reader to:

- Understand the rules and procedures of the casino table game of roulette.

- Become familiar with the rules of play, dealing procedures, and payout odds of the money wheel or Big 6.

- Identify dealer errors associated with the Big 6 game.

- Understand the playing rules and dealing procedures of Caribbean stud poker.

- Become familiar with the playing rules and dealing procedures of baccarat.

INTRODUCTION

Whenever James Bond enters a casino, he invariably gravitates to the baccarat table or the roulette wheel. Both of these games, as well as the remaining table games, are discussed in this chapter.

ROULETTE

The game of roulette is fairly simplistic and yet it offers an exciting gaming venue. The roulette wheel (see Figure 4.1) is spun counter-clockwise by a

Figure 4.1
Roulette Wheel (From "The Sheraton Gaming Guide," courtesy of the Sheraton Desert Inn, Las Vegas, an ITT Sheraton Resort & Casino)

Action at the Roulette Table *(Courtesy of Harvey's Resort Hotel/Casino, Lake Tahoe, Nevada)*

roulette dealer who simultaneously spins a small, white ball clockwise around the inside top rim of the wheel. There are grooves or indented spaces numbered 1 to 36 plus a zero and a double-zero space for a total of 38 possible numbers on the American-style wheel. European roulette only features the single zero. The ball eventually will fall into one of the numbered slots, and this determines the winning number.

Prior to the commencement of the game, players buy stacks of roulette chips or "wheel chips," which are different in size and color from other casino chips. Normally, six colors are used for roulette chips: red, white, yellow, green, blue, and brown. Players receive their own color to clearly designate which player is making a particular wager. Since roulette chips do not have an imprinted dollar value, the dealer will take a player's color, place it on the rim of the wheel and cap it with a numbered plastic lammer button which indicates the dollar denomination. For instance, to indicate *dollar* chips, a lammer with a "20" on it is placed on the rim chip, which denotes these chips are worth $20 per stack. Casinos do not allow players to play with cash and will have the dealer exchange cash for roulette chips. The dealer is required to insert the currency through a slit in the table into the table drop box using a paddle to force the money into the slit.

With chips in hand, players place their wagers on numbers appearing on the grid layout, or they can choose to bet on red or black (the background colors behind the numbers on the wheel) or "odd" or "even" (i.e., whether the spun number is an odd or even number). Casinos categorize roulette bets as either "outside" or "inside" bets. Some of the outside bets are: betting 1 through 18 or betting the even or odd. The inside bets include:

- *Straight-up bets.* Betting one of the 38 possible numbers, which pays 35:1.
- *Split bets.* A two-number bet, that pays 17:1.
- *Row bets.* Betting on three numbers in a row, with an 11:1 payoff.
- *Basket.* Wagering on 0, 00, or 2, with a 6:1 payoff.

Players can also make "corner" and "double-row" bets.

Once all bets have been made, the dealer will announce, "No more bets," and will place the roulette ball on the track found at the top of the inside rim of the wheel. The dealer snaps the ball with his fingers and waits until the ball drops into one of the numbered spots on the roulette wheel. The dealer calls the number and places a plastic lammer button marker on the winning number or on top of chips found in the grid square of the winning number. Next, the dealer collects all losing bets—casinos train all dealers to collect losing wagers prior to paying off winning wagers. In collecting losing bets, dealers use two hands to gather the chips and "sweep" the chips into the dealer's apron (aka mucking apron). This process is referred to as mucking. Games

Action at the Roulette Wheel *(Courtesy of Trump's Castle Casino Resort, Atlantic City)*

with heavy chip action will employ a second dealer known as a mucker or apron dealer who collects then sorts won chips by color. Recent technology has witnessed the introduction of a "chip chunker" which automatically sorts and stacks chips by colors, thus eliminating the need for the mucker.

Finally, winning wagers are paid and the marker is removed from the winning number. Other game procedures are listed below:

1. **Calling large bets.** Usually, large customer wagers require the dealer to call out the amount to the pit floorperson (note that the roulette table or wheel is typically contiguous with the twenty-one table in U.S. casinos, although it may be found in its own pit in European casinos).

2. **Protecting the game.** Past-posting, capping, and pinching are frequently attempted during a roulette game, and dealers must maintain close scrutiny of the game at all times. Dealers working with an agent have been known to rig or "gaff" the wheel to make it stop on certain numbers. Floorpersons are responsible for protecting the casino against this scam. Casinos instruct dealers to alternate the speeds when spinning the ball, since some players have actually been able to clock the number of spins of the ball, increasing their chance of predicting where the ball will land.

3. **Maintaining a good game pace.** This simply involves efficiency in spinning the wheel (without long delays in between spins), accepting, collecting, and paying off bets in an expeditious manner.

4. **Customer service.** Customer service involves friendly and congenial explanation of game rules and handling customer questions and disputes with a professional and courteous demeanor.

THE MONEY WHEEL OR BIG 6

Popularized in carnivals and charitable fund-raising events, the money wheel or Big 6 has been a gaming attraction since casinos have been in existence (see Figure 4.2). Gaming at the Big 6 is conducted at a wheel, circular in shape, usually not less than 48 inches or more than 66 inches in diameter. The rim of the wheel is divided into 54 equally spaced sections, with each section displaying monetary bills as indicated below:

23 sections containing a $1.00 bill

15 sections containing a $2.00 bill

8 sections containing a $5.00 bill

4 sections containing a $10.00 bill

2 sections containing a $20.00 bill

1 section containing the name of the casino or a special logo

1 section containing a picture of a joker or a special bonus logo

Figure 4.2
Big 6/Money Wheel (From "The
Sheraton Gaming Guide,"
courtesy of the Sheraton Desert
Inn, Las Vegas, an ITT Sheraton
Resort & Casino)

Wagering is conducted by players who can either stand or sit at stools in front of the Big 6 wagering table/layout. The table cover is clearly marked with insignias of a $1.00 bill, $2.00 bill, $5.00 bill, $10.00 bill, $20.00 bill, the casino or special logo, and the joker or bonus logo. Betting is conducted by patrons placing wagers on any of the indicated insignias.

The casino establishes payout odds as well as minimum and maximum allowable wagers, which are posted conspicuously at each Big 6 table. Figure 4.3 provides an example of how payout odds might be displayed for the Big 6.

The minimum wager for any insignia is usually $1.00, and maximum wagers must conform to established house rules posted at the table. Big 6 dealers are advised through written game policy and procedures that any deviation from established table limits must be approved by management.

Rules of Play and Dealing Procedures

Prior to spinning the wheel, the dealer ensures that all bets have been made and are clearly placed on designated insignias. The dealer announces, "No more bets," and spins the wheel. Big 6 procedure requires that the wheel complete at least four revolutions to constitute a valid spin. Additionally, dealers are trained to alternate the spinning speed with each succeeding spin. Should a player inadvertently interfere with the spin, the dealer must immediately

Winning Wagers	Payout Odds
$1.00 insignia	1 to 1
$2.00 insignia	2 to 1
$5.00 insignia	5 to 1
$10.00 insignia	10 to 1
$20.00 insignia	20 to 1
Casino name or special logo	40 to 1
Joker or bonus logo	40 to 1

Figure 4.3
Big 6 Payoff Odds

stop the wheel and advise all players that there is an invalid spin by announcing, "No spin; all bets are off." The wheel is equipped with a plastic or wooden clapper at the top of the wheel which serves two purposes. First, it acts as a denomination pointer when the wheel has stopped, and, second, the clapper's hitting against the wooden pegs protruding out from the wheel (wooden pegs are found on the lines between each denomination on the wheel) causes the wheel to slow and eventually stop on one denomination. If the clapper comes to rest between two numbers upon completion of the spin, it is declared a "No spin" and the wheel is rerotated. Upon completion of the spin, the dealer first collects all losing wagers and inserts them in the table drop box. Winning wagers are then paid according to the casino's payoff odds. Wagering is made with casino chips, and casinos do allow cash wagers if so specified in the internal control procedures and/or approved by a pit supervisor.

At first glance, it might appear that the responsibilities of a Big 6 dealer are uncomplicated compared to dealers of other table games. Since a careless, inattentive, unskilled dealer can cause serious financial loss at this game, Big 6 dealer training and supervision are especially important. Following are several dealing errors associated with the Big 6 game:

1. Failing to collect losing bets
2. Accepting late bets
3. Not calling out winning bets
4. Not paying attention to the game and allowing past-posting, capping, or pinching of bets. Many times this happens when the dealer spends inappropriate time watching the wheel and not the players at the table and their bets.
5. Allowing players to place unapproved objects on the table, which could lead to a cheating opportunity.

6. Failure to notify the floorperson of bets which exceed the maximum table limits. The table limits specify a minimum wager (e.g., $1 per hand) and a maximum (e.g., $1,000 per hand). Wagers above these limits must either be approved by the floorperson or, in the case of an exceedingly high wager, the pit boss or even the casino manager.

7. During a "dead" game (one where there is no ongoing action with customers), failure to spin the wheel in order to attract potential players

The Big 6 does not attract the large sums of money wagered at baccarat or craps, but *it is one of the most consistent money makers and game winners for the casino*. Many casino executives, when asked if they could personally own any table game in the casino, respond with "The Big 6" because of its consistent winning formula.

CARIBBEAN STUD POKER

The game of Caribbean stud poker achieved initial popularity among cruise line casinos and in the early 1990s was successfully introduced throughout American casinos. The game is based on the basic rules of stud poker while allowing players to participate in a progressive jackpot. However, unlike poker-room-style play, players do not compete against each other but their hands compete against the house, thus making this particular poker game a table game and not a card game by definition.

Rules of the Game

A Caribbean stud table is similar to a twenty-one table with six or seven spots or player positions (see Figure 4.4). However, the table layout provides three separate betting areas: the ante bet, the call bet, and a single slot for betting on the progressive jackpot. Whether the casino utilizes one or several tables, a prominent feature of this game is an electronic progressive meter displaying the jackpot as it grows and any other message the casino wishes to display. The game is played with a standard deck of 52 playing cards with all jokers removed. The dealer follows standard house procedures for dealing a hand-held deck; however, unlike most other card games, in the game of Caribbean stud poker the cut is not offered to the players and only the dealer is allowed to cut the deck.

To begin a hand, the dealer, while shuffling the deck, announces, "Place your ante and progressive bets, please." As indicated above, players have an opportunity to wager up to three separate bets.

Ante Bet. This is the player's opening bet and must be made in order for the player to participate in the game and the progressive jackpot. The bet is placed by the player on the designated ante area of the table and must be within table limits established by the casino.

Figure 4.4
Caribbean Stud Poker Table (Courtesy of Trump's Castle Casino Resort, Atlantic City)

Progressive Jackpot Wager. A player wishing to participate in the progressive jackpot does so by inserting a dollar chip into the coin slot located in front of the ante bet area. This wager is treated as a side bet, meaning that the dealer's hand has no bearing on the outcome of the wager.

Once the dealer has confirmed all players' ante and progressive bets and before the cards are dealt, the dealer presses a "play" button which drops all chips wagered on the meter into a table drop box and, simultaneously, activates the lights by each active slot as well as on the control panel which confirms the wagers. This activity also locks out any additional progressive wagers for that particular hand. With all ante bets made and the progressive wagers dropped into the table drop box, the hands are ready to proceed. Five cards are dealt face down to the players in front of their corresponding coin slots and may not be touched by the players until the dealer pushes the five cards to them. During the deal, the dealer receives four cards face down with the fifth card turned face up. Cards remaining after the deal are placed face down in the discard rack.

Once all cards have been distributed and remaining cards discarded, the players look at their hands and decide if they will call or fold. "Call" means they wish to remain in the hand and "fold" indicates a player's desire to drop out of the hand.

Folding the Hand. Players throw in their hands—fold—if they feel they cannot beat the dealer's hand. To fold a hand, the player's cards are placed face down to the player's right of the ante bet. The dealer spreads each of the folded hands, the cards still remaining face down, to verify that there are five cards, takes the ante bets, and discards the hand. Should the player have made a progressive bet, this bet is forfeited on a folded hand. Game procedure stresses that a dealer must not turn over and read a folded hand.

Call Bet. This is the final bet to be made by players. A call bet is made if players believe their hands can beat the dealer's hand. Game rules require the call bet to be exactly twice the amount of the player's ante bet. Once call bets are made, players place their cards, face down, to the left of the call bets.

The Dealer's Hand

After all fold and call decisions have been made, the dealer turns over the remaining four cards of the dealer's hand and places the hand in order from the highest ranking card on the left to the lowest on the right. For play to continue, the dealer's five cards must have at least a combination of ace/king or better. These additional rules also apply:

1. If the dealer does not have a qualified hand (ace/king, one pair, two pairs, etc.), even money is paid to those players who made an ante bet. After paying each player's ante, the dealer spreads each player's hand face down to verify five cards, and, once verified, those cards are placed in the discard rack. Once all cards are collected, the dealer presses the "End" button to unlock the jackpot bet and proceeds to reshuffle the deck. It is important that players' hands are not exposed if the dealer's hand does not qualify for play. Players are responsible for notifying the dealer if they have a winning bet on the progressive jackpot.

2. If the dealer's hand qualifies for play, it will be compared with the players' hands and the highest-ranking poker hand between the dealer and each player is declared the winner. If a player's hand beats the dealer's hand, that player is paid even money on the ante bet. Should the player have made a call bet, that wager is paid on a bonus schedule posted at the table in clear player view. As an example, the bonus payment to be made on a winning call bet would be determined on the basis of the following card combinations:

One pair	Even money
Two pairs	2:1
Three of a kind	3:1
Straight	4:1
Flush	5:1
Full house	7:1

Four of a kind	20:1
Straight flush	50:1
Royal flush	100:1

Progressive Jackpot Winners

In order to be eligible as a progressive jackpot winner, a player must have made the progressive side bet. Qualifying hands for a progressive payout include flush, full house, four of a kind, straight flush, and royal flush, and the progressive jackpot payout schedule could be paid as follows:

Royal flush (any suit)	100% of the progressive meter
Straight flush (any suit)	10% of the progressive meter
Four of a kind	$100
Full house	$75
Flush	$50

Typically, a progressive jackpot will be in the hundreds of thousands of dollars, so the incentive for a big payday induces a significant number of gamblers to play this game.

An important aspect of the game is the fact that a progressive bet is considered a side bet and will be paid to the player even if the dealer does not have a qualifying hand or if the hand qualifies and beats the player's hand. Further, if a player is not participating in the progressive jackpot and has a flush, full house, four of a kind, straight flush, or royal flush, the call bet will be paid based only on the associated odds of the bonus payoff chart and not on the progressive meter.

Since a progressive jackpot can reach extremely large amounts, conformance to strict game procedures is required of dealers and floor supervisors, exemplified by the following progressive jackpot guidelines.

To be eligible for meter payouts, a player must have made the progressive side bet. If the hand is eligible for the progressive jackpot, the dealer must immediately summon a floor supervisor for verification of the qualifying hand. In the case of a straight flush or royal flush, the hand must also be verified by the casino shift manager or the casino manager and may be subject to eye-in-the-sky scrutiny. After verification of the player's hand is completed, the dealer activates a button on the game control panel corresponding with the hand. In turn, the floor supervisor inserts and activates a verification key on the control panel to deduct the amount of the payout from the progressive meter. In the case of a straight flush or royal flush, the shift or casino manager will have the key to reset the meter. A royal flush payout will cause the meter to reset at a seed amount predetermined by the casino. The player is then paid out of the table rack or from a table fill provided by the casino cage. Game control procedures also require completion of a progressive jackpot log, to which any payoff from the progressive meter must be recorded. Information recorded to this log includes: date, time, shift, table number, winning hand, amount paid (both numerical and spelled out amount), dealer signature, pit boss or floor supervisor signature, and shift or casino manager signature (on straight or royal flushes).

Although Caribbean stud poker is a relatively new game on the casino floor, it has generated a great deal of player interest and represents the increasing influence technology has exerted over casino operations.

BACCARAT

The most elegant game in a casino is baccarat. The classic European casino features an ornately decorated baccarat room complete with crystal chandeliers, thick, plush wall-to-wall carpeting covered with expensive oriental rugs, bouquets of potted, fresh flowers, tea served from silver tea sets, and baccarat dealers adorned in tuxedos, catering to the highest rollers entering the casino. No other casino game can match the pure James Bond touch of baccarat.

Rules and Procedures of the Game

Baccarat is a table card game played by one or more players (see Figure 4.5). Although there are only 12 positions or player spots on the baccarat layout, the game could be played with more. Eight decks of cards are used and are dealt from a shoe. Face cards and 10s have no value per se, and the suits of the cards do not impact play. Aces count as 1. The highest or best hand in baccarat is 9, and the closest to 9 is the winner.

Unlike other casino card games, one player is offered the shoe by the baccarat dealer and this player, known as the banker, draws the cards from the shoe. The banker will draw two hands from the shoe, with one hand referred to as the banker's hand and the other as the players' hand. Each hand is dealt two cards. As the banker draws the first card from the shoe, it is given or slid face down to one of the baccarat dealers known as the croupier, caller, pole, or stick, who then announces, "No more bets." The banker deals another card, which is placed under the lip of the shoe. The same dealing sequence is done with two more cards. The two cards under the lip of the shoe are the banker's hand and the two cards dealt to the croupier are the players' hand.

Players can bet on either hand as follows. The players' hand is acted on first. The croupier slides the players' hand to the customer with the highest wager on the players' side counter-clockwise from the shoe. Next, the croupier states "Players' hand," and the player, after turning over the cards, slides them face up to the croupier. The croupier places these two cards next to each other on that portion of the table marked "Player" and then calls out the numerical total. The value of the hand is determined by the sum of the last digits. For example, if there is a 10 and 3 the total is (0 + 3 =) 3 and the croupier would

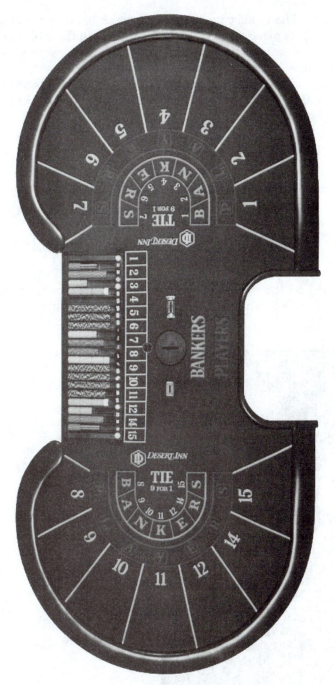

Figure 4.5
Baccarat Layout (From "The Sheraton Gaming Guide," courtesy of the Sheraton Desert Inn, Las Vegas, an ITT Sheraton Resort & Casino)

say, "Players show 3." The banker now tosses the bank hand to the croupier, face up, and the croupier places these cards side-by-side on the table layout in the "Banker" spot. The croupier now calls the total, "The bank shows ————." Only one other card *may* be drawn per hand as explained below.

Players wagering on the players' hand may draw a third card based on the following (generally, if there is no 8 or 9 total for either the bank or the players' hand, a third card is drawn):

Hand Value	Hand Action
0–5	Draws a third card
6 or 7	Stands
8 and 9	A "natural," and the banker cannot draw. A natural on either the players' or bank's draw ends the hand.

Players wagering on the bank's hand draw a third card based on the following. If the hand value is from 0 to 2, the banker's hand draws the third

Baccarat Table *(Courtesy of the Sheraton Desert Inn, Las Vegas, an ITT Sheraton Resort & Casino)*

card. If the players' hand stands, the banker's hand will draw the third card if the total is from 3 to 5. The banker's hand stands on 6 or 7. Some other special rules apply:

1. If the value of the banker's hand is 3, the banker's hand draws the third card when the players' hand is 0 to 7 or 9. Conversely stated, in this instance, the banker's hand would stand if the players' hand is 8.
2. If the value of the banker's hand is 4, the banker's hand draws the third card if the players' hand is 2 to 7, and stands otherwise.
3. If the value of the banker's hand is 5, the banker's hand draws the third card if the players' hand is 4 to 7, and stands otherwise.
4. If the value of the banker's hand is 6, the banker's hand draws the third card if the players' hand is 6 or 7 and, again, stands if this is not the case.

The placement of the banker's or players' third card on the layout is done in an exact manner. The first two cards are placed vertically in their appropriate spots on the layout, while the third cards are placed horizontally next to the hand. After the third cards are dealt, the croupier will direct all players to stand or draw. Once the hand is finished, the used cards are discarded into a "box" or a "can" in the middle of the table. The banker/player maintains control of the shoe as long as this person continues to win. The shoe is passed to the right to the next person. Customers pay a 5 percent commission or vig on all winning bank wagers while no commission is taken from winning wagers on players' hands or on a tie. If there is a tie (i.e., the values of the hands are the same), the players may either withdraw (i.e., a push exists) or increase their wagers. Casino commissions are either paid at the end of the hand or, more often, at the completion of play.

Baccarat Organizational Structure

Figure 4.6 is the organization chart for the baccarat department. This gaming division is headed by a baccarat manager who reports to the casino manager or shift manager. The baccarat manager is responsible for all operations, including the efficient operation of the baccarat game, hiring and disciplinary matters, prevention of cheating by players or employees, and securing top-notch players. Although casinos establish table limits for baccarat, it is not unusual for these limits to be raised for the ultimate high-rollers. Win and loss deviations are so dramatic that most casinos report this game's revenue separately from the total of all other casino games.

The shift manager is the direct game supervisor and is responsible for the conduct of the game during an assigned shift.

Three dealers operate a baccarat game. The croupier, as explained previously, directs the game and advises the banker when to deal and when to draw or stand. Two "base" dealers sit behind the money rack and secure lost wagers,

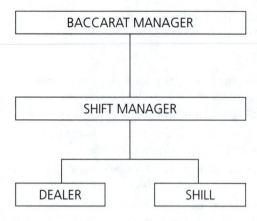

Figure 4.6
Bacarrat Organization Chart

pay winning wagers, and "mark the vig" on the bank winners. Finally, some casinos employ baccarat shills who wager with house money and are primarily used when a single player wishes to play the game. At one time, Las Vegas casinos would only employ attractive females as baccarat shills who would also act as escorts for high-rollers wishing to go to dinner or a show in the showroom.

In baccarat, the advantage is 1.17 percent on bank hands and 1.37 percent on player hands after the vig.

Baccarat, the most elegant game in the casino, still has a special niche in the total gaming operation strategy. As a matter of fact, many casinos have moved the traditional baccarat game into the twenty-one pit via a faster, low-stakes version of the game known as mini-baccarat, which operates basically according to the same rules.

Although it is not suitable for every casino setting, baccarat in the right setting almost becomes a must-see attraction and truly offers the high-level approach to gambling.

OTHER TABLE GAMES

In addition to twenty-one, craps, roulette, the Big 6, Caribbean stud poker, baccarat, and mini-baccarat, other table games might include pai-gow, Red Dog, pai-gow poker, Let It Ride, and a series of other games that, in the final analysis, offer table card players a full variety of game options and challenges geared to virtually everyone's taste and pocketbook.

DISCUSSION QUESTIONS

1. What is the difference between American- and European-style roulette?
2. Why does the game of roulette utilize various chip colors?
3. Define the following roulette terms:
   a. Wheel chips
   b. Lammer button
   c. Split bet
   d. Mucking
   e. Chip chunker
4. Why is close game scrutiny required of roulette dealers?
5. Describe the spacing used on the money wheel or Big 6 game.
6. List several dealer errors associated with the Big 6 game.
7. Where did the game of Caribbean stud poker achieve its initial popularity?
8. How is Caribbean stud poker unlike poker-room-style play?
9. What is the prominent feature of a Caribbean stud table?
10. How does a player participate in a Caribbean stud poker progressive jackpot? Why has this become an incentive to players?
11. What is the role of the "banker" in the game of baccarat?
12. Describe the organizational structure of a baccarat pit.
13. What are the principal duties of a baccarat croupier?

5

SLOT OPERATIONS/ THE SLOT DEPARTMENT

 LEARNING OBJECTIVES

This chapter will enable the reader to:

- Understand how slot machines have evolved over the past one hundred years.

- Become familiar with the functions and characteristics of reel and video slot machines.

- Define terminology common to the daily operation of a slot machine department.

- Identify methods by which casino operators acquire slot machines.

- Become familiar with the organization plan of a slot department as well as personnel responsibilities.

- Discuss strategies utilized in floor planning of a slot department.

- Describe slot revenue functions and cycle.

- Become aware of slot marketing and merchandising strategies.

The authors of this book wish to thank International Game Techonology for its assistance and support in writing this chapter. Their research and information proved invaluable in the compilation of data for this chapter.

INTRODUCTION

The crashing of coins into metal trays, bells ringing, lights flashing, and the announcement of another lucky jackpot winner—such are the sights and sounds of a slot department. In anticipation of winning that promised jackpot, men and women, yuppies and senior citizens are attracted to slot machines in casinos throughout the world. Little was it realized when the first slot machine was introduced toward the turn of the nineteenth century the profound impact they would cause on casino gaming.

Rapidly changing technology, sophisticated marketing promotions, an ever-increasing customer base, and the fact that slots are the leading revenue generators in the casino industry are just a few of the reasons for the importance of understanding the operation of a slot department (see Figure 5.1).

THE EVOLUTION OF SLOT MACHINES

Charles Fey, a young Bavarian immigrant to San Francisco, is credited with introducing the first slot machine in about 1895. The device, which accepted and paid out nickels, enjoyed a modicum of local success. However, it was not until the development of Herbert Mill's "Liberty Bell" in 1930 that slot machines were distributed nationally, with locations primarily in taverns and fraternal clubs. The death knell for this fledgling product was sounded during

Figure 5.1
Slot Carousel (Courtesy of the Excalibur Hotel/Casino, Las Vegas, a Circus Circus Enterprise)

Action at a Slot Machine *(Courtesy of the Sheraton Desert Inn, Las Vegas, an ITT Sheraton Resort & Casino)*

this time period as a result of a federal movement to not only declare the machines illegal but to prohibit their shipment across state lines. The exception to this prohibition was the state of Nevada, where legalized casino gaming existed since 1931. However, from 1931 until the decade of the 1980s, slot machines for Nevada casinos were not a primary revenue source. The decade of the 1980s marks a dramatic turn of events in slots operations as a result of two major innovations: stepper motor technology and video poker.

1. Stepper motor technology. Stepper motor technology allowed expansion of the physical number of stops on a machine's reel strip, resulting in greater play versatility than had been possible with previous models. Consequently, a greater number of games were now offered along with more player options, bigger jackpots, and credit play. Casinos came to realize that machine maintenance cost was drastically reduced since fewer machine parts and mechanics were required to keep the devices operational. In addition, machines now played considerably faster, resulting in increased slot revenue and win.

2. Video Poker. The introduction of video poker allowed players decision-making options not offered by reel slots. By the mid-1980s, video slots achieved overwhelming success, and by the early 1990s, Nevada casinos were reporting that more than 50 percent of their slot mix consisted of video poker machines.

The decade of the 1980s witnessed further innovations, notably: the appearance of higher-denomination machines offering customer options of $1, $5, $25, $100—and even $500 games; increasingly higher jackpots, and progressive machines wherein the jackpot continuously increases based on coins played in the machines, resulting in payoffs in the millions of dollars. While slot machines continued to improve through new computer technology, they were also changing in appearance. New graphics, brighter colors, sleeker shapes, and attractive signage were integrated, offering players more variety of machines and greater excitement.

As the casino industry entered the decade of the 1990s, slot devices were now surpassing the combined revenues of the once-dominant table games, accounting for upwards of 70 percent of total gaming revenue for a great number of operations.

ANATOMY OF A SLOT MACHINE

Just as computers evolved through successive generations, slot machines have experienced a similar transition. While newly designed machine exteriors stimulated greater customer appeal, advanced technology vastly improved functional systems and subsystems as machines progressed from mechanical to electromechanical to microcomputer-controlled devices.

Figure 5.2 illustrates the IGT (International Game Technology) S-Plus Spinning Reel slot machine, while Figure 5.3 provides an illustration of the IGT Players Edge-Plus Video Poker/Video slot machine. Both models are microcomputer-controlled devices interfacing such functions as coin acceptance, coin dispensing, game statistical data accumulation and accounting, player switches, and indicators. Critical game data are stored in random access memory, with the entire microcomputer system residing on a single printed circuit board housed in a lockable enclosure.

The functional subsystems of the devices illustrated are described below.

Power System

The machine's power cord supplies voltage for both AC power distribution and DC power supply. AC power distribution services the fluorescent lighting system, coin hopper motor, video color monitor, and the step-down transformer used for DC power supplies necessary to operate the microcomputer system.

Coin-in System

The major components of the coin-in system consist of the coin receptacle, coin comparitor, and coin acceptor. The coin receptacle is the exterior slot that

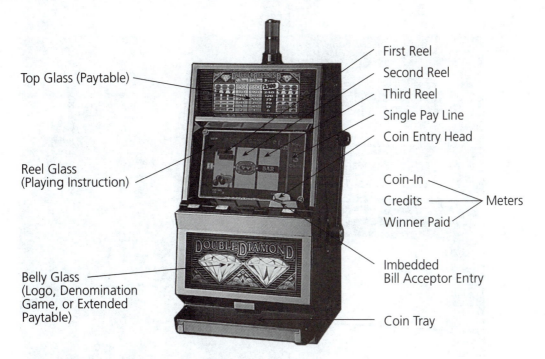

Figure 5.2
S-Plus Spinning Reel Slot Machine (Courtesy of International Game Technology)

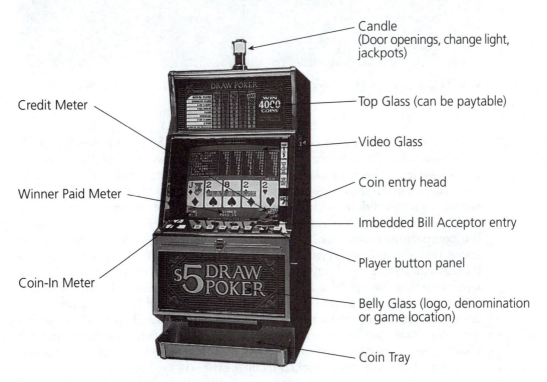

Figure 5.3
Video Poker Slot Machine (Courtesy of International Game Technology)

S-Plus Slant Top Slot Machine *(Courtesy of International Game Technology)*

allows the player to insert coins or slot tokens into the machine either singly or sequentially. The coin comparitor is often referred to as the heart of the coin-in system. This is an electrical device within the machine that detects, by physical comparison, one specific kind of coin or token. Utilizing principles similar to a metal detector, the magnetic properties of the incoming coins or tokens are compared to the properties of a reference coin or token residing in the comparitor. Coins that match are allowed to enter the machine, while those that do not are rejected to the payout tray. The coin acceptor is a mechanical device residing within the machine that accepts coins or tokens. Upon entering the machine beyond the coin comparitor, valid coins or tokens are scanned by optical sensors, which relay an electrical coin-in pulse to the computer, indicating that a valid coin or token has properly passed the optical sensors. Coins are accepted in this manner until the maximum number allowed for the particular game is reached, at which time the coin-in system is deactivated and any additional coins or tokens will be rejected.

Coin-out System

The coin-out system is responsible for paying out the number of coins owed a player, and consists of the slot hopper and associated control and monitoring devices.

Interfacing with the coin-in and coin-out system is the slot hopper—a container inside the machine that holds and dispenses coins. Coins or tokens entering the machine are initially routed to the slot hopper until an electrical sensor signals a "hopper full" condition, at which point the computer activates an electromechanical coin diverter. This action causes coins or tokens to bypass the slot hopper and to be dispensed directly to the drop bucket located inside the stand directly underneath the machine. These buckets are routinely retrieved through a process called the "hard drop."

As previously mentioned, a slot machine's coin-out system is responsible for paying out coins owed to a customer. Monitoring circuits are designed to function with noncredit machines (winnings are paid immediately) or credit machines (winnings are retained until the player activates the cash-out button or switch). Activation of the cash-out switch causes the slot hopper to dispense

Players Edge-Plus Upright Video Poker
(Courtesy of International Game Technology)

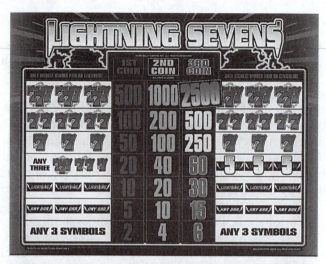

Bally Gaming Lightning Sevens Slot Machine *(Courtesy of Bally Gaming, Inc.)*

coins or tokens through the machine coin exit chute. Existing coins are optically scanned while the computer is comparing coins and tokens to be paid with the number actually paid. Upon completion of pay-out, the hopper drive sends a signal causing the pay-out to shut down.

Should the cash-out system malfunction, the slot hopper's monitoring circuit senses that no coins are leaving the hopper because it is either empty or jammed. This condition results in an automatic shutdown, or the machine placing itself "out-of-order," at which point signals are activated summoning an attendant to remedy the problem.

Player Input

Whether a spinning reel slot or video poker machine, initiation of customer play is a function of the device's player input system, offering the following functions:

- Spinning reel slot machines: Coin insertion with player option of betting one coin or maximum coins; activating (spinning) the reels by pulling the machine's handle or depressing the "spin" button; pressing the button to collect winnings or to summon a change attendant.
- Video poker machines: In addition to the play functions listed above, additional play options are integral to video poker machines, such as: hold 1-2-3-4-5 cards; deal or draw to a new hand or to cards held.

The machine's handle is considered the most important player input function. As originally designed, this mechanical device caused reels to be activated or spun. With today's machines, however, the slot handle is merely a switch that simulates the "feel" of a mechanical handle. Upon insertion of the first coin or token, the handle selenoid is computer-activated, allowing the player to pull the handle. Pulling the handle activates an electrical switch, which signals the computer that the handle has been pulled. When the game is not being played, an electric selenoid locks the handle mechanism, preventing the handle from being pulled. Contrary to what some people believe, jerking or

Players Edge-Plus 13-Inch Video Reel Slot *(Courtesy of International Game Technology)*

slowly pulling the handle of a computer-activated machine will not alter the outcome or increase the chance of winning.

Player Status Displays

Visual and audio functions are included to provide the player with a constant game status. Utilization of stepper lamps, line lights, and illuminated switches provide visual information of the number of credits accumulated, the number of coins bet, and the number of coins won. For example, coins inserted in a single payline slot activate lighting of a stepper lamp indicating first coin, second coin, third coin, and so on, as each coin is inserted. Line lights are used in multiple payline machines signifying the lines that will be paid to the player as each coin is inserted. Illuminated player switches (e.g., "spin reels," "cash out," etc.) act as prompts or reminders to players to push the appropriate button. Machine sounds, including coin-in sounds, reel spin sounds, and win and jackpot sounds, are computer generated and serve to prompt the player and add game excitement.

Bally Gaming California Dreamin' Slot Machine
(*Courtesy of Bally Gaming, Inc.*)

Player Outcome Functions

A slot's computer software package is designed to generate reel stop information, evaluation of winning or losing combinations, whenever a winning game has occurred, and the amount won. In the final analysis, game outcome is determined by numbers randomly generated by the computer. IGT's informational and instructional manual summarizes this computer function as follows: "The computer 'knows' which symbols are on which stops on the reels; the computer randomly generates stop numbers representing the game outcome; the exact number of pulses to 'spin' the reels from their current positions to the game outcome positions is known, and the motors are driven to this position; the motion and stopping of the reels is monitored and reported to the computer."

Game Accounting

Coins in, coins out, and coins diverted to the drop are critical items of revenue information, and the generation of this information is an integral function of a slot device accounting system. Depending on individual machine manufac-

Large Screen Players Edge-Plus Upright Video Poker Machine *(Courtesy of International Game Technology)*

turers, this important measuring activity is performed by slot meters internal to the machine. As an example, machine design might utilize nonresettable counters functioning much like the odometer of an automobile as a measurement of coins in, often referred to as the "hard meter." This type of game accounting system utilizes a secondary system to store coin-in, coin-out, and coin drop data, known as the "soft meters." In any event, a fundamental purpose of slot meters is to provide a measurement of slot activity, with meter readings taken and recorded during the process known as the "hard drop." Compilation of this data allows for a comparison of the actual performance of the machine to theoretical performance.

Machine Security

Security features incorporated in the design of a slot machine to deter cheating activities are of prime concern. Since the first slot device was introduced to the present time, slot cheats have used ingenious methods and devices to "rip off" machines. Consequently, manufacturers expend considerable effort and expense in designing and installing security systems to include the following features:

- Optical sensors transmitting signals whenever the slot door is open
- Coin-in optics sensors to defend against machine "stringing" (coins attached to strings for retrieval, allowing for free play)
- Rejection of lead slugs (machine slugging) through utilization of a coin comparitor
- Utilization of hopper optics to prevent "fishing" of coins through the coin exit chute
- Sensing devices to detect deliberate attempts to reposition machine reels
- Computer software features designed to detect malfunctions and security violations, resulting in the machine being placed out of order, displaying an error message, or triggering the "candle" (the lamp atop the machine) to flash (alerting the slot attendant to investigate the problem and take corrective action)
- Currency acceptors that reject counterfeit bills and create a guillotine effect after the bill has been scanned and accepted, to prevent stringing

Nonfunctional Parts and Other Terminology

Although not integral to a slot machine's functional subsystems, the following slot terms are common to this department's operation:

- **Belly glass.** Lower glass on the door, which shows the denomination, paytable, and/or game theme.
- **Bowl.** A steel tray attached to the machine stand top to collect coins paid out by the machine.

- **Chase lights.** Low-voltage strips of lights under program control that blink in series to simulate movement.
- **Cycle.** The total number of possible symbol combinations on a slot machine, or the total number of possible card combinations on a poker machine.
- **Expanded paytable glass.** Lower glass on a machine that shows an extension of the upper paytable glass.
- **Game sheet.** A graphic display and the payback statistics of the game program installed in a slot machine.
- **Link.** Two or more machines connected to a progressive meter.
- **Multiple game.** The winning amount on one coin multiplied by the number of coins played.
- **Paytable glass.** Top and/or bottom glass that shows the payoff table for that machine.
- **Progressive.** One or more machines where a percentage of the wager is added to the jackpot amount.
- **Touchscreen.** New technology that allows customers to play the machine by touching the slot machine's video screen.

Slot Machine Acquisition

Whether opening a new casino or maintaining an existing facility, the acquisition of the proper mix of slot machines represents a major management financial decision. Basically, casinos are afforded three options: purchase, lease/purchase, and lease participation.

Purchase. Slot machines may be purchased directly from the manufacturer for cash, resulting in favorable cash discounts, or by a manufacturer-financed deal. Depending on the strength of the casino's financial statements, manufacturers will finance from 50 percent to 80 percent of the purchase at negotiated interest rates. A major advantage of a cash purchase is that the casino optimizes gross daily margins since it retains all revenue generated. The major disadvantage is that the casino must commit a sizable portion of start-up capital.

Lease/Purchase. Machine acquisitions are based on fixed payments per machine over a negotiated period of time. The gross lease payment, including interest, is calculated in advance of machine installation. After total payments reach an anticipated level, a percentage of payments is applied to the purchase contract, enabling the casino to buy out the lease. The obvious advantage to this arrangement is the substantial reduction in initial capital investment. A disadvantage is the loss of cash discounts and the reduction from gross revenue per machine resulting from lease payments.

Lease Participation. Many slot manufacturers and distributors will negotiate a smaller machine downpayment, to receive a percentage of the daily slot drop until full payment of the machine is reached. Typical lease participation agreements are 70/30 or 60/40, with the casino retaining the larger share. This acquisition arrangement usually requires the least amount of up-front money. The disadvantage is that the manufacturer or distributor becomes, in effect, the casino's partner until the machines are paid off.

Major Sources

Slot machines are available through numerous manufacturers and distributors. Since it is beyond the scope of this text to provide a complete description of all manufacturers, discussion will be limited to the following:

Bally Manufacturing. This name has been paramount in the slot machine industry for over sixty years since the production of its first mechanical slot in the 1930s. The company is credited with mass production of electromechanical machines in the 1960s and introduction of the first electronic slot in the 1980s. The company pioneered microprocessors in the technology of slots.

Bally Manufacturing innovations include: machine upgrading from multiple to single-card technology, resulting in increased slot reliability and reduced service time; an internal bill acceptor located directly over the coin slot, featuring only one moving part for reliability and a quick-removing acceptor head for easy clearing of jams; and an interactive, multi-gametouch screen video machine featuring up to ten game play options.

International Game Technology (IGT). With well over 200,000 slot machines operating in casinos throughout the world, IGT is positioned as the industry's single largest slot manufacturer. In 1986, IGT introduced "Megabucks" slot progressive machines to the Nevada market, which featured multimillion-dollar jackpots. Soon to follow were other wide-area progressive systems including "Quartermania," "Nevada Nickels," "Fabulous Fifties," and "High Rollers." The company further positioned itself as a primary supplier of casino management products for slots operations. Its "Smart System" is a computerized slot marketing tool allowing casinos to identify players, record slot play levels, develop customer demographics, and perform automated slot accounting.

Aristocrat Leisure Industry. This is an Australian-based firm involved with the slot industry for over forty years. It ranks second to IGT in sales of slots worldwide, and only Bally Manufacturing has been in existence for a longer period of time. Its models have enjoyed exceptional popularity among Native American gaming operations.

Other major slot manufacturers include Universal, Sigma, and Williams.

Open 24 hours a day, seven days a week, Grand Casino Mille Lacs has over 1,400 loose video slots to choose from. *(Courtesy of Grand Casino Mille Lacs Hinckley, Minnesota)*

SLOT DEPARTMENT ORGANIZATIONAL STRUCTURE

Figure 5.4 indicates the organizational structure of a casino slot department. The director of slot operations (slot manager) is responsible for the daily operation and administration of the slot department and reports directly to the casino manager. Slot revenue functions (i.e., slot drop, slot weigh and count, slot audit, and coin form control) fall under the jurisdiction of the casino controller, resulting in required separation of duties.

Slot Manager. The slot manager reports to the casino manager or shift manager and is responsible for overall supervision of the slot department, determining slot mix, number and placement of machines on the casino floor, and ensuring that machines are properly maintained. This person is authorized to conduct investigations into slot machine manipulations and approval of large slot jackpots. Further duties include resolving customer disputes that may arise within the department, preparation of department work schedules,

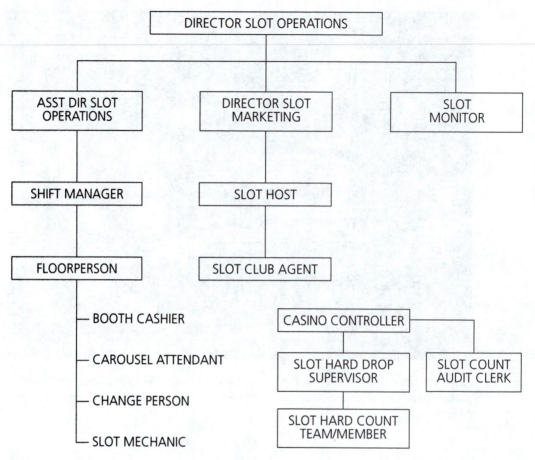

Figure 5.4
Typical Slot Organization Chart

maintaining documentation relating to removal and replacement of machines, coordinating purchase of new machines, and ensuring compliance with department policies and procedures to properly safeguard assets.

Assistant Slot Manager. This person assists the slot manager in operation of the slot department, performs duties as assigned, and assumes slot manager responsibilities as required.

Slot Secretary. The slot secretary reports to the slot manager and is responsible for preparing required reports relating to slot operations, preparing department work schedules, and maintaining the slot department office.

Slot Shift Manager. This person reports to the slot manager and is responsible for supervising slot operations during an assigned shift, ensuring that all

(Courtesy of Harvey's Resort Hotel/Casino, Lake Tahoe, Nevada)

procedures are followed in accordance with casino policy. While exercising supervisory authority over employees, the shift manager ensures adherence to employee work schedules and monitors employee-customer relations. Duties further include monitoring and signing jackpot payout slips, in accordance with approved policies; coordinating with slot technicians to ensure efficient machine maintenance; training and evaluating shift personnel; and recommending to the slot manager improvements within the department.

Slot Floorperson. The floorperson reports to the slot shift manager and is responsible for overseeing slot operations during an assigned shift, including: front-line supervision of slot employees on the casino floor (but does not normally have the authority to hire and terminate); handling money transfers from the casino cage to change persons and carousel attendants; overseeing hand-paid jackpots made by change persons to casino patrons; approving and overseeing slot hopper fills; promoting good customer relations and handling customer complaints; clearing minor currency acceptor jams and other minor repairs to slots prior to calling a slot technician; and notifying the slot manager when a major jackpot is won.

Booth Cashier. The booth cashier reports to the slot floorperson and is accountable for the slot booth bankroll. Responsibilities include dispensing change to casino patrons; replenishing change persons' banks; maintaining records of slot fills and transfer of funds to the casino cage; receiving loose coins from patrons and placing these in coin counter/jet sorter, then giving the customer the amount indicated on the counter's meter; and providing the slot person with currency for hand-pay jackpots.

Carousel Attendant. This person reports to the slot floorperson while performing the following duties: maintaining a change bank and selling change to customers from a designated slot carousel; and balancing the carousel change bank at the end of the shift.

Slot Change Person. This person reports to the slot floorperson and is responsible for selling coins and tokens to customers; counting and auditing the assigned change bank at the beginning and end of a working shift; participating in hand-paid jackpots to customers; and demonstrating a friendly attitude when interacting with customers, often "celebrating" jackpots with winners.

Slot Technician. The slot technician reports to the slot repair manager and performs slot machine repairs and preventative maintenance, monitors accuracy of slot machine pay-outs, analyzes schematics of slot machines, handles computer chip and microprocessor board changes, and maintains a log of all machine problems and repairs and verifies incidences of machine tampering.

Director of Slot Marketing. This person reports to the slot manager and is responsible for developing flyers, brochures, and other advertising material to promote the slot department; coordinating slot tournaments and the slot club; and, with the cooperation of the casino marketing director, assisting in customer development.

Slot Host. This person assists with all promotional activities pertaining to the slot department. He or she is responsible for developing and maintaining customer goodwill in responding to customer requests and resolving any customer problems that may arise and promoting membership in the casino's slot club.

Slot Hard Drop/Count Team Member. Team members remove and transport slot coin drop according to required procedures. Team member duties include: emptying hoppers of slot machines and transporting coinage to the designated slot-drop room; working with other team members who verify each others' work; and counting or weighing coinage and recording same on slot drop audit forms or entering data on the designated computer terminal. The slot hard drop team may be under the direction of a slot drop supervisor, who reports to the casino controller.

Slot Count Audit Clerk. The audit clerk reports to the slot audit supervisor and performs the following duties: testing and operating the coin weigh scales;

auditing the scales weigh tape to ascertain that all slots are accounted for in the drop; and reconciling the weigh/wrap and entering the drop by denomination to prescribed documents or records.

Slot Monitor. The slot monitor is responsible for monitoring ongoing slot activity via a computer linkup and makes notations of jams, calls slot technicians for repairs, and notes door openings on slot machines, current revenue earnings for each machine, and which machines have had a significant number of fills. Many casinos will shut down a machine that requires three or more fills throughout the day, absent large jackpots, and review the machine's system of tampering or cheating devices.

Floor Planning the Slot Department

Whether planning a new casino or expanding the existing facility, the management team will expend considerable time and energy in designing the slot floor plan and slot mix. Floor planning a slot department requires the combined efforts of a manufacturer's design department and the casino slot manager. Utilization of high-technology computer-aided design tools dramatically reduces the time required in formulating the initial floor plan. International Game Technology uses a state-of-the-art autocad, three-dimensional computer simulation to this end. The resultant rendering provides a specific matrix indicating the floor location of each machine as well as machine type, denomination, cabinet style, and game theme. The design matrix is used in planning construction of the facility by indicating electrical wiring required for machine installation and lighting and floor treatments. Prior to finalizing the floor plan, a decision will have been reached regarding selection of machine manufacturer(s) and optimum slot mix.

The ideal slot mix means the selection of a combination of slot machines that will offer the greatest customer appeal. The slot manager must consider factors that include coin denominations, variety and type of machines, pay-off schedules, blend of video slots and reel slots, and proper location of machines on the casino floor. In formulating a decision-making model to arrive at the ideal mix, the following factors are considered.

Ratio of Reel Machines to Video Machines. Research conducted by IGT indicates that a successful equipment mix for opening a new casino is approximately 80 percent reel spinning slots to 20 percent video poker slots. The preponderance of reel slots is based on an analysis of new casino jurisdictions indicating that customers are more familiar with reel spinning slots. As a casino establishes a customer base, video slots tend to attract increased play as patrons become more familiar with the play features of the machines. Since slot mix is not static, management must remain constantly aware of changing customer preferences and adjust machine ratio accordingly. As is noted in Chapter 10, Casino Marketing, Las Vegas casinos responding to the local customers' preferences now feature more video poker machines than reel slots!

Coin Denomination. With a decision finalized regarding equipment mix, management next focuses attention on denomination mix of its machines. Options include machines accepting 5 cents, 25 cents, 50 cents, $1, and higher, as well as machines accepting single-coin play, two-coin play, three-coin play, and five-coin multiple play. As with equipment mix, no exact formula or science exists to aid in the decision. However, a denomination matrix will include machine variety appealing to a wide customer base. Assuming that a new startup casino plans to open with 1,000 machines, the machine configuration may be structured to conform with the following percentages:

Denominations	Total Number	Total Percentage
5¢	100	10%
25¢	600	60%
50¢	50	5%
$1	200	20%
High denominations	50	5%
Total	1,000	100%

From the above, it is readily discernible that 25-cent (quarter) denomination machines should constitute the highest percentage (60). Analysis of statistics available from the Nevada State Gaming Control Board reveal that quarter slot machines won more money for Nevada casinos than did twenty-one, roulette, and craps tables combined. Gaming jurisdictions throughout the United States reflect extremely favorable results generated by quarter slots. Popularity of these slots is attributed to affordability of play and enticement of sizable jackpots.

By now it is apparent that achieving the optimum slot mix is a constantly evolving process based on changing machine technology, customer preferences, and management's desire to achieve predetermined win objectives.

Machine Placement. The slot floor plan includes the exact location of each gaming device by type and denomination, considering: aisle space, customer traffic flow, carousel locations, placement of slot change booths, and relationship of machine locations to the live gaming areas. The slot department interior design must also include number and location of progressive jackpot machines, appropriate customer seating, interior signage, utilization of themed slot "belly glass," and slot cabinetry. The ultimate placement of machines will determine customer traffic flow throughout the department. Banks of machines requiring customer flow to proceed past the machine fronts, rather than machine sides, is customary. This placement, along with machine variety, creates an opportunity for customer impulse play. As previously mentioned, slot floor layout is not static. Initially, machines of similar type and denomination may be grouped together. Quarter, dollar, and five-dollar carousels offer points of attraction. Centralizing progressive machines dominated by brightly lit progressive jackpot signage stimulates customer play, especially as the size of the jackpot increases. Based on daily analysis of machine performance, revenues may be increased simply by moving a group of machines to a different floor location, and this is customary in the casino business.

Placement of a bank of dollar video poker machines, for example, in close proximity to quarter videos may encourage customers to upgrade their play. Machines may be placed in interest groups (e.g., "Deuces Wild" video poker, "Jokers Wild" video poker, bonus poker, double-bonus poker). Reel slots offering various game themes also lend themselves to this type of floor placement.

Proper floor planning and machine mix are critical to a slot department's ultimate success. Initial decisions may not be 100 percent correct. However, the slot manager must be cognizant of changing machine appeal and customer preferences and be willing to change the mix based on revenue results.

SLOT REVENUE FUNCTIONS

A single slot machine located on the casino floor represents an independent revenue center. Obviously, a casino that offers a thousand or more devices is positioned to generate several millions of revenue dollars during a fiscal period. The slot revenue cycle, to be described, is subject to the strictest internal control regulations and adherence to written policies and procedures.

Prior to the casino's opening, or the addition of new machines, the initial requirement is to bank each machine with coin denominations as prescribed by the management team. As with decisions regarding slot mix and machine selection, initial slot bankrolls vary among casinos. However, the following chart serves as a guideline to the process of the original hopper fill:

Denomination	Original Hopper Fill
5¢	$100
25¢	250
50¢	300
$1	400
$5	500

Slot change booths, carousel stands, and change person banks are also funded as a prelude to customer activity. The cashiering function of a slot department is a straightforward process since all monetary transactions conducted with slot players are considered "par," that is, customer currency is exchanged for coin or slot tokens.

SLOT DEPARTMENT ACTIVITIES

Slot Hopper Fills

A slot hopper fill is the process of replenishing coinage to the machine's hopper. A large jackpot or series of cash payouts will cause a hopper to be emptied, requiring a hand-fill to be made. The process requires adherence to strict regulatory procedures. The machine's hopper is considered sensitive equipment and can only be accessed by designated personnel who must obtain the key to open the device. A slot floorperson verifies the need for a machine fill and prepares a Request for Fill form, indicating date and time, machine number, denomination, and amount of fill requested. The completed signed request form is presented to a designated area, usually the casino cage, for processing. A cashier reviews the request form for completeness and required signatures and prepares a Slot Fill form, indicating date and time, fill designation, machine number, amount of fill, signature of person authorizing and making the fill, cashier signature, and, depending on established procedures, any other signatures. The original copy of the Slot Fill form is retained by the cashier for documentation of the transaction, while the duplicate copy, along with the bagged coinage, is given to the slot floorperson. The floorperson fills the machine with a change person and security officer witnessing the fill, who also sign the duplicate copy attesting to their participation in the transaction. The original and duplicate copies are ultimately routed to the accounting department for examination and retention. Whenever a slot fill transaction is performed using manually prepared documentation or performed by a computer, written procedures must not only be available but strict compliance with these procedures must be followed.

Slot Drop

The slot drop is a process of retrieving slot drop buckets from the stand beneath the machine and transporting the coinage to a designated area. The casino will establish a slot drop schedule and assign personnel as a team to perform this activity. Large operations must conduct the drop daily, while smaller casinos may "drop" machines two or three times a week. The slot drop team consists of at least three individuals (at least one of whom is independent of the slot department), and the members are rotated based on days off. Prior to commencement of the slot drop, team members secure empty buckets from a storage area, place the required number on a portable cart, and proceed to place the empty buckets in front of each slot cabinet.

The drop team supervisor and team members meet at a predetermined time to obtain keys to the slot drop cabinets (and currency acceptor drop box release keys, if applicable, described later in this chapter). The keys are secured in a double-lock key cabinet, with access requiring the presence of a casino supervisor and security officer. Release of the required keys to the drop team is documented by participants in a key control log.

Having secured the required keys, the drop team follows a specific machine route and proceeds to open each slot drop cabinet. As cabinets are opened, each bucket is tagged with the machine number, removed, and placed on the cart. Machines equipped with currency acceptor drop boxes are opened and boxes exchanged for empty boxes. (Note: Removal of currency acceptor boxes may take place at a time other than the slot drop.) An empty bucket is placed in the cabinet area, the cabinet door is locked, and the team continues the process.

After all slot drop buckets have been placed on the portable cart, the team, accompanied by a security officer who has observed the entire drop, transports the coins to the count room. Access to the coin count room is restricted until at least three slot count team members are present. As with all sensitive areas and keys, strict access procedures are required for gaining entrance to this area.

Slot Count

The slot count (or weigh) normally commences immediately after the drop team delivers the drop contents to the coin count/wrap room, and may be performed by the same individuals completing the slot drop. However, during this process, a representative of the accounting department is required to be present in order to observe and record the slot weigh. A coin weigh scale is used to weigh and convert coins to dollar amounts, with the scale tested for accuracy by the slot count team before the commencement of each count. The test is performed using various test weights or precounted coins and documented on a scales weigh tape. Assured of the accuracy of the scale for each coin denomination, the count begins, with coin denominations weighed separately. A slot team member displays the slot machine number tag to the accounting clerk operating the scale. The accounting clerk enters the machine number into the scales count-recording console, after which the team member dumps the coinage into the coin scale. The weigh results for each individual slot machine are automatically converted to dollar amounts and recorded manually to a Count Sheet or, in a computerized system, automatically recorded. At the conclusion of the weigh, the accounting clerk and a count team member sign the Count Sheet and a Slot Summary Report. A summarization of the totals on the Count Sheet is prepared by the accounting clerk.

Slot Coin Wrap

Immediately after coins are weighed, the coin wrap commences. Coinage is wrapped and reconciled separately from other coinage and not comingled with coinage from the next drop collection. At least two members of the count team are involved in removing wrapped coin rolls from a conveyor and inserting them into cans designed to contain specific coin denominations. With all coinage now "canned" or "racked," a designated supervisor is notified who is responsible for reconciling the coinage wrap. Satisfied with the accuracy of the coin inventory, the count team members and designated supervisor sign a requisite document authorizing transfer of the coins into coin room inventory.

Currency Acceptor Drop

A currency acceptor is a device contained within a slot machine that allows the machine to dispense coin or credits for selected paper currency. Currency acceptors utilized by a slot department represent a drop location, in addition to the coin hopper. As previously mentioned, removal of the currency acceptor drop boxes may occur at the same time as the scheduled slot drop or be scheduled as a separate procedure. In any event, strict procedures are followed comparable to the slot drop. Drop box release keys are secured from a double-lock key cabinet and documented with required signatures in a key control log, and as drop boxes containing currency are removed, they are exchanged for empty boxes. Full boxes are placed on a cart and immediately transported to the soft-count room. During the process of the soft count, assigned team members open the boxes, count and verify the currency, and record the results. Following the conclusion of this count, the accounting department compares the "bill in" meter reading to the currency acceptor drop account, resolving any discrepancies prior to the preparation of slot statistical reports.

Ticket Printers

Some casino jurisdictions require a ticket printer as a substitute for the coin hopper, requiring slot winners to be cashed out by an attendant or at a separate terminal responsible for validating tickets for payment. Coins inserted in a printer-equipped device are routed directly to the drop with no coin payout made directly to the player. When a player desires to "cash out" and activates a control button, the machine prints and dispenses a ticket indicating the credits won, dollar value of credits won, ticket number, and machine number. The customer must present this ticket at a designated control area for payment.

SLOT AUDITING

Within the decade of the 1990s, computer technology has impacted not only slot machine functions but also audit procedures required for effective monitoring of a slot department. Regularly scheduled procedures utilizing computer slot-monitoring systems are capable of verifying the continuing accuracy of coin-in meter readings as recorded in slot statistical reports. Weigh scale interface systems allow the accounting department to compare the slot weigh tape to the system-generated weigh as recorded to the slot statistical reports. Proper utilization of applicable computer software packages provides a casino auditing department with a viable tool to: compare projected theoretical slot performance to actual performance, identify significant deviations in wins and losses, and perform customer tracking, which indirectly helps the casino with its slot marketing.

Internal and External Slot Marketing

External slot marketing strategies are planned to attract customer patronage to the facility through media such as newspapers, radio, television, billboards, and direct mail. Media messages typically conveyed focus upon size of jackpots paid (mega jackpots, progressive amounts of possible jackpots, photos of winners and amounts won, and frequency of winners). Advertising enticements such as "loosest slots," "hottest slots," "Our machines return 97.5%," "the newest millionaire," and so on, serve to whet the appetite of prospective customers.

Internal slot marketing strategies are structured to encourage and increase slot activity while a customer is in the casino through the use of slot merchandising and promotion.

Slot Merchandising

The slot department represents a key merchandising opportunity. Occupying more than 50 percent of casino floor space, it has customers continually wind-

Players bet on miniature simulated horses and jockeys racing around a track in "Royal Ascot." *(Courtesy of Grand Casino Mille Lacs Hinckley, Minnesota)*

Live video craps has at least 44 different ways to win on a single roll of the video dice. *(Courtesy of Grand Casino Mille Lacs Hinckley, Minnesota)*

ing their way through aisle after aisle of machines. Vivid machine graphics, flashing neon, the sheer number and variety of machines stirs a customer's sense of sight and hearing resulting in impulse play. Considerable research has been conducted to determine the most effective merchandising techniques, which include: visual appeal (i.e., overhead signage with lights and colors, distinctive machine graphics and colors); theming machine groups and carousels (i.e., dollar progressive carousels, banks of "Deuces Wild," "Jokers Wild," bonus video machines, etc.; and coordinating machine belly graphics with the overall casino theme.

Slot Promotions

Slot promotions are proven methods of creating customer excitement and giving the customer another reason to play at your casino rather than the competition's. Promotion strategies are as varied as offering free cocktails to slot players to expensive automobile give-aways. Examples of promotions include: paycheck cashing, food discounts, discount coupon books, hourly drawings, double jackpot payoffs for limited time periods, prizes for jackpots over specified amounts, slot and video poker tournaments, slot club membership, and special promotions featuring unique give-aways such as automobiles, trucks, vacation trips, and so on.

As important as slot merchandising and promotions are in developing a successful slot department, in the final analysis, management must develop a continuing awareness of the psychology of slot players in attempting to determine why slot machines are so popular. Obviously no one answer will suffice, although consideration of the following factors should be considered:

- The way the game looks and sounds
- Customer perception of entertainment value
- Large progressive jackpots
- Smaller jackpots but greater hit frequency
- High payback percentage
- A specific game's popularity
- Repeat customers who stay longer and expect their gaming budget to last

 ## SUMMARY

The slot department is the new, shining star for casino operations. Once a mere ancillary component of casino gaming, it now represents the premier source of revenue. Slot technology has dramatically changed over the years, and today's machines are computer-driven and highly interactive with touch screens, bill acceptors, and push buttons. Machine design and ergonomic concerns have resulted in multiple configurations, colors, light attractions, and slot themes. Slot machines of the future will likely feature debit cards or some other form of cashless/coinless option and rely on virtual reality special effects to take customers to the next level of satisfaction and excitement.

 ## DISCUSSION QUESTIONS

1. What two major innovations caused a major turn of events in slots operations?
2. What are the three major components of a slot coin-in system?
3. What is the function of a slot hopper?
4. What methods do casinos typically use to acquire slot machines?
5. Discuss the organization structure of a slot department.
6. What are the primary duties of a slot floorperson?
7. What is meant by the "ideal" slot mix, and what factors are considered to achieve this mix?
8. Discuss procedure to be followed for a slot hopper fill.

9. Explain the purpose of the slot drop.

10. Discuss reasons why casinos have opted for installation of currency acceptors with their slot machines.

11. What advantages are gained by a casino's slot department in utilizing ticket printers as a substitute for hoppers?

12. What are the primary strategies of a slot marketing program?

13. Explain why a slot department has become the number one generator of casino revenue.

14. Discuss the differences between internal and external slot marketing.

6

OTHER GAMING REVENUE DEPARTMENTS

 ## LEARNING OBJECTIVES

This chapter will enable the reader to:

- Be familiar with the organization structure and personnel responsibilities in the operation of a bingo department.

- Understand rules of play and operating procedures of the game of bingo.

- Be familiar with the organization of a casino sports and race book department.

- Understand methods of conducting sports and race book wagering.

- Be familiar with the organization structure and personnel responsibilities in the operation of a poker department.

- Identify several of the more popular poker games offered at casinos.

- Be familiar with the organization structure and personnel responsibilities in the operation of a keno department.

- Understand the rules of play and operating procedures of the game of keno.

In addition to table games and slots, casinos depend on other casino departments for their gaming revenue. Specifically, a full-access casino operation also offers bingo, sports and race book operations, poker, and keno.

BINGO

Since its inception, the game of bingo has been perceived as a form of entertainment and recreation rather than gambling. Estimates of bingo players in the United States range from 50 to 60 million, resulting in revenue generation of approximately $6 billion annually. Historically, bingo games were, and continue to be, operated by churches and other charitable, non-profit organizations as well as Native American tribes. Therefore, a distinction must be made between charitable and casino-style bingo, as well as "Indian Bingo" not offered in a casino setting.

Legalized casinos operating bingo rooms or gaming departments have adopted modern innovations and technology to improve the game. One is the use of throwaway paper pads in place of the traditional reusable playing boards, thus eliminating the need for plastic markers. These pads are marked using felt-tipped pens which daub a red blot on the called number. Electronic equipment is used for ball selection and verification of winners via a bingo board reader.

This section focuses on procedures typically utilized by casinos in the operation of bingo, including departmental organization, bingo card sales, game play, and closing procedures.

Grand Casino Mille Lacs offers casino Bingo in its 400-seat Bingo area *(Courtesy of Grand Casino Mille Lacs Hinckley, Minnesota)*

Organizational Structure

Figure 6.1 indicates the three levels of authority and responsibility for a casino bingo operation.

The director of bingo operations (bingo manager) reports to the casino manager or shift manager and is responsible for supervising bingo games as well as enforcing policies and procedures relating to the operation. Further responsibilities include reviewing gaming results and statistics, following up on variations and exceptions related to these statistics, hiring and disciplinary procedures related to employees, and maintaining high standards of customer service. The bingo manager has access to such areas as the bingo cashier's cage, the bingo office and storage area, supervisors' keys, and the bingo bankroll. Additionally, the manager has signatory authority for the following documents: the Currency Exchange Slip, the Cashier's Sales Report, the Sessions Sales Summary, the Caller's Payout Control Sheet, the Cash Payment Control Sheet, the Daily Sales Summary, and the Key Control Log.

The bingo shift manager reports to the bingo manager and is responsible for the enforcement of policies and procedures related to the bingo operation as well as supervising bingo games in progress. The bingo shift manager has access to sensitive areas and signatory ability identical to those of the bingo manager.

Bingo agents report to the bingo shift manager and are responsible for bingo card sales and performance of the caller and verification functions during bingo games. The caller is the person who sits in the front of the room and announces the selected bingo numbers to the bingo players. The verification function requires bingo agents to walk around the room inspecting winning cards or generally answering questions asked by players. It should be noted that standard procedures do not allow agents to perform selling and verification functions at the same time during bingo games. Agents are given access to

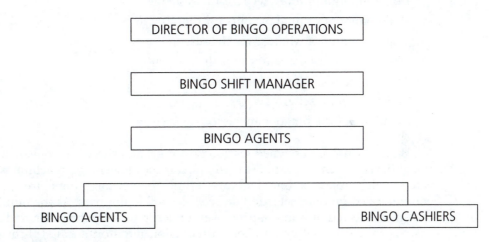

Figure 6.1
Bingo Organization Chart

the bingo cashier's cage and seller's bankroll only when authorized and may likewise have signatory authority for the various forms as directed.

Game Rules and Operating Procedures

Prior to the start of shift play, the bingo manager or bingo shift manager signs out the bingo keys and bingo bank trays at the casino cage and issues cash drawer banks to assigned agents. The responsible manager, bingo agents, and an accounting clerk conduct an inventory of bingo cards, which establishes the basis for the day's revenues through an initial recordation to a Sales Summary Sheet. Bingo cashiers inventory the cards for their respective windows by listing the count on a Bingo Card Sheet as well as recording cash received. This procedure allows for a determination of cash overages or shortages at the end of the shift. Bingo cards or "packs" are sold at a designated area within the bingo room and documented on a Session Sales Report, which indicates the following information: date, shift, session, dollar amount of sales, seller's name and signature, and a bingo supervisor's signature. At the end of each session, an inventory is taken of bingo cards or packs that have not been sold. The resulting count is then subtracted from the opening inventory to determine units sold. This inventory count will be recorded to the Sales Summary Sheet, which should correspond to the Individual Count Sheet as recorded by the sales cashiers.

A review of the Cashier's Sales Report reveals the following information:

Date

Shift

Session

Dollar amount of total sales for the session

Dollar amount of total payouts for the session

Dollar amount of win/loss for the session

Win/loss-to-sales percentage for the session

Total number of players for the session

Signature of all sellers

Signature of the bingo manager or supervisor

Bingo agents are assigned session positions, and these are done on a rotational basis. When the game is ready to start, a blower-type machine is activated which releases one ball at a time, or if computers are used, a computerized random selection device selects the numbers. As the number is drawn or selected, it is announced over a microphone by the caller, and many casinos show the ball or number on television monitors located throughout the bingo room. If the casino is using a ball system, each used ball is placed in a bingo ball rack which lights the corresponding number on bingo display boards located throughout the casino; thus, players can easily verify any and all numbers called throughout the game.

The caller announces a number together with a letter from the word "Bingo" until a player completes a row or sequence on the card. For instance, the caller will announce "B4" or "Under the letter B, number 4." If a player calls out "Bingo," a verification agent will check the card and verify the accuracy. Some casinos will then have the agent show the card to other players for verification or the agent will call the numbers out loud to the caller who repeats the numbers over the microphone for everyone to hear. Other casinos may use computerized, electronic cards to mark and verify numbers. If balls have been placed on a rack, the caller checks to make sure all the balls correspond with the called numbers, and once this is accomplished, the caller announces the payout amount and records the amount on the Payout Control Sheet. The caller then releases all balls from the bingo rack, which are automatically returned to the bingo machine. Once verification has been completed, an agent proceeds to the bingo cage to collect the jackpot for the player.

Other systems require winning sheets to be shown on a television monitor for customer viewing. In this procedure, a floor verifier calls the winning card (aka face) to the bingo caller, who enters the numbers into a computer system causing the bingo face to appear on a television screen with the winning pattern highlighted and the last number called displayed.

Each casino formulates a payout authorization policy appropriate to its operation, as exemplified below:

Payout Range	Required Authorization
$1 to $1,200	Bingo manager or bingo shift manager
$1,201 to $3,000	Bingo or shift manager and casino shift manager or pit manager
$3,001 or more	Bingo or shift manager and casino shift manager

Policy will also require that IRS Form W-2-G be prepared for winnings of $1,200 or more or that IRS Form 10425 be prepared if the winner is a non-U.S. citizen.

Closing Procedures and Bingo Audit

Stringent procedures and controls are required for session and shift closing as well as for the bingo audit. As has been indicated, each operation will determine appropriate procedures to be included in its system of internal controls. Session closing requires totaling the Payout Control Sheet. Additional requirements include arriving at a net sales figure, counting and verifying all cash banks, safeguarding, and signing all related documents.

Shift closing necessitates recordation by the shift supervisor of a final payout to a Game Log/Payout Sheet, requesting fills as required, counting down all receipts, recording all money on a cashier's report, and transferring all funds to the casino cage with a security officer escort.

The bingo audit is performed by the accounting department under the supervision of the casino controller. Discovered discrepancies are reported to the controller and the bingo manager. The audit consists of reviewing bingo documents and totaling session revenue and payouts by shift to arrive at a daily win and any cash variances. Payouts are compared to game prize limits on a random basis and variations reported on designated report forms. With the review of all bingo documents completed, appropriate recordation of the bingo department's financial activities are entered on the casino's accounting records.

Bingo remains one of America's favorite games and is used by casinos mainly as a means of attracting customers for other games (e.g., slots). Many casinos, in fact, use bingo as a loss-leader to this end. One of the main attractions of the game is the social interaction that occurs. Casinos actually foster "bingo clubs" as repeat customers meet and play on a regular basis. One final note on the game: Jackpots have reached surprisingly large amounts, and what was once a low-stakes game has become a casino game where substantial amounts can be won for relatively small wagering amounts.

SPORTS AND RACE BOOK OPERATIONS

Over the past twenty years, Las Vegas casinos have allocated a major portion of their casino floorspace to sports and race book operations. As indicated in Chapter 1, sports books handle wagers on sporting events, while race books cater predominantly to horse racing. Las Vegas sports books attract their heaviest wagering for the Super Bowl football game and will realize more than $50 million in wagering on such events as the college basketball NCAA tournament. Race books have one of the best theoretical casino-win percentages at 18 percent and can generate profits of $250,000 a month at a major Las Vegas hotel.[1] Combined, these two gaming revenue centers represent not only a lucrative addition to the casino's bottom line but also an exciting, user-friendly crowd attraction. Figure 6.2 depicts the typical employees found in a casino race and sports operation.

Sports Book Wagering

Sports books in Las Vegas casinos are a couch potato's dream come true. Televisions dominate the decor, cocktail servers are readily available, and a good hot dog stand is within an arm's reach. Football, baseball, basketball, hockey, golf, tennis, and virtually any other major sport are constantly being shown on large-screen televisions in a party atmosphere. Add to this the ability to wager on games, and you have the makings of a very thrilling wagering and entertainment experience.

The majority of sports book wagering occurs on NFL and college football. One of the more popular betting venues is parlay tickets or cards. Literally

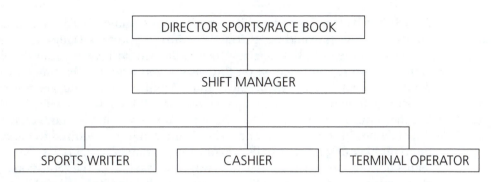

```
┌─────────────────────────────────────┐
│      DIRECTOR SPORTS/RACE BOOK       │
└─────────────────────────────────────┘
                    │
        ┌───────────────────────┐
        │     SHIFT MANAGER      │
        └───────────────────────┘
                    │
     ┌──────────────┼──────────────┐
┌──────────────┐ ┌──────────┐ ┌──────────────────┐
│ SPORTS WRITER│ │ CASHIER  │ │ TERMINAL OPERATOR│
└──────────────┘ └──────────┘ └──────────────────┘
```

Figure 6.2
Sports Book Organization Chart

printed on cardboard, parlay tickets offer a high return or odds factor to the bettor. A football parlay card will list a series of college and professional teams that will be opposing each other during the upcoming week. The book's odds-maker sets a pointspread for each game. For instance, if the Dallas Cowboys are going to be playing the Pittsburgh Steelers, the oddsmaker might make Dallas a 7-point favorite. This game would then be listed on the ticket: "Dallas at

Sports Book Counter *(Courtesy of the Excalibur Hotel/Casino, Las Vegas, Nevada, a Circus Circus Enterprise)*

PITTSBURGH [the home team is capitalized] +7." Since Dallas is favored by 7 points, Pittsburgh would be "getting" 7 points. If you took Dallas and "laid the 7 points," you would be wagering that Dallas would beat Pittsburgh by *more than 7 points*. If you wagered on Pittsburgh, you would be betting that Dallas would not beat Pittsburgh by more than 7 points. Note, you are not betting Pittsburgh to win the game; in fact, you would still win the wager if Pittsburgh *lost* the game but lost by less than 7 points. A parlay ticket would then list additional games in the same manner. The bettor would be required to bet a minimum number of games, usually two or three, and may wager on as many as ten teams or even more. The more teams wagered, the higher the return on the bet. As an example, a ten-team parlay might offer odds of 100:1 or 150:1, compared to 4:1 for a three-team parlay. A parlay wager is won only if all teams cover the pointspread. A ticket with a six-team wager must result in six winners, and many casinos have a policy that ties equate to a no-win. In order to avoid ties, casinos will create ½-point lines (e.g., +3½ points). If a minus sign appears in the pointspread, this means that the team is a favorite and giving away that many points. In our previous example, if Pittsburgh was playing Dallas at Dallas, the game would appear as follows: "Pittsburgh at DALLAS –7." Thus, Dallas would be giving away or "spotting" Pittsburgh 7 points.

In addition to parlay tickets, casinos offer "teaser tickets" and straight bets. A teaser adds or subtracts a large number of points to the pointspread to entice or tease action either way on games; the tradeoff for the bettor is reduced odds or less return than a parlay ticket. Finally, sports books offer straight-bet wagers on individual games, and the normal payoff is 11:10. Unlike with parlay tickets, ties result in a push, with neither the casino nor the bettor winning.

Casinos make money on wagers by charging a commission or vig. Lines are set to ideally create an even distribution of wagers (i.e., half the money on Dallas and half on Pittsburgh), and, under these circumstances, the casino hypothetically cannot be financially hurt. If too much money is being wagered on one side, the casino will lower or raise the line for affected games. Professional gamblers carefully monitor line movements hoping for a "middle" or will shop various sports books looking to "middle a bet." A middle involves the placing of two wagers on the same game when two different lines have been established. In our Pittsburgh versus Dallas example, let's assume that one book establishes Dallas as a 7½-point favorite while another book establishes Dallas as a 9½-point favorite. Actually, a middle may occur at the same book if the line is sufficiently moved. The bettor would take Dallas and lay the 7½ points at one book and then take Pittsburgh (aka "the dog" as in underdog) and the 9½ points at the other book. The player, by placing the bet at the first book, believes that Dallas will win the game by more than 7½ points. The wager at the second book or at the higher line is that Pittsburgh will not lose by more than 9½ points. Remember, by taking Pittsburgh, the player is not betting that Pittsburgh will win. This middle wager is analyzed as follows: The bettor is betting that Dallas will win by more than 7½ points but not by more than 9½ points. If Dallas wins by 8 or 9 points, the bettor has middled the bet and wins both wagers (i.e., the Dallas wager at the first book was covered since Dallas won by more than 7½ points and the Pittsburgh wager at the second book was also won since Dallas did not win by more than 9½ points).

Additional bets at sports books include "money-line," "over-or-under," and "proposition" wagers. A money-line on the Dallas–Pittsburgh game might appear as "Dallas –140" and/or "Pittsburgh +125." The "–140" establishes a ratio between the wager amount required to the payoff if the player wants the favored team. As an example, a bettor would be required to wager $140 in order to win $100. If the plus number is taken, the player would only be required to wager $100 to win $125. Note that there are no points involved with this wager, and the wager is only won if the wagered team wins. Ties are treated as a push. This wager is extremely popular when there is no clearcut favorite in the game or a bettor believes that the dog can upset the favored team.

An over-or-under bet is based on the total points scored in a game. On our Dallas–Pittsburgh game, the book might believe that both teams have strong defenses and will establish a low point total. Players then would simply bet that the total points scored would either be *over* or *under* the total. Over-or-under wagers result in an 11:10 payoff. Baseball over-or-under wagers are based on total runs; hockey games are posted as total goals; basketball is listed as total points.

Proposition wagers (aka side bets or off-the-board bets) are perhaps the most intriguing wagers at a sports book. The book will accept individual propositions on a game, a boxing match, or the like. The following propositions may be established for a heavyweight championship fight:

1. The champion will win by a knockout (2:1).
2. The challenger will win by a knockout (10:1).
3. The fight will not go the distance (i.e., all 15 rounds) (3:1).
4. The fight will go the distance (4:1).

Propositions on the Super Bowl usually include which team will score first, which player will score the first points of the game, the total number of rushing yards for a star running back, and so on.

Sports book wagering caters to a large population base that follows sports as a hobby. Each person is wagering his or her knowledge of a game as superior to the book. If a book believes that too much money is being wagered on a particular game or that the basis for the original line has been changed (e.g., the star quarterback gets hurt and cannot play in the game), the book will "circle" the game and put a limit on additional wagers. "Wise guys" (i.e., smart bettors or those who believe they have inside information) look for advantages in a game and will go as far as checking the weather conditions on game day, believing that one side will have an advantage if there is inclement weather. Many players subscribe to touting services or private oddsmakers who provide "inside" information or statistical analysis on games for a fee. The amount and type of data available through reputable touting services are impressive, including a particular team's historical record against its next opponent; its record at home or on the road; or its record when they play on Monday night before a national television audience. It's easy to see why people who follow sports as a hobby find a great measure of appeal in sports betting . . . they are betting they know the sport better than the casino.

Race Book Wagering

The majority of racetracks feature pari-mutuel wagering on horse races. In pari-mutuel wagering, the winners divide the total amount bet less the house commission. Bettors may place a bet on a single race, betting a horse to come in first (aka win), second (aka place) or third (aka show).

A horse *must* finish first for a payoff on a "win" wager. However, a bettor wins a "place" wager if the horse finishes first or second, and the "show" wager is won if the horse finishes first, second, or third. If a horse is eliminated prior to the start of a race, it is considered a "scratch" and all wagers on that horse are voided.

In addition to wagering on a single horse, also known as a straight wager, race books offer the following combined bets:

1. Daily Double. This is a two-race, parlay wager, which requires the bettor to successfully pick the winner in two consecutive races, usually the first two races of the day at a racetrack. This type of wager pays significantly more than a straight wager but is much more difficult to win.

Race Book Area *(Courtesy of Trump's Castle Casino Resort, Atlantic City)*

2. Exacta Wager. This is a wager on a single race, and the bettor must successfully pick the first- and second-place horse *exactly* in the race.

3. Trifecta Wager. A trifecta is won when a bettor successfully picks the first-, second-, and third-place horses in order in a particular race.

4. Quinella Wager. This is a variation of the exacta bet in that the bettor is attempting to pick the two horses that will finish first and second or second and first in any race offered on the board. One advantage to the bettor in this situation is that although the win and place horses must be correctly selected, they do not have to finish in the order wagered as long as they both finish first and/or second.

POKER

When one thinks of gambling, an image of a poker game comes to mind. This is the ultimate player-to-player challenge. The game combines skill, wagering strategy, nerves, and the ability to bluff under the right circumstances.

Poker is not considered a table game *per se* since players are wagering against each other rather than the casino. Figure 6.3 shows the employees found within this gaming department. Poker is under the supervision of a poker manager who runs the room, maintains the integrity of the game, hires and disciplines employees, has complementary authority, and can initiate investigations into game misconduct by a player or employee. The assistant poker manager and shift managers run the room in the absence of the poker manager. Poker dealers, in addition to dealing the game, may act as a brush-person, one who entices passersby to join the game, or as a shill, an employee who gambles with house money and is not allowed to keep any winnings (as opposed to employees known as proposition players who wager with their own money and can offer raises as well as call bets).

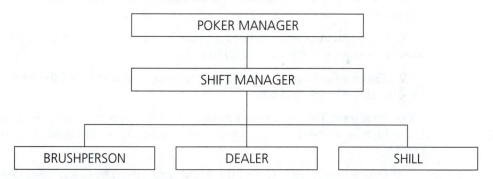

Figure 6.3
Poker Organization Chart

There are numerous forms or styles of poker games. This section will briefly analyze several of the more popular games offered at casinos.

Draw Poker

This is one of the basic forms of poker. Players are dealt five cards and are allowed to discard three of these cards and draw three new cards. Each player is required to put money into a pot (ante), and the pot increases through a series of raises. As one player raises the stakes, other players, looking at their hands, may call or accept the raise and then raise themselves or fold by throwing in their cards. Hands win based on the following combinations, given in rank order:

1. Royal flush. This is the highest hand in poker. A player with a royal flush possesses an ace, king, queen, jack, and 10 all of one suit. In those extraordinary times when two players have a royal flush, a true rarity, then suit rank determines the winner (spades ranks highest, then hearts, followed by diamonds and clubs).

2. Straight flush. A straight flush occurs when a player has five cards in numerical sequence in one suit and the sequence is not 10 through ace. If more than one player has a straight flush, the highest numerical straight flush wins the hand.

3. Four-of-a-kind. Four aces represents the highest four-of-a-kind total, and should there be more than one equally high four-of-a-kind, suit rank determines the winner.

4. Full house. Simply stated, this is three-of-a-kind (e.g., three queens) combined with two-of-a-kind or a pair (e.g., two 9s). This hand is also referred to as a full boat. If there is more than one full house, the highest three-of-a-kind determines the winner, and if these tie, then the highest pair wins.

5. Flush. A flush is five cards all in the same suit, regardless of numerical sequencing.

6. Straight. A player realizes a straight when the five held cards are in numerical sequence but in multiple suits.

7. Three-of-a-kind. As the name suggests, this is three of the same cards: three 7s, three kings, and so on.

6. Two pair. This is two sets of two of a kind; if more than one player has it, the highest numerical pair wins, and if a tie exists, the other pair is compared.

7. One pair. A pair is two of the same cards, such as two queens or two 9s. If more than one player has it, the highest numerical pair wins.

8. No pair. In the event that none of the players has any of the above hands, the winning hand is the hand with the highest ranking card. First the numerical ranking is compared, followed by, in the case of a tie, the suit ranking. The ace of spades outranks the ace of hearts; a 10 is higher numerically than a 9, and so forth. (See Figure 6.4 for the sequence of hands.)

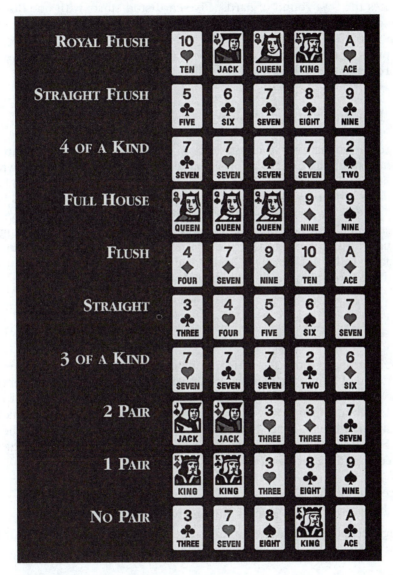

Figure 6.4
Sequence of Hands in Poker (Courtesy of Harvey's Resort Hotel/Casino, Lake Tahoe, Nevada)

Stud Poker

Stud poker has multiple variations, such as five-card or seven-card stud. The number (e.g., "five"-card) indicates the total number of cards dealt per hand. Also, unlike draw poker, players cannot discard and draw cards in stud poker. Stud poker requires an ante, and there is wagering or raises after the dealer distributes the first round of cards. Five-card stud starts with one downcard and the remaining cards dealt face up by the casino dealer. In seven-card stud, the dealer first distributes two downcards and one upcard (aka the "door-card") prior to the betting rounds. Each additional card dealt in seven-card stud is referred to as "fourth street," "fifth street," and so on.

Texas Hold 'Em and Omaha Poker

These poker games involve cards dealt to the players as well as boardcards that can be mutually used to improve hands. Players are dealt two downcards in Texas Hold 'Em, followed by a series of betting rounds. With each betting round, a new boardcard is added. At the end of the hand (aka the "show-down"), players may use both individual cards and three boardcards, one individual card and four boardcards, or may "play the board," disregarding their individual cards in favor of the five boardcards. In Omaha Poker, four cards are initially dealt, all face down, and at the showdown, each player must play two of these cards along with three boardcards.

KENO

The final gaming revenue department of a casino is keno. Basically, this game is a variation of bingo; the keno board contains 80 numbers, and players mark keno tickets trying to predict which of the 80 numbers will appear of the 20 selected numbers per game. Keno, however, is more extensively marketed internally than bingo. Keno boards are found on walls not only in the keno lounge but also in the main casino, restaurants, and casino lounges. The game has three appealing factors for players:

1. Ease of play
2. Low wagering stakes, usually starting with one dollar per game
3. A significant return on investment. A person picking four out of four numbers can win $150 on a one-dollar wager.

In addition to regular keno, casinos offer "way" or combination tickets by which multiple number combinations can be wagered.

Figure 6.5 is the organization chart of employees working in the keno department. This gaming center is headed by an executive known as the keno

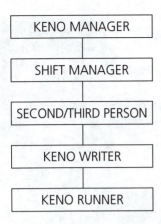

```
┌─────────────────────┐
│    KENO MANAGER     │
└─────────────────────┘
           │
┌─────────────────────┐
│    SHIFT MANAGER    │
└─────────────────────┘
           │
┌─────────────────────┐
│ SECOND/THIRD PERSON │
└─────────────────────┘
           │
┌─────────────────────┐
│    KENO WRITER      │
└─────────────────────┘
           │
┌─────────────────────┐
│    KENO RUNNER      │
└─────────────────────┘
```

Figure 6.5
Keno Organization Chart

manager who reports to the casino manager or shift manager. The keno manager is responsible for staffing the department, ensuring that games are called in an expeditious yet accurate manner, establishing jackpot and payout amounts, and developing external and internal marketing programs as keno promotions. Larger operations may also employ an assistant keno manager but normally rely on shift managers, one per shift, as administrative assistants to the keno manager. Casinos feature a keno lounge where customers can sit and watch the balls being drawn for each game and personally hand their tickets in at the keno counter. Employees working in the keno lounge are sec-

(Courtesy of Harvey's Resort Casino/Hotel, Lake Tahoe)

Dining Area *(Courtesy of Grand Casino Mille Lacs Hinckley, Minnesota)*

ond/third persons, keno writers, and keno runners. The actual game is supervised or run by employees sometimes referred to as second or third persons. They initiate the game, call the selected ball numbers over a microphone, close games, and verify large jackpot winners. Keno writers accept tickets and wagers from customers seated in the keno lounge. They also make payoffs on normal jackpot amounts. Keno runners circulate throughout the entire casino, restaurants, bars, and lounges accepting tickets from customers who want to play keno but choose not to sit in the lounge. Runners accept tickets and wagers from these customers, submit the tickets and wagers to the keno writers, and make payoffs on winning wagers. Computerized keno operations print a list of winning tickets with corresponding jackpot amounts, facilitating the runners' job.

Keno has the same basic appeal as bingo but is a faster-paced game and offers an alternative form of gaming.

 ## SUMMARY

As can be seen, a casino offers multiple gaming alternatives with a wide spectrum of appeal to all styles of gamblers. In addition to gaming departments, many casinos receive revenues from nongaming departments such as restaurants, guestroom rentals, lounges and bars, showrooms, entertainment centers such as bowling alleys and movie theaters, theme parks and rides, kids' arcades, gift and retail shops, lease arrangements with national chains (e.g., McDonald's, TCBY, Burger King), and photo concessions. The Circus Circus Hotel and its other Las Vegas properties, the Luxor and Excalibur Hotels, feature massive arcades to attract families. The Circus Circus Hotel/Casino additionally features live circus acts over the casino, including trapeze artists and highwire acts.

To add to the excitement of gaming, Las Vegas casinos have added other entertainment attractions such as the 33-acre theme park at the MGM Grand Hotel/Casino; Circus Circus's Grand Slam Canyon, a domed indoor theme park; an erupting volcano at the Mirage Hotel/Casino; a pirate ship battle at the Treasure Island Hotel/Casino; an outdoor tropical island setting complete with exotic birds and massive waterfalls at the Tropicana Hotel/Casino; and the new Stratosphere and the $65 million computerized Fremont Street Experience. Las Vegas has also added the New York, New York Casino which duplicates downtown New York City, Hilton's new theme park based on the popular television and movie series "Star Trek," and Bally's duplicate of the city of Paris, complete with a five-story Eiffel Tower. It's no wonder that casino gaming has made the transition into the entertainment field and reached the golden years of prosperity.

   ## DISCUSSION QUESTIONS

1. Describe the organizational structure of a casino's bingo department.

2. What, in your opinion, is the future of bingo departments as a casino revenue center?

3. Describe the organizational structure of a casino's sports and race book department.

4. Define or explain the following sports book terms:

a. Parlay card	**f.** Money line
b. The "vig"	**g.** Over or under bet
c. Dallas +7	**h.** Proposition wager
d. Teaser ticket	**i.** "Circle" game
e. Middle a bet	**j.** "Wise guy"

5. Define or explain the following race book terms:

   a. Pari-mutuel wagering

   b. Place and show wager

   c. Trifecta wager

   d. Quintella wager

   e. Daily double

6. Describe the organizational structure of a casino's poker room.

7. Describe various forms or styles of games offered by a casino poker room.

8. Name three appealing factors offered to patrons for the game of keno.

9. Describe the organizational structure of a casino's keno department.

10. What is the role of a keno runner?

ENDNOTE

1. Joe Marroso, *Race and Sports Books: Theory and Practice*. Clark Community College, Las Vegas, Nevada.

7

CASINO CAGE OPERATIONS

 ## LEARNING OBJECTIVES

This chapter will enable the reader to:

- Discuss reasons why the cashier's cage is referred to as the casino's "nerve center."
- Describe the organizational strategy and structure of a casino cage.
- Identity types of equipment, facilities, and layout typical of a casino cage.
- Discuss contiguous areas of the cage as part of a cage supervisor's accountability.
- Understand duties, responsibilities, and skills required of cage personnel.
- Explain the function of Central Credit Inc.
- Discuss the impact of Title 31 of the Bank Secrecy Act on cage operations.
- Discuss the cycle of bankroll and revenue accountability as an integral part of a system of internal controls.

INTRODUCTION

Where can I cash in chips I have won at the gaming tables? Will the casino cash my personal or payroll check? Can I establish casino credit privileges?

Who takes care of and accounts for all that money that seems to endlessly flow through the casino? For an answer to these questions—and many more—attention in this chapter is focused on the role of the casino (cashier's) cage.

THE CASINO'S "NERVE CENTER"

The cashier's cage is often referred to as a vital "nerve center," the heart or hub of casino operations. On a shift-by-shift, day-by-day basis, it is charged with performance of many vital functions, as follows:

1. Bankroll custodianship and accountability. Bankroll requirements of a casino consist primarily of currency, coinage, and gaming chips, which must be accurately inventoried and closely monitored. Custodianship and accountability of the daily bankroll and revenues generated is vested in the casino cage. One can imagine the extent of documentation and controls required of a cashier's cage in accounting for hundreds of thousands and even millions of dollars on a daily basis!

2. Servicing the casino pit(s). A major function of the cashier's cage is to service the casino pit by: providing table chip fills requested by a gaming supervisor; receiving table chip credits as authorized by a gaming supervisor; processing customer credit instruments (markers or "IOUs") transferred to the cage; supplying and tabulating table game activity; and providing relevant information to casino supervisors to ensure timely communication.

3. Relationship to casino departments. The casino cage interfaces with virtually every revenue and nonrevenue department of the casino. Not only are direct services provided to the gaming pit areas, but cash banks are prepared for issuance to other gaming and nongaming revenue centers (e.g., hotel banks, restaurant and bar banks, and keno, bingo, and sports and race book departments). Daily shift revenues from these various departments are transmitted to the cashier's cage for recording to a daily revenue form prior to preparing funds for a bank deposit. The security department is typically responsible for assigning officers to conduct the transporting of gaming chip fills and credits. The accounting department is the recipient of the voluminous paperwork generated by the cage on a daily basis. The surveillance department monitors cage activities with camera coverage and is responsive to cage requests for reviewing taped transactions occurring in the cage. The slots department utilizes the cashier's cage for issuance of slot fills and hand-paid jackpots as well as for issuing wrapped coins to customers or exchanging customer coins for cash.

4. Documentation of Transactions. The cashier's cage is responsible for preparation of countless forms evidencing revenue generation as well as accurate inventory of the casino's daily bankroll. Implementation of and conformance to sound internal control procedures to ensure the safeguarding of the casino's assets is a serious obligation incumbent upon the cashier's cage.

ORGANIZATIONAL STRATEGY

It is obvious that the duties and functions of the cashier's cage require a highly qualified and competent staff in the performance of assigned duties. Staffing is a logical consequence of an organizational strategy manifested by an organization chart. When determining the organizational plan for the cashier's cage, attention might be directed to a study conducted by the Nevada Society of Certified Public Accountants resulting in the following recommendation:

"In regards to the segregation of functions and duties, the committee recommends that *organization* of the accounting and *cashiering functions* should be aimed at preventing the fraudulent conversion or substitution of casino assets. As a general rule, responsibility for accounting for assets should be vested in the accounting department, while responsibility for the *custodianship* of these assets should remain with the *cashier's office*. Furthermore, the assets controlled by one group should be physically separated from those controlled by another, and appropriate accounting records should be maintained to show each group's accountability."

The casino management team develops the organization chart for the cashier's cage that will best serve its operational needs. As with all organizational strategies, responsibilities are identified and communicated and authority is entrusted, and performance accountability is an expected outcome. Figure 7.1 depicts an organization chart structure for a large casino.

Typical Structure for a Large Casino

Note the role of the chief financial officer/controller as supervisory authority over the cage manager and responsible for the establishment of adequate cashier cage internal controls that are in compliance with the state's gaming regulations. The cage manager thus reports to the CFO/controller and is accountable for the cage bankroll, hiring and terminating cage personnel, as well as ensuring effective daily operations of the cage.

In conformance with a basic principle of internal controls regarding separation of duties, the functions of casino credit and collections are assigned individually to a credit manager and a collection manager. While both individuals report to the cage manager, the credit manager exercises responsibility for customer credit approval while the collection manager is responsible for the collection of outstanding customer obligations. Implicit in these responsibilities is the tenet that the individual who authorizes customer credit privileges must not be the same person collecting the debt.

Note further that the coin room manager who supervises the hard-count team also reports directly to the cage manager rather than the slot manager. Key duties of the coin room manager are supervision of the slot drop and count as well as exercising control over uncounted coinage during the drop.

Staffing the cashier's cage necessitates appointment of shift managers or supervisors who perform the duties and responsibilities of the cage manager

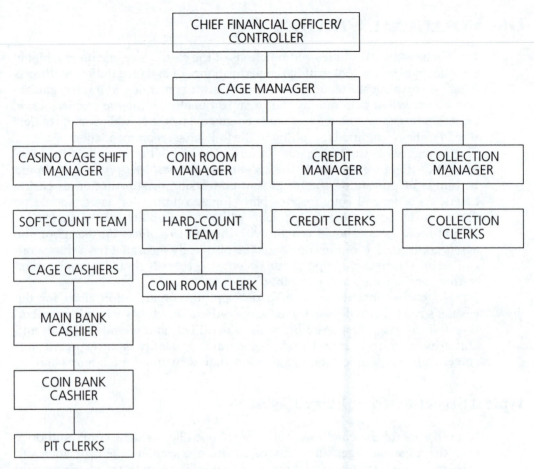

Figure 7.1
Casino Cage Organization Chart

in his or her absence, including responsibility for the physical custodial control of all assets held in the cashier's cage during the assigned shift. Personnel typically reporting to the cage shift supervisor include "front-line" cage (window) cashiers, the main bank/vault cashier, the coin bank cashier, the soft-count team supervisor, pit clerks, and if utilized, fill and credit bankers.

Once an organization plan has been determined and job descriptions written, attention now turns to the physical location of the cashier's cage on the casino floor, equipment requirements, and cage security.

STRUCTURE OF THE CASINO CAGE

Size of the casino, proximity to "live" table games, and customer access are certainly considerations in floor planning the cashier's cage. As casinos increase in size, satellite cages are constructed to facilitate requirements of the main cage. Historically, the main cashier's cage is located toward the rear of the casino and away from entrance and exit doors. Imagine the temptation facing a customer who has "cashed out" at the window, walking past gaming tables and rows of slot machines to indulge in "one more hand" or "one last play" at the tables or machines! A number of structural possibilities exist. A small casino might possibly offer two customer windows and one employee window, requiring window cashiers to engage in a great variety of transactions. Large casinos are more specialized, with cashiers assigned specific responsibilities of conducting customer transactions, such as check cashing, exchanging gaming chips for currency, issuing and receiving revenue banks, preparing table gaming fills or receiving table game chip credits, conducting customer credit transactions (Markers/"IOUs"), and completing myriads of paper (computer) transactions related to the revenue cycle.

Some cages utilize metal bars or shatterproof plexiglass windows separating customers from cashiers, while other cage designs are "open"—offering a wide, unprotected counter area from which customer and employee transactions are conducted. The use of protective barriers in the cage and manned security booths in close proximity to the cage is obviously intended as a deterrent to cage robberies.

Cage Robberies

For many years, Nevada gaming operators functioned with the perception that a cage robbery was highly unlikely. Believing in the deterrent effect of the presence of a large security staff and total casino surveillance coverage and that no individual(s) would be so rash (owners in the decades of the 1940s through 1960s had their own methods of meting out punishment), as well as in line with new, sophisticated casino decor and ambiance, casino operators began removing protective cage bars. However, during the mid-1990s, Las Vegas casinos became the targets of a series of cage robberies. These incidents caused casino management to revitalize security policy and procedures, and in some casinos, protective cage bars began to reappear. Since casinos are provided with adequate insurance coverage and no longer utilize armed, uniformed security officers, a basic mandate to cage personnel is not to jeopardize lives should an attempt to rob the cage occur.

Accessibility

Entrance to the cage interior must not only provide maximum protection but be limited to authorized personnel. An electronic door entry system is often used, activated by a cashier from inside the cage or a security officer located in a booth outside the cage. Entrance at other casinos may require displaying an identification badge to a surveillance camera; upon verification of that individual's identity, a surveillance operator activates the electronic mechanism for entry. Nevada State Gaming Regulations strictly prohibit "secret" entrance or exit doors. A standard policy should require a security officer to escort unauthorized personnel into and out of the cage. Unauthorized personnel include equipment repair representatives, service personnel, VIP guests being toured through the facility, consultants retained by the casino, or independent gaming inspectors.

Cage Facilities and Equipment

A first-time visitor to a modern casino cage will be immediately impressed with the array of computer terminals, business machines, cabinetry, safe deposit boxes, and the staff efficiency necessary to operate this nerve center twenty-four hours a day, seven days a week. Following is an overview of the layout, facilities, and types of equipment typically found within a casino cage.

Computer Terminals. Computer technology has impacted daily operations in large and small casino cages, requiring cage personnel to possess requisite computer skills. Requests for gaming chip fills or credits can be initiated with terminals located in the pit areas linked directly to the casino cage. Instantaneous customer credit information can be accessed through Central Credit Inc. databases. Documentation relating to table game activity (e.g., table opener and closer figures, fills, credits, and marker transactions) are electronically recorded to a master game report form. Obviously, the adoption of high-tech computers has dramatically improved the speed and accuracy of casino cages while allowing cage managers to become more effective decision makers.

Alarm Systems. Silent alarm systems located at window cashier stations, when activated, can be detected at the casino security office, in the surveillance room, and by local police. Cashiers must be familiar with policies and procedures to be followed should these alarms be activated.

Surveillance Cameras. Fixed and pan-tilt-zoom (PTZ) cameras are mounted in strategic locations within the cage, with monitoring conducted by the surveillance department. In addition to camera coverage of all transactions conducted between cashiers and patrons, all fills and credits are viewed and videotaped by a fixed or dedicated camera activated by a motion-sensitive switching mechanism. An obvious purpose of this intensive surveillance is protection of the cage assets and to investigate any suspected wrongdoing on the part of cage personnel. Reviewing videotapes also provides assistance to the cage in locating errors that may have occurred resulting in shortages or overages.

Safe Deposit Boxes. Casino patrons wishing to safeguard personal valuables are directed to the cashier's cage where the customer is requested to complete and sign a data form. Two keys are required to access the box—one given to the customer and the other retained by the cage—and *both* keys are required to remove the box from safe deposit. The customer may be charged a key deposit, which is refunded at the time of the key's return. Should the customer lose the key, the safe deposit door lock must be drilled, since the cage key alone will not open the door lock. Strict procedures are required by cashiers for customer identification and data form signatures.

Keyboard or Panel. Strict controls must be utilized and enforced in issuance and retrieval of keys allowing access to sensitive equipment, devices, and rooms. Typically, the cage is entrusted with this responsibility. Cage personnel maintain a written log sheet, located in a locked panel box within the cage interior, to document movement of keys to authorized requestors.

Fill/Credit Slip Dispensing Machine. As stated previously, many casinos utilize computer-generated fill/credit forms transmitted directly from the pit to the cage. Lacking this type of system—or in the event of computer failure—a lockbox dispensing machine requiring hand-written fill/credit forms is used. For example, Nevada Gaming Regulations stipulate, "All fill and credit slips shall be serially numbered in forms prescribed by the Board [Nevada Gaming Control Board], and shall be purchased in triplicate in a continuous series utilizing the alphabet, so that no gaming establishment may ever utilize the same number or series—which series must be inserted in a consecutive order *in a machine* that permits the original and duplicate to be utilized by the establishment in accordance with the detailed rules for each type of slip set forth hereafter, and will only permit the third copy to be retained intact in a continuous unbroken form."

Time and Date Stamp Machine. Should transactions or documents require investigation, a basic audit technique is to understand when the transaction occurred. Consequently, cage procedures require the insertion of fill/credit slips, customer checks, markers, documents, and the like into a machine that imprints the date and time of the transaction. A cage axiom states: "If in doubt, date and time stamp it."

Jet Sorters. Customers wishing to cash in coins or gaming tokens dispensed by a slot machine are normally served by change booths located throughout the casino. However, as a further customer service, as well as to assist the slots department, the casino cage may also provide coin-cashing services. Cups of coins offered by the customer are "dumped" into the jet sort, and upon activation, the machine sorts and counts the coins and registers a clearly visible dollar amount for payment.

Adding Machines/Calculators. The volume of forms and reports requiring completion by cage personnel requires skill, proficiency, and accuracy in working with these devices.

Phone Systems. Wall-mounted or desktop phones are standard equipment items. Systems are designed so that by simply lifting the receiver and pushing a designated number, the caller is immediately connected with the needed casino supervisor or executive.

Work Counters. To facilitate the work routine, wall or self-standing counters are located to the sides and/or rear of the cage and away from cashier or service windows.

Storage Cabinets. Above and below work counters or on wall areas are located locked storage cabinets for supplies, forms, documents, reserve gaming chips, and other items entrusted to cage personnel for storage and retrieval.

Miscellaneous. Currency (vacuum) counters, check encoders, counterfeit currency detectors, microfilm machines, word processors, and many more items of equipment are standard items to be found in the modern casino cage.

OTHER CAGE AREAS

Certain areas or rooms, although not included as part of the "main cage," fall under the supervision or accountability of the cage manager/cage shift supervisor. Figure 7.1 indicates a line of supervision to the main bank cashier, soft-count team, and hard-count team. Since these positions are involved in the casino's daily revenue cycle, a further review of these functions is necessary.

The Main Bank (Vault)

Supervised by a main bank (vault) cashier, this entity is responsible for custodianship and accountability of the casino bankroll. The main bank issues all window cashier banks and casino revenue banks, as well as receiving all shift ending revenues. In essence, the main bank serves as a conduit for the casino bankroll and is responsible for balancing all inventories entrusted to its care and completing requisite revenue forms attesting to proper safeguarding and reporting of assets. Main bank functions may be conducted within the main cage, but the integrity of assigned responsibilities must be separated from the activities of other cage personnel.

The Soft-Count Room

At the completion of each casino shift, gaming table drop boxes are unlocked from the tables, placed on a portable, secured cart, and directly transported to the highly secured soft-count room. This process is conducted by a minimum of three designated individuals conforming to strict internal control procedures. Casinos utilizing slot machine currency acceptors will designate time of removal and procedures for removing these devices for transport to the soft-count room as well. Access to the soft-count room is highly restricted and monitored by the surveillance department. At a time prescribed by the casino's system of internal controls, the soft-count team enters the room, and under surveillance monitoring, begins and completes the process known as the "soft drop." Each table drop box is opened and its contents emptied on the surface of a clear plexiglass table. The team, each with a specific assignment, proceeds to sort, count, and record the drop box contents to a form known as the Master Game Report form or "Stiff Sheet." When the contents of all boxes, from all three shifts, have been recorded and money verified, contents of the currency acceptor boxes are also counted, verified, and recorded to a Slot Currency Report form. Upon completion of the soft drop, the main bank or vault supervisor is notified. Entering the soft-count room, the supervisor reverifies all funds and accepts the funds into the main bank inventory, after signing required documentation.

The Hard-Count Room

Coins and tokens are removed from slot machine buckets at a prescribed time designated by the casino's system of internal controls in a process known as the "hard drop." Coins and tokens removed from slot cabinets are loaded on portable carts by the hard-count team (a minimum of three individuals) and transported to a designated hard-count room. As with the soft-count room, entry to the hard-count room is strictly limited and monitored by surveillance cameras. The hard-count team sorts, wraps, verifies, and records all coins and tokens. After canning or racking coins and tokens, the coin room manager receives, signs for, and accepts the coinage into coin room inventory, after which resultant accounting procedures accept the coinage into main bank accountability.

CAGE CASHIERING

All casino cage employees, whether assigned as window cashiers, fill/credit bankers, or vault cashiers, must be skilled and proficient in handling gaming chips and currency.

Gaming Chips

Nevada Gaming Regulations define gaming chips as being "representative of value used by casinos in gaming play which may be exchanged by a gaming patron for cash in the amount stated on the chips in accord with the rules of the casino." Casinos utilize various chip denominations ranging in value from $1 to $1,000. Nevada Gaming Regulatory agencies require casinos to submit chip designs, colors, and logos for regulatory approval. Once approved, the casino proceeds to have the chips manufactured and receive them for inclusion to bankroll accountability.

Assume that a casino will use gaming chip denominations and colors indicated in the chart below:

Color*	Chip Value
Pink	25¢
Gray	$1
Red	$5
Green	$25
Black	$100
White	$500
Gold	$1,000

*Colors represented in this chart do not represent a standard color scheme used by the casino industry. However, it seems that casinos uniformly utilize red for $5 chips, green for $25 chips, and black for $100 chips.

Racks and Rack Values

Gaming chips are stored in cage inventory in plastic racks subdivided into five trays (tubes or stacks) containing 20 chips each. Thus, a full rack of chips always contains 100 chips. The following chart illustrates the value of a stack and rack of chips:

Color	Chip Value	Value per Stack	Value per Rack
Pink	25¢	$ 5	$ 25
Gray	$1	20	100
Red	$5	100	500
Green	$25	500	2,500
Black	$100	2,000	10,000
White	$500	10,000	50,000
Gold	$1,000	20,000	100,000

Chip Cutting

When conducting chip transactions or recording chip values to cage inventory reports, a cage employee must demonstrate skill and accuracy in the performance of these tasks. A great deal of practice is required to master techniques of "sizing" and "cutting" stacks of chips. Remembering that one stack of gaming chips always contains 20 chips, two basic rules may be helpful:

1. For chip denominations of $1, $5, $100, and $1,000: Cut five chips out of the stack and make four cuts.

$1 chips: Cut 5 chips = $5 value × 4 cuts = $20 stack

$5 chips: Cut 5 chips = 25 value × 4 cuts = 100 stack

$100 chips: Cut 5 chips = 500 value × 4 cuts = 2,000 stack

$1,000 chips: Cut 5 chips = 5,000 value × 4 cuts = 5,000 stack

2. For chip denominations of 25¢, $25, and $500: Cut four chips out of the stack and make five cuts.

25¢ chips: Cut 4 chips = $1 value × 5 cuts = $5 stack

$25 chips: Cut 4 chips = 100 value × 5 cuts = 500 stack

$500 chips: Cut 4 chips = 2,000 value × 5 cuts = 10,000 stack

Currency

Cage cashiers are responsible for handling thousands of dollars in currency during the course of a working shift. Responsibilities typically include: operating a window cash bank containing various currency denominations; receiving gaming chips from customers in exchange for currency; cashing personal and payroll checks and travelers checks; receiving payment on customer markers; and preparing currency for recording to window bank check-out forms or to the main bank inventory form. These job requirements necessitate knowledge of "clips" and "straps" of currency.

Clipped and Strapped Currency

Currency is "clipped" and "strapped" by denominational value. For example, 25 one-dollar bills make a clip, and strapping four clips together results in a strap value of $100. (Note: A "clip" refers to a paper clip inserted over the left-hand corner of the bills. A "strap" is a paper currency strap sealed around the money. Cage policy requires cashiers who strap currency to initial and date the strap.)

The following chart illustrates clip and strap values:

Denomination Amount	# of Bills Clipped	Clip Value	# of Clips to a Strap	Strap Value
$1	25	$ 25	4	$ 100
$5	20	100	5	500
$10	25	250	4	1,000
$20	25	500	4	2,000
$50	20	1,000	2	2,000
$100	25	2,500	2	5,000

CUSTOMER CREDIT PRIVILEGES

Casinos in Nevada and Atlantic City extend millions of dollars of gaming credit to patrons, which, in turn, necessitates stringent credit and collection procedures. Nevada State Gaming Regulations define a "marker" or "IOU" as "a form evidencing that a patron has received gambling credit from the establishment." To assist casino credit managers, collection managers, and cage managers in the burdensome task of customer credit, many casinos throughout the world utilize the services of Central Credit Inc.

Central Credit Inc.

Central Credit Inc., located in Las Vegas, Nevada, has been gathering and distributing gaming credit information for the international gaming industry since 1956. The company has positioned itself as the world leader in storage and retrieval of credit information, utilizing a database in excess of 3 million patrons and 90,000 companies. Casinos offering check-cashing and gaming credit privileges to its customers are equipped with a computer-to-computer network providing instant transmittal, and updating of information.

As subscribers to Central Credit Inc., casino cages and credit/collection offices are offered services including, but not limited to, the following:

1. **Gaming credit reports.** These are comprised of information previously recorded from other casinos and gaming establishments, including: date of application, limit requested or granted, last action, highest action, bank ratings, last inquiry (date and type), outstanding receivables, discrediting information, paid items, customer status.

2. **Daily reports.** These contain notices of gaming returns and paid items of those individuals established with the casino. This report may additionally contain: reports of lost or stolen travelers checks; chip information; warnings on lost, stolen, or abused credit cards; alerts from banks, law enforcement agencies, and other subscribers.

3. **Collection manager's report.** This provides the casino with an edited report on customers who have negative credit/check-cashing information. Central Credit's database continues to monitor these customers and generates a report with any new activity.

4. **List processing.** This allows casinos who are inviting players to the property to receive a report on the credit status of each individual prior to arrival.

5. **Registration of returned items and payments.** Returned items, including paid items and write-offs, are reported by subscribers, allowing this information to be logged into Central Credit's database. This cooperative reporting protects subscribers from cashing further checks and provides daily updating of patron accounts.

6. Travelers check information. The database stores up-to-date reports of lost and stolen travelers checks and allows cashiers to process customer checks through the system for verification.

7. Chip description. Central Credit provides information concerning the description and status (as reported) of gaming chips used by its Nevada subscribers. The information consists of individual denomination descriptions and holds or warnings reported by the proprietary casino.

8. Check cashing information. Through its Cash-No-Card and Check Guarantee options, the risk of customer personal check cashing is reduced. Accessing the system allows cashiers to determine where checks were previously presented, including the date, time, amount, and whether the check was cashed or turned down.

TITLE 31 OF THE BANK SECRECY ACT

In 1985, the U.S. Treasury Department ruled that casinos fall under the definition of a financial institution, thus extending the Bank Secrecy Act of 1970 to include casinos. Consequently, casinos in Nevada, Atlantic City, and Puerto Rico were subject to reporting certain cash transactions required by Title 31 of the Bank Secrecy Act under the following definition: "Each casino shall file a report of each deposit, withdrawal, or exchange of currency, gambling tokens or chips, or other payment or transfer, by, through, or to such casino which involves a transaction in currency of more than $10,000." Interpretation of this act includes coverage of multiple currency transactions which "shall be treated as a single transaction if a casino has knowledge that they are by or on behalf of any person and result in either cash in or cash out totaling more than $10,000 during any twenty-four period."

The enactment of this legislation was intended primarily as a means of preventing money laundering and now required casinos, like banks, to report the identities of individuals making cash transactions of more than $10,000. Casinos in Atlantic City and Puerto Rico immediately complied with the act by reporting all requirements directly to the Treasury Department. However, Nevada gaming operators, fearing direct involvement by the federal government into Nevada gaming, sought an exemption to the act. As a result of extensive negotiations with the Treasury Department, Nevada was successful in obtaining the sought-after exemption. Regulation 6-A, a self-regulation model, was written for the Nevada gaming industry and accepted by the Treasury Department. Enforcement of Regulation 6-A was entrusted to the Nevada State Gaming Control Board, with copies of all reports forwarded to the Treasury Department.

Failure to comply with the Bank Secrecy Act can result in severe penalties including fines, imposition of prison terms on the people involved, and revocation of the casino's license. Since its enactment in 1985, casinos in Nevada and Atlantic City have been fined several millions of dollars—not as a result of attempted money laundering but largely because of human error and inadequate training of casino cashiers. Regulatory agencies of each state have authority to levy fines for noncompliance.

Compliance requirements and rules of the Bank Secrecy Act and Nevada's Regulation 6-A are complicated and require intensive training on the part of casino cashiers to avoid violations. Basically, cashiers must be versed in two types of transactions: prohibited and reportable.

The following transactions, per Nevada Regulations 6-A, are strictly *prohibited*:

- Cash-for-cash exchange with a patron, or on behalf of a patron, where the exchange involves more than $2,500.
- Issuance of a check (or other negotiable instrument) for cash to a patron in excess of $2,500. The one exception would be issuance of a check for casino winnings (e.g., a patron winning a large slot jackpot could be issued cash or a check for his or her winnings).
- Issuance of a check or wire transfer for winnings to a third party. (The issued check or wire transfer must be in the name of the third party.)

Reportable transactions are those that are legal but require cashiers to complete complex reports, and typically involve transactions in amounts over $10,000. Nevada cashiers, for example, must be knowledgable in completing Currency Transactions reports, Currency Transaction Incident reports, and Multiple Transaction Logs. A review of Nevada's Gaming Regulations 6.030, 6.040, and 6.050 will be helpful in emphasizing not only the complexity but also the basic requirements of the regulation. Specific concerns of reporting requirements by cashier's cages include:

- Sale of more than $10,000 in chips for cash in a single transaction.
- Redeeming more than $10,000 in chips for cash, in a single transaction, that were not won or wagered.
- Accepting more than $10,000 in cash as front money or for safekeeping.
- Accepting more than $10,000 in cash as payment on markers.
- Any receipt or disbursement of more than $10,000 in cash not specifically covered.
- Redeeming of more than $1,000 worth of another casino's chips for cash.
- Cash payoff when a player wins on a wager of more than $10,000 (in chips or cash).
- Redeeming more than $10,000 in chips or cash that was won or wagered.

BANKROLL AND REVENUE ACCOUNTABILITY

Casino gaming is a cash-intensive business requiring strict adherence to casino cage procedures and controls. A gaming licensee's system of internal controls is designed to achieve the following objectives:

- Safeguarding of assets
- Reliability of financial records
- Execution and recording of transactions in accordance with casino policies
- Access to assets only in accordance with casino policies
- Records complete and sufficiently accurate to permit periodic comparisons of assets on-hand versus book value.

The above objectives are manifested in procedures utilized by the cashier's cage to effectuate bankroll and revenue accountability. It is beyond the scope of this chapter to provide detailed methodology. However, an overview of three important documents will provide the reader an insight to the process.

The Master Game Report

Nevada Gaming Regulations define the Master Game Report as "a form which includes for the shift opening and closing chip inventories and fills and credits." This form, also known as the "Game Sheet," "Hard Sheet," or "Stiff Sheet," serves several purposes:

1. As a control document, it accounts for all gaming fill and credit transactions as well as table opening and closing inventories for each casino shift.
2. It is used by the soft-count audit team in calculating table and shift gaming results (win or loss).
3. It is a source document for the accounting department for preparation of the daily management report.
4. It is relied upon by internal and external auditors in determining proper recording and documentation of table revenue.

Although the format of the Master Game Report may vary among casinos, a common formula is utilized:

Table opening inventory
+ Table chip fills
– Table chip credits
– Name credits (markers/IOUs)
– Soft drop
= Table inventory accountability
– Table closing inventory
= Net game results (win/loss)

The process to initiate and complete the Master Game Report may be summarized as follows:

1. The pit supervisor records the opening shift table gaming chip inventory to a table opener/closer document. Table fills and credits made during the shift as well as table closing inventory are also recorded to support documents. Copies of all documents are inserted in appropriate table drop boxes, and copies of all documents are routed to the cashier's cage for recordation to the Master Game Report. Utilization of a computer terminal in the pit allows the supervisor or pit clerk to directly input transactions to the terminal, which electronically records all entries to the Master Game Report for retrieval by the cashier's cage.

2. All copies of support documents are retained by the cage, and in absence of a computer system, the transactions as recorded on the support documents are entered, in ink, on the Master Game Report.

3. At the time scheduled for the soft-count audit, the soft-count team obtains the Master Game Report from the cashier's cage, along with all support documents. In the soft-count room, the team opens table drop boxes, recovers copies of documents in the drop boxes, compares all entries recorded by the cage to the report form, records the soft drop to the report form, and compares table results.

4. At the conclusion of the soft-count audit, all Master Game Report forms along with support documents are routed to the accounting office.

5. The main bank or vault supervisor receives and verifies the soft drop from the soft-count team and accepts and records these funds to the casino bankroll.

Main Bank Inventory Form

The Main Bank Inventory form serves several important purposes:

1. It indicates the actual amount of cage inventory (i.e., currency, chips, coin, markers, customers' checks, etc.) at the start and the completion of a shift.

2. It serves to transfer inventory accountability from one shift to the next succeeding shift. In other words, the ending inventory of one shift automatically becomes the opening inventory for the next shift.

3. It provides details of every inventory category entrusted to cage custodianship.

Casino Revenue Summary Form

All revenue and expense transactions handled by the cage for the graveyard, day, and swing shift (i.e., the *business cycle*) are summarized on the casino Revenue Summary form. This form serves the following report functions:

1. It summarizes all revenue and expense transactions occurring during the daily cycle.

2. It supports the accuracy of the cage inventory as reported on the Main Bank Inventory form. For example, the Revenue Summary reports the daily bankroll beginning balance, adds all daily revenues, subtracts all daily expenses, and arrives at an ending bankroll control figure, which is the *expected* amount of the cage bankroll. This expected balance is compared to the total of the Main Bank Inventory amount—the *actual* bankroll—and, optimally, the two figures agree. Disparity between the two amounts is carried as an inventory overage or shortage.

3. As a transmittal document, it is used by the accounting department for recording daily revenues and expenses to the journals.

4. As a control document, it monitors transactions affecting bankroll increases or decreases.

 ## SUMMARY

In the introduction to this chapter, the casino cage is described as the financial nerve center for casino gaming transactions. Not only does the cage play a vital role, but the application of internal controls is especially essential to this entity. Additionally, it should be evident that proper cage procedures require a systematic approach based upon forms utilization, signatory controls and authorization, and separation of functions and duties—all of which lead to an easily tracked audit trail and solid internal controls. The cage is an extension of the financial controller's office and shares fiduciary responsibility for maintaining the financial well-being of the operations. Therefore, a systematic approach to cage operations is not only important, it is imperative if the business is to be successful.

 ## DISCUSSION QUESTIONS

1. Explain why the cashier's cage is referred to as the "nerve center" or "heart" of the casino.
2. Describe the organizational structure of a casino cage.
3. Where is the casino cage typically located and why?
4. What control procedures or policies would you recommend as a defense against cage robberies?
5. Discuss the importance of surveillance camera coverage in a casino cage.
6. What is the function of a fill/credit dispensing machine?
7. What purpose is served by a cage's main bank or vault?

8. Explain the purpose of the soft-count and hard-count rooms.

9. As a casino cage manager, what skills or proficiencies would you require of a window cashier?

10. Explain why extending gaming credit to a casino patron is considered a privilege.

11. What role does Central Credit Inc. play within the gaming industry?

12. What impact did the enactment of Title 31 of the Bank Secrecy Act have on the gaming industry?

13. Identify three major report forms used in a casino revenue cycle to effectuate bankroll and revenue accountability.

8

THE SECURITY AND SURVEILLANCE DEPARTMENTS

 ## LEARNING OBJECTIVES

This chapter will enable the reader to:

- Describe the organizational structure of a casino security department.
- Explain the duties and responsibilities of security department personnel.
- Discuss attributes and skills that contribute to effective daily operation of a security department.
- Describe the organizational structure of a casino surveillance department.
- List the functions required of a surveillance department.

INTRODUCTION

"Player down on BJ6". . . "Unruly player disturbing customers on Craps 1". . . "Monitor customer play on BJ1". . . "Slot player needs to be 86ed. . . ." To the novice, these phrases may sound strange, but to personnel in the security and surveillance departments, they are the language and directives that are integral to the efficient operation of these key components of a casino.

This chapter examines the role of a casino's security and surveillance departments. Succinctly stated, these areas are responsible for protecting the casino's assets, upholding the integrity of the operation through effective law and order, assuring compliance with gaming regulations, and maintaining a safe environment for guests and employees.

THE SECURITY DEPARTMENT

The word "security" implies a safe or secure feeling, and in essence, this is the overall mission of the security department. Safety and security have multiple applications and can become a complex assignment for a casino. Therefore, the organizational structure and procedures established for the security department often determine its measure of success and effectiveness. Figure 8.1 depicts the organization chart for a typical casino security department.

Director of Security

Depending on the operation's size, the director of security may have an assistant director(s), and the ranks of captain, lieutenant, and sergeant may be utilized based on departmental responsibilities.

The director of security reports to the general manager or, in some cases, the casino manager. This person is responsible for the administration of the security department and ensures that it operates in accordance with approved policies and procedures. The director determines departmental staffing and employment requirements, including firearms proficiency, customer relations skills, and knowledge of police/security procedures; establishes or approves shift schedules and assignments; creates or maintains departmental training requirements, including safety adherence programs and emergency/crisis management procedures; carries out the role of security in internal control procedures; assumes the legal authority of the security department both with

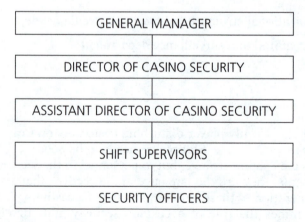

Figure 8.1
Security Department Organization Chart

customers and employees; carries out procedures for criminal background investigations of job applicants and for safeguarding this information once secured; and carries out procedures by which the casino interacts with city, county, state, and federal police agencies.

Shift Supervisors

Security shift supervisors report to the director of security or the assistant director if one has been appointed, and are responsible for directing security activities on their respective shifts. As the director of security focuses more on administration, shift supervisors are primarily involved in the operations portion of the security department. Operational duties include establishing roving patrols of security officers to ensure the safety to guests; overseeing officers' involvement with the casino internal control procedures; providing a safe work environment for employees; keeping a vigilant eye for safety hazards and unsanitary working conditions; preventing guests who are intoxicated from creating a public nuisance; and ensuring a drug-free casino environment.

Security Officers

Security officers are analogous to a city's police force and in many ways perform similar functions. A qualified security officer must not only possess the technical job qualifications (familiarity with firearms, detention and apprehension techniques, etc.), he or she must also serve as a public relations representative for the casino. Perhaps more than any other employees, security officers are engaged by guests seeking assistance, directions, or general information about the property. Therefore, security personnel must possess excellent communication and customer service skills. Recently, several casinos have chosen not to have their indoor security officers wear the traditional police uniform or carry a weapon, opting instead for a more business-style appearance (i.e., suit coats or blazers). Philosophically, this removes the appearance of an armed police force, which can be somewhat disconcerting to some guests.

A list of duties for security personnel includes:

1. Maintaining law and order in the casino, including apprehending lawbreakers or those involved in criminal activities.
2. Ensuring that safety and emergency procedures and policies are intact, and reporting any unusual occurrences to the shift supervisor.
3. Escorting cash transfers from the casino to the cage, and escorting guests who have won considerable sums of money to their car, airport, etc.
4. Assisting the casino cage and pit in transferring table chip fills and credits.
5. Removing drop boxes from table pit games and delivering them to the casino cage where they are placed in a secured area for the soft-count team.

6. Replacing removed drop boxes from table games.

7. Guarding the casino cage and preventing robberies or assaults of cage personnel and other secured assets.

8. Acting as public relations representatives for the casino by assisting guests with questions.

9. Providing emergency medical assistance and treatment (i.e., CPR) to guests and employees in distress.

10. Assisting the slot department by witnessing the replenishment of slot booth bankrolls, hand-paying large jackpots won by slot players, performing slot machine hopper fills, and assisting with the slot drop.

11. Controlling or preventing access to restricted or sensitive areas of the casino, including the casino cage, hard-count room, the time office, loading/shipping/receiving dock, guestrooms, food and liquor warehouses, and administrative and executive offices.

12. Maintaining the masterkeys for the casino and ensuring that no authorized persons have access to these keys.

13. Conducting the duties of timekeeping in the time office for casino workers, including monitoring punch-in procedures and issuing payroll checks to employees.

14. Escorting employees to parking areas, especially during the nighttime.

15. Assisting local police authorities investigating criminal activities.

16. Visually checking to make sure no minors are engaged in gaming activities in the casino.

17. Preventing youths from loitering in or around the casino.

18. Ensuring that the casino's "Serving Alcohol With Care" program is being followed by bartenders and cocktail servers, and preventing guests who are "under the influence" from driving.

19. Maintaining crowd control, including emergency evacuation procedures in the event of fires, bomb threats, robberies, acts of God, or other such crisis situations.

20. Directing vehicular traffic onto and off the casino property so as to prevent accidents and traffic jams, and citing violations of city or county traffic laws, including misuse of fire lane access and disabled parking.

21. Ensuring observance of county, city, state, and federal codes or laws, including fire laws and building codes.

22. Remaining familiar with the department's security manual, which outlines procedures for handling fire emergencies, building evacuations, holdups and robberies, deaths on the property, accidents, conditions resulting from natural disasters, elevator emergencies, power outages, casino camera outages, threats from terrorists, and medical emergencies.

23. Conducting inspections of employee lockers and package or purse checks as employees exit the property via the time office.

Finally, the security department in a casino faces several special customer service challenges: Not only may they be required to handle intoxicated or unruly guests, but this situation may be compounded if the guest is irate over losing a wager or money to the casino. Hence, tactfulness and proper emotional restraint play a significant part in the attitudinal profile of security officers. Add to this the fact that we are living in an extremely litigious society, and the security department is faced with the potential of being sued for excessive or unreasonable force used by one of its officers in apprehending or detaining an individual guilty of trespassing or similar type of activity. Additionally, the failure of the security department to properly conduct criminal background investigations on job applicants can lead to negligent hiring lawsuits. If a casino fails to demonstrate ordinary care in doing a background check on a new employee who has a criminal record (e.g., a history of assault convictions) and this employee assaults a guest or coworker, the casino could be sued for negligence in its hiring procedures.

Besides negligent hiring, casinos face another form of litigation which can be based on poor security procedures. Let's assume that a security officer detects a casino worker who is under the influence of alcohol and, as a favor to the employee, decides not to the report the incident as is normal procedure. Two nights later, the security officer discovers that the same employee is intoxicated on the job again, and after listening to the employee admit that he has a drinking problem, decides to give the employee "one more chance" on the promise that the employee will not report to work intoxicated in the future. In our scenario, the employee does report to work drunk and, due to his condition, seriously injures a guest. If an attorney representing the guest discovers that the casino knew the employee had a drinking problem and condoned it, the casino could be sued for negligently retaining the employee. Negligent hiring and retention judgments have cost businesses millions of dollars. A security officer who is unaware of the law or fails to follow established procedures can be the cause of such a lawsuit.

THE SURVEILLANCE DEPARTMENT

In examining the surveillance or "eye-in-the-sky" organizational structure, the first observation is that this department, contrary to expectation, does *not* report to the casino manager. Figure 8.2 depicts the organizational structure of a casino surveillance department indicating a reporting line of the Director of Surveillance to the General Manager. Figure 8.3 indicates the reporting responsibility of the surveillance department directly to the Tribal Gaming Commission. Rather, the surveillance department acts as a check and balance on the casino. The other control mechanism on the casino is internal audit, which reports directly to the chief financial officer or the casino controller. Allowing the casino manager to have authority over either of these departments invites potential cases of collusion, and a separation of authority and power represents sound and effective internal control procedures.

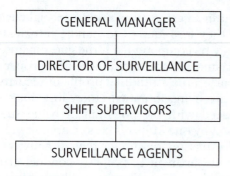

Figure 8.2
Surveillance Department Organization Chart

The first surveillance rooms in Las Vegas casinos featured an extensive network of catwalks over the casino where eye-in-the-sky personnel would visually view the gaming pits through one-way smoked glass in the ceiling of the casino. Today's surveillance rooms no longer rely on this observation technique, opting instead for high-technology video cameras with zoom and wide-angle lenses, color television monitors, computers capable of instantly reproducing photographs of suspected cheaters, and computer linkups to the slot tracking system, which allows surveillance employees to note any cases of tampering. VCRs line the walls of a modern surveillance room, and this department maintains a video library of their observations which can be used by the casino department for review purposes. Because of the importance and confidentiality of this data, surveillance rooms are often protected by a double-lock security system, and most rooms include a halogen gas fire prevention system.

Surveillance Functions

The primary function of the casino's surveillance department is detection of theft of company assets and theft from the gaming tables, slot machines, the

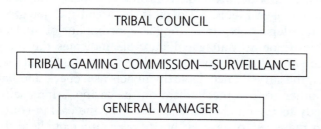

Figure 8.3
Tribal Casino Surveillance Department Organization Chart

cage, and all other revenue areas of the casino. Accomplishment of this objective requires highly trained personnel; some casinos promote or use former table game or slot personnel who have first-hand knowledge of the games, while others prefer individuals with excellent observation skills.

Surveillance observations are done either with dedicated cameras permanently fixed on key revenue areas of the casino, such as table games, megabuck progressive slot machines, and the casino cage, or scanning cameras which randomly rotate and videotape less-critical areas of the property. Should a scam be detected, surveillance will initiate contact with the casino manager's office and call government regulators who will arrest the cheaters. In the state of Nevada, cheating a casino is a felony. Videotapes used in the detection of the crime are used in court by the casino and the state government as *prima facie* evidence of fraud. It is noted that should surveillance detect a player counting cards at a blackjack table, the pit will be advised and most casinos will ask the player to leave even though card counting is not a crime. Although it is impossible to catch every thief or slot cheat, especially with the high-tech devices now being used by the scam artists, casino surveillance departments historically have uncovered the major portion of scams, and certainly, the presence of cameras in the casino, albeit disguised via smoked glass, acts as a reminder that surveillance is on the watch.

The surveillance department is often viewed as a one-dimensional department, when, in fact, it performs numerous other services for the casino. As an example, this department frequently assists the casino with player ratings. Table game supervisors rate players' action based on four criteria: buy-in amount, duration of play, average wager, and largest wager. Surveillance tapes are then used to test the accuracy of these ratings and might be used to help create a more objective set of criteria for rating a particular player. Additionally, surveillance may be used to determine the quality of play of a certain player. Many casinos believe that because a particular player has consistently "beat the house" or is on a long-term winning streak, this player can't be beat. First, probability distribution and the odds of the games are or should be in favor of the house, and if these are intact, the casino *must* eventually win. Yes, some players *must* win based on the same mathematical premise. Therefore, prior to succumbing to the belief that a particular player cannot be beaten and asking this good player to leave, surveillance should be utilized to determine if this player is merely applying excellent basic strategy and money management in the game. If so, the casino risks chasing away a good player who, eventually, can be beaten.

What are the requirements to work in surveillance? As stated previously, it may not be necessary to have been a dealer in order to work surveillance; however, eye-in-the-sky personnel must completely understand the rules of all casino games and the basic technology of slot machines. Further, a thorough comprehension of internal control procedures is mandated, and these employees must be able to recognize the standard cheating techniques. This includes recognizing customers as well as employees guilty of procedural misconduct. Surveillance must understand all other gaming department procedures so that they will spot deviations in cage procedures or improper soft-count team procedures. A well-organized casino will take steps to assist surveillance in the performance of its duties, such as having the soft-count table made of clear plastic laminate to improve observations and reducing the number of banners or height of slot machines carousels that may cause viewing impediments. Slot machines can be arranged so as not to create blind spots or difficult viewing angles for surveillance. Many casinos now use an autocad computer software package that creates a three-dimensional computerized picture of the casino as seen by surveillance. These and other similar steps can significantly reduce potential problems for the surveillance department.

Finally, casinos can use the surveillance department to identify employees who are doing a great job. Imagine introducing a surveillance tape into a training session showing a casino dealer providing excellent customer service or representing the ideal dealing procedures.

SUMMARY

The surveillance and security departments of a casino are truly the glue of the organization. Their failure can result in economic loss for the casino, legal liability, poor public relations—a dysfunctional organization. There is an old saying that the best casino security is security that is not obvious. There is still a lot of truth to this; surveillance and security should perform their respective functions in a nonintrusive but always vigilant manner. In so doing, customers will be able to feel secure while enjoying their casino experience.

DISCUSSION QUESTIONS

1. What is the primary function of a casino's security department?
2. Describe the organizational structure of a security department.
3. List several daily duties performed by a casino security officer.
4. Explain the importance of a written casino security procedures manual.
5. Why must security personnel be knowledgeable in civil and criminal liability law?
6. Describe the organizational structure of a casino's surveillance department.
7. Explain the functions of a surveillance department.
8. As a surveillance director, what specific skills or qualifications would you require of your surveillance personnel?

9

HUMAN RESOURCES MANAGEMENT IN THE CASINO INDUSTRY

 ## LEARNING OBJECTIVES

This chapter will enable the reader to:

- Examine the concepts and principles involved in casino human resources management.
- Outline guidelines for establishing a strong HRM program.
- List the key components included in an HRM mission statement.
- Explain procedures used in developing an HRM system.
- Identify important federal laws dealing with discrimination in the workplace.
- Understand the function of the employee recruitment, interviewing, and hiring process.
- Provide reasons for the importance of developing and utilizing casino job descriptions.
- Describe important HRM personnel administration forms required for successful management of casino departments.
- Explain proper procedures required of casino supervisors to properly discipline employees while documenting corrective action taken.

Introduction

"Dummy up and deal." "The only reason we don't hire monkeys as twenty-one dealers is that they can't explain insurance." "If you don't like it here, don't let the door hit you in the butt on your way out." How many times over the years were casino employees subjected to this type of treatment and managerial attitude? For how many years were casino workers regarded merely as payroll liabilities? What message was sent to job applicants who found the personnel office in the rear of the casino, next to the trash compactor by the loading dock? Unfortunately, for years casino workers were not highly regarded by many members of management, often seen as a necessary evil, and certainly not viewed as an asset or a human resource. Today, attitudes have changed; employees have become valued assets, and the concept of human resources management is being fully embraced by the industry. This chapter examines the concepts and principles involved in casino human resources management (HRM) as well as guidelines for establishing a strong HRM program.

What Is Human Resources Management?

Human resources management can be defined as recognizing employees first and foremost as human beings deserving fair and reasonable treatment and, secondly, as a resource that if properly tapped can provide the competitive edge. This is *not* to suggest that employees should be treated well because it is good for business! Rather, employees should be treated fairly because they are human beings deserving fair and reasonable wages, hours, and working conditions. Absent an equitable system, an organization invites needless turnover, excessive absenteeism, poor morale, increased pilferage, poor customer service, and a shrinking bottom line. It took the gaming industry years to realize that one of the main keys to success is . . . the employees. A casino may spend millions of dollars on decor, themes, and marketing but fail with the delivery of the product through poor customer service due to poor human resources management. In the final analysis, we must realize that it all comes down to how well our employees do their jobs. With this in mind, let us examine the steps that can be taken to develop a strong product delivery system to our guests through our employees.

Start with a Human Resources Mission Statement

Chapter 2 emphasized the need for an effective *business* mission statement. In conjunction with this, casino operators must take an equal amount of time to structure and write a human resources (HR) mission statement. It is amazing that so few businesses have accomplished this task. An HR mission statement is the company's published philosophical expression and attitude toward its employees. It is a manifestation of how it feels about its employees and what values it holds dearest or most important. There are a number of key components that should be included in the statement:

1. **The concept of team or family.** Running any business takes coordination of effort and a common direction—teamwork. An analogy can be drawn to passengers on an airplane or people on an elevator. Everyone is heading in the same direction but there is no communication or cohesiveness. Group dynamics is virtually nonexistent under these circumstances. People in these situations feel no sense of kinship nor have any meaningful long-range goals other than reaching their desired stop or destination. Employees working without a team effort are like airline passengers. They have a general goal in mind (i.e., do my job so I can get paid) or some vague concept of where the business is going but really do not share or communicate any mutual goals. Many casinos operate this way with a loose conglomerate of individual departments all in motion but not tied to a unified, organizational goal. They are classic examples of individual and not team efforts. Eventually, lack of teamwork leads to a dysfunctional organizational or departmental situation. Can you imagine sending a football team onto the field without plays (i.e., a mission statement) and no sense of why they are on the field? The chances of this team being successful are minimal. In a sense, the players have merely been programmed for survival and not success. Contemporary managers are coaches and mentors and need to build and lead teams of employees. In the final analysis, we must realize that it all comes down to how well our employees do their jobs and how well they pull together as a team or with a sense of family.

2. **Goal-setting.** Goal-setting needs to be done at two levels: short-term and long-range goals. Managers must clearly articulate what needs to be accomplished today, this week, or this month, and where the company will be in a year or five years if the goals are attained. Goals must be achievable and realistic since unattainable goals lead to frustration and a "what's-the-use" attitude.

3. **Expectancy theory.** A typical business plan explicitly or tacitly enumerates the goals of the company. Employees are asked to provide good service and work hard for the good of the business. The HR mission statement must address the expectancy theory: What's in it for the employees?! Why should employees work hard beyond ensuring that the business succeeds so they may receive a paycheck? Is the message, "Work hard or you will be discharged"? If this is overtly stated or implied, management has created a negative basis for its employee relationship. Rather, the concept of gainsharing or sharing the company's gains must be expressed. Ideally, the HR mission statement should talk about mutual success for the casino and employees.

4. **Customer service.** The gaming industry is part of the hospitality industry, and as such, its foundation rests on successful customer service. The importance of customers must be emphasized, noting that everyone's success will be determined by the quality of service rendered.

5. Trust. Trusting and empowering employees not only leads to a sense of well-being, but it also lays the cornerstone for a successful HRM program. Allowing employees to "own" their jobs leads to a vested interest mentality. One of the great apprehensions of casino workers is job security. Once employees believe they are trusted in their jobs, they will trust in management. This is an extremely strong bond that serves as a benchmark for measuring quality managers or leaders. Supervisors who have conveyed a sense of trust in their employees will receive the same type of trust from their workers.

6. Value statement. The Preamble to the United States Constitution makes a value statement about government's attitude toward people: "We hold these truths to be self-evident, that all men are created equal. . . ." An HR mission statement should embody the company's values. What are your business ethics? What does the company believe in, and what values do you want your employees to share?

7. Pride. The core essence of an HR mission statement is a message about pride in workmanship, oneself, and the company. A casino and its employees will be successful when everyone feels pride about their workplace, careers, and working conditions. Pride is manifested in multiple ways: pride in one's appearance and one's uniform; pride in the beauty, ambiance, and aesthetics of the casino decor; pride in how the business is prospering; pride in the company's involvement in the community. It is easy to detect this type of pride; employees will show it in their demeanor and how they speak about the operation.

The following represents a possible mission statement that achieves all or most of the above-stated HR mission statement goals: "We recognize employees as our M.I.P.s (Most Important People), and by working and communicating together as a team we are seeking to achieve the maximum success for our employees, the company, and our customers by empowering and trusting our staff to deliver extraordinary customer service. Together, we will grow as a family and a company . . . a company and a team we can all be proud of and enjoy."

DEVELOPING AN HRM SYSTEM

Having completed an HR mission statement, it now makes sense that a plan be designed to implement the professed philosophical concepts. This is known as creating a human resources management system. It is imperative that the system permeate every employment practice and all aspects of personnel administration. Specifically, an HRM system must include a consistent approach to:

- the employee recruitment process
- the selection process (interviewing)
- the hiring process (including the orientation session)

- the casino's training program
- employee appraisal and evaluation procedures
- employee discipline procedures
- the separation process

The next section of this chapter analyzes how each of the above components can be injected into the personnel administration and HRM system.

RECRUITMENT

Recruitment is the process of attracting qualified job applicants. An HRM system dictates that recruitment focus on the "best-qualified" job applicants. The best candidates, first, share the values of the organization and then meet the task requirements of the job as specified in the job description. Specifically, a job applicant who can deal two more hands per hour than a second candidate, but is looking to steal from the employer, is *not* the best candidate for the job. Prior to the recruitment of any job applicant, casinos must first design a job application that addresses the following criteria: legal concerns and format.

Legal Concerns

The use of discriminatory language on an application form (words or terms that are discriminatory in appearance) can serve as *prima facie* evidence against the casino in a discrimination lawsuit if the hiring profile creates an adverse impact on members of a group protected by the civil rights laws in the United States. The U.S. Equal Employment Opportunity Commission (EEOC), the federal agency that administers the U.S. civil rights laws, uses the term "chilling effect"—an employment practice that dissuades members of a protected group from even applying for a job or contradicts the concept of equal employment. Wording on an application form can cause a chilling effect. For example, an application form that lists casino jobs only using the male gender in the job title (e.g., box*man*, floor*man*) might not only be viewed as *prima facie* evidence but may also cause a chilling effect. Simply stated, the message is, "Females need not apply," whether or not this is the intent. During the 1970s, a number of Las Vegas casinos were charged with discriminating against females. One of the defenses used by the casinos was a lack of application flow. The EEOC countered by showing that a number of hiring procedures were blatantly anti-female, including the personnel forms used by casinos (i.e., gender bias on application forms, job descriptions, newspaper job advertisements, etc.). Thus, numerous females testified that there was no sense in even applying for the jobs since the message was obvious on these employment forms and in the actual hiring profiles at this time. Only males were hired as "floorman," "boxman," "stickman." Hence, discrimination existed from the application and recruitment process through the actual employment period.

In order to prevent lawsuits during the application/recruitment process, casinos must understand the federal laws dealing with discrimination in the workplace. Additionally, many states have more stringent requirements or added employer requirements, and these also must be applied.

United States Civil Rights Laws

The Civil Rights Act of 1964. Title VII of this law prohibits discrimination in *any* employment practice (hiring, discharge, promotion, benefits) based on race, color, religion, national origin, and/or gender. It should be noted that employment practices based on a bona fide occupational qualification (BFOQ) do not violate Title VII. As an example, normally an application form noting gender preference or using gender in job titles would be potential evidence of discrimination. If, however, the reason for gender use was to comply with a county or state law (i.e., some states prohibit members of one gender from giving massages to members of the opposite gender), then there is a job-related, nondiscriminatory, bona fide occupational qualification for the job and this would justify the use of gender. Application forms should refrain from the following types of questions to avoid possible conflicts with Title VII provisions of the 1964 Civil Rights Act:

1. Requesting title (Mr., Mrs., Ms.) when asking for someone's name.

2. Requesting gender (unless there is a BFOQ).

3. Inquiring into a person's national origin (i.e., "In what country were you born?"). If the casino is desirous of knowing foreign language skills, then the question should be phrased: "What languages do you speak, read, or write?" Regarding eligibility to work in the United States, an application question can be framed to ask, "If hired, can you provide the legal documents required by the Immigration Service certifying your eligibility to work in the United States?"

4. Asking about religious denomination or membership in religious organizations. Questions seeking information on needed days off for religious holidays are not advised.

5. Requesting a photo during the pre-employment period (this may be a way to determine a person's race or color).

The Age Discrimination in Employment Act (ADEA) of 1968. This law prohibits discrimination in any employment practice against individuals 40 years of age and older. Questions to be avoided on an application form include "Date of birth" or "How old are you?" If the casino requires a minimum age, then the question should be framed as follows, "This casino requires that all workers be at least 21 years of age. If hired, can you provide proof that you meet this minimum age requirement?" As you can note, the phraseology of questions becomes critically important in relation to potential discriminatory practices. Another example would be inquiries into an applicant's education. If the application form asks applicants to list all schools attended, starting with high school, as well as the dates attended, it would be relatively easy to determine someone's current age (i.e., most people graduate from high school at age 17 or 18). The preferred format for this question is, "Total years of education." Finally, it is important to realize that discrimination within age groupings over 40 is likewise prohibited. A casino that hires workers 40 to 45 years of age thinking it has complied with the law will still be at risk if the hiring profile indicates that no one over 45 has been hired.

The Employee Pregnancy Act of 1978. In 1978, President Carter signed this amendment to the 1964 Civil Rights Act. Basically, this law prohibits employment discrimination based on a female's pregnancy or anticipated pregnancy. The law also requires that employers' policies on temporary medical conditions be applied to pregnant workers. Therefore, application forms should not ask questions relative to current or anticipated pregnancy, number of children, whether a female applicant has adequate daycare, and similarly styled inquiries.

The Civil Rights Act of 1991. Another amendment to the 1964 Civil Rights Act, this law allows for punitive damages. Employers with 500 or more employees are exposed to the maximum amount allowed by this law, $300,000.

The Americans with Disabilities Act of 1993. It is estimated that there are nearly 43 million Americans with a disability, and this law is intended to provide equal employment opportunities for a labor group that for many years was either generally ignored or stereotyped as handicapped individuals who could not produce at the same level as other employees. The Americans with Disabilities Act (ADA) now protects qualified individuals with a physical or mental disability. In order to be considered qualified, the applicant must be able to do the essential or critical functions of the job with or without a reasonable accommodation. The essential functions of the job are those tasks that require the greatest amount of time or occupy the vast majority of the employee's time. The essential functions of a blackjack dealer are dealing the cards, shuffling the cards, accepting wagers, paying off wagers, verifying table fills and credits, and maintaining strong customer relations. Remove these functions, and the job of a blackjack dealer ceases to exist. As noted, ADA covers physical and mental disabilities. These disabilities are legally defined as those which substantially limit one of life's major activities such as walking, seeing, hearing, talking, and so on. Examples of disabilities covered by the ADA are cerebral palsy, multiple sclerosis, cancer, heart disease, mental retardation, learning disabilities, epilepsy, and diabetes. The law makes it clear that a person is covered by the ADA even if medication stabilizes or puts the disability in remission. For instance, an individual with diabetes would still be covered even though the use of insulin completely controlled the ailment. Thus, coverage under this law is extended not only to individuals with a present disability, but also to those with a history of a disability and those who are regarded as being disabled even though no disability exists (e.g., a person with a disfigurement). Also, the law protects those who associate with individuals with a disability covered by the ADA. A good example of this would be an employee who works with AIDS patients on a volunteer basis, since AIDS is an enumerated disability under the law. It was stated that qualified employees with a disability are protected if they can do the essential functions of a job with or without a reasonable accommodation. The phrase "reasonable accommodation" is interpreted as something that can be done, with or without an expense, to help the employee do the essential functions of the job without creating an undue hardship on the business (i.e., it costs too much or is too difficult to do). As an illustration, assume that a person who uses a wheelchair applies for a job as a blackjack dealer. A review of the application indicates that this person dealt all table games for eight years at some of the finest casinos in Las Vegas, thus meeting and exceeding the requirement of being able to do the essential functions of the job. Due to an automobile accident, this person now uses a wheelchair, and as a result, can no longer reach the blackjack table. A reasonable accommodation for this employee would either be lowering the blackjack table or building a ramp up to the table. Both accommodations are easily done, and neither results in an undue hardship for the employer (i.e., too expensive or difficult). In fact, many casinos *have* lowered their gaming tables to accommodate not only employees but also customers with a disability. If a casino is concerned that a particular job might pose a significant direct threat to the job applicant, it should secure an outside medical opinion rather than arbitrarily determine that the person should not be hired.

Casinos need to avoid any questions on an application form directed at determining a person's health. These include, "Have you ever had any of the following illnesses?" "Have you been hospitalized within the past ten years?" "Are you currently under a physician's care or on any medication?"

The ADA also is aimed at raising consciousness about individuals with disabilities. The law uses the word "disabilities" rather than "handicapped" since the latter term's derivation is "beggar with cap in hand." The arrangement of words in the title of this law is significant; the word "Americans" appears prior to "Disabilities," indicating that the emphasis should always be placed on the person and not the disability. ADA sensitivity requires that employers use the following references to disabilities during the pre-employment period:

Use	*Do Not Use*
Vision impairment	Blind (unless the person has a total loss of sight)
Hearing impairment	Deaf (unless the person has a total hearing loss)

Use	Do Not Use
Down Syndrome	Mongoloid
Small stature	Dwarf
Cancer survivor	Cancer victim
Person who uses a wheelchair	Wheelchair user Restricted to a wheelchair
Person who uses a cane	Must use a cane

In the realm of "Legal Concerns", applications can achieve two more goals for casinos: first, establish an employment-at-will relationship with workers, and, second, secure permission to verify the job applicant's previous employment, criminal background, and other job-related issues.

Employment-at-Will

The principle of employment-at-will establishes the following basis for the labor-management relationship: As the employee has the right to quit without justification and/or advance notification to the employer, so also does the employer reserve the right to discharge the employee without cause or advance notification. Many states have laws prohibiting the discharge of employees without cause, while others adhere to the concept of employment-at-will. One of the historic cases in gaming history dealing with this concept involved the Las Vegas Hilton, which discharged 38 casino dealers based on the Hilton's belief that they were employed at-will. The dealers filed a class-action or joint lawsuit claiming that they were wrongfully discharged and used four legal defenses:

1. Statutory remedy. They claimed the Hilton violated the federal civil rights statutes, since all the dealers were males and over 40 years of age.

2. Implied contract. Although no written contract existed between the casino and the workers, the dealers believed there was an implied contract. This was based on the premise that when they were hired, their employee handbook specified the reasons for discharge, and absent one of those reasons, the implication was, you would not be fired. Thus, the employees stated that an implied contract existed since they were not terminated for one of the reasons in the handbook.

3. Covenant of Good Faith and Fair Dealing. This is an English commonlaw principle which merely means that employers should not deal in bad faith with their employees and should treat them fairly.

4. Emotional distress. Initially, the dealers received a $38 million jury award, which increased to $42 million when interest and legal fees were added. Upon appeal, this amount was reduced to $4.5 million.

> I understand that the ABC Casino is offering no contract for employment and that my employment is at-will, which means I can quit at any time with or without justification, and with or without prior notification to the employer; and the employer may terminate my services at any time, with or without just cause and with or without prior notification. I further understand that no employee, agent, or representative of the ABC Casino, other than the Casino Manager or Chief Executive Officer, has the authority to enter into any agreement for employment for any specific amount of time or make any agreement contrary to the foregoing language. It is additionally understood that any contrary agreement with the Casino Manager or Chief Executive Officer must be done in writing. Finally, no other company document such as an employee handbook, application form, etc., represents a contract of employment and should not be relied upon by me as such.
>
> _____   _____
> (Signature)   (Date)

Figure 9.1
Employment-at-Will Statement

As a result of this case and other similar-type awards, employers have modified application forms specifying, where legally permissible, that the employment-at-will principle does exist. Figure 9.1 is an employment-at-will statement appearing on the back of a casino employment application form.

Release of Claims/Waiver of Liability

The application form can be used to address one other legal concern, that of securing background information about job applicants. Casinos need to be wary of invasion of privacy and defamation lawsuits that can result from improper securement or disclosure of information about job applicants and employees. Employers can avoid this exposure by having job applicants grant permission to do background checks and absolve the employer from liability in so doing. This is referred to as securing a release of claims or waiver of liability. Figure 9.2 is a sample of a release of claims found on a casino application form.

As a final note on this particular topic, the EEOC guidelines on pre-employment inquiries direct employers not to include questions on an application form dealing with arrests. Rather, criminal history questions should be limited to convictions.

I understand the following:

    I have been advised that the information I provide is needed by the ABC Casino to assist them in making an employment decision regarding my application with this casino, and, in accordance with my right to privacy, I am not obligated to sign this form but do so voluntarily with the understanding that a copy of this Release Form will be made available to me upon request.

    I hereby authorize the ABC Casino and any of its wholly owned subsidiaries to obtain any and all information about me from previous or current employers, educational institutions, credit-reporting agencies (if this information is deemed job-related), law enforcement and gaming regulatory agencies, or individuals relating to my background, history, and past activities. I understand that this information may include verification of grades and degrees/diplomas received from schools, history of renting or home ownership, job performance, and any conviction record I may have. I also authorize the ABC Casino to disclose this information to its designated representatives who will be involved in determining my employment eligibility.

    I further release all directors, officers, agents, employees, or other representatives of the ABC Casino from any and all liability damages caused by the access or use of the information secured through this Release of Claims Form.

_____   _____
(Signature)   (Date)

Figure 9.2
Release of Claims Form

Format

The second consideration in developing an application form is the format. There are several principles that apply:

- *Readability.* The print on the application form should be sufficiently large and easy to read. Terms and expressions used on the form should not be overly complicated or difficult to understand. Finally, if the form is photocopied in-house, the copies should be clear, not blurred, and easy to read.

- *Appearance.* The appearance of the form makes a statement about the organization. Is it professional in appearance? Are the main topics in bold print or highlighted?

- *Conciseness.* Application forms should avoid long, drawn-out questions. Excessively long forms tend to be tedious and burdensome.

All questions on the application form *must* be answered. If an applicant has omitted information or dates of employment, these answers should be obtained from the applicant. Employers have been sued for negligent hiring simply because they did not exercise ordinary care in securing all information on an applicant or failed to verify information provided on the application form. Casinos should likewise not permit the submittal of a resume in lieu of an application form. Resumes are often typed by professional services, ensuring correct spelling and grammar. Having a person complete an application form will not only reveal discrepancies between the form and the resume but will also reveal the applicant's spelling ability, grammar, and penmanship.

Questions that should be asked on an application form are:

1. Applicant's name
2. Address/phone number
3. Previous employment or related experience
4. Educational background, special training, seminars attended, and degrees/diplomas
5. Eligibility to work in the United States
6. Ability to meet minimum age requirements
7. Special skills (e.g., typing, computers, foreign languages, military training)
8. Conviction record
9. List of references
10. Position desired
11. Narrative section. This section may be used to determine the person's career goals or it may pose a "think" question.

With the application form reviewed, the employer can activate the recruitment process.

Internal and External Recruitment

The goal of recruitment is to create a flow of qualified applicants, and in order for this to happen, the casino must properly disseminate information about job openings. This can be done through internal and external recruitment.

Internal Recruitment

Internal recruitment or promotion from within is an extremely popular and prevalent procedure in the gaming industry. Many casino managers started as dealers and through a series of promotions rose to the executive level. Promotions are a great incentive for joining and staying with a company and certainly serve as an employee motivator and morale booster. There are some negatives associated with this practice. If a casino only promotes from within, parochialism develops, in which everyone was trained in the same manner and thinks along established company lines. The inherent flaw is the possible exclusion of "outside" thinking and new ideas or approaches. Additionally, if the company is not in a growth mode, waiting for a promotion may take an extraordinarily long period of time, resulting in demotivation of the workforce. The key to internal recruitment is making incumbent employees aware of the openings and assessing their abilities based on current, accurate data. To accomplish the first goal, casinos post employment openings for a minimum of 72 hours in the human resources department, at the time office, in the employees' dining room, or in any other area frequented by the workforce. The second goal requires employers to upgrade employee personnel files with new skills gained by employees since they originally completed their application forms. Many properties use a Skills Inventory form which acts as an updated addendum to the application form (see Figure 9.3).

External Recruitment

External recruitment is the marketing of employment opportunities to outside/external candidates. This is normally done through advertisements in the "Help Wanted/Employment Opportunities" section of newspapers; listings in trade journals; campus recruitment (Harrah's Casinos and Mirage Resorts presently have casino management development programs, and target graduating seniors from universities as candidates); minority/affirmative action groups; government agencies such as the state employment security department; or notices posted with churches or religious organizations and at military bases. New gaming jurisdictions often specify that a percentage of the workforce must be regional, since one of the governmental goals in legalizing gaming is the creation of new jobs.

INTERVIEWING

A successful recruitment campaign will result in a flow of qualified candidates for a job. There are two essential tools gaming managers can use to achieve a successful interview: working from a job description and having a formalized interview plan.

Job Descriptions

For years, casinos wrote job descriptions and placed them in a binder, where they became company archives and dust collectors. The Americans with Dis-

Thank you for your interest in the position opening of _____
which was posted in the Human Resources Department from (date) to (date).

The ABC Casino Corporation is dedicated to the policy of promotion from within, and in order for us to have the most current information on you since your original application form was completed, we are asking you to provide us with an update.

Please list any new skills, training, education, experience, or expertise acquired since you originally completed your application form or since completion of your last Skills Inventory Form. Examples include computer training; new foreign language skills; seminars attended; classes taken at a university, college, vocational training institute, or dealing school; training obtained through the ABC Casino; awards or recognitions; community services provided; training on office equipment or any other types of equipment related to the current job opening; or any other information that will help us to base our decision on the most current and accurate information about you.

_____

_____

_____

_____

_____

_____

_____

_____

_____

_____

_____   _____
(Name)   (Signature)

EMPLOYEE ID#: _____

CURRENT DEPARTMENT: _____

CURRENT SUPERVISOR: _____

DATE: _____

Figure 9.3
Skills Inventory Form

abilities Act, although not specifically requiring employers to create job descriptions, has caused employers to unearth their job descriptions, since they can be used as a basis for a defense against a charge of discrimination if prepared prior to the advertising of a job. The ADA has additionally caused a dramatic change in job description formats. Current forms now list essential and nonessential job functions separately, indicate the duration or percentage of time required to perform each task, and detail much more exact information about the job, including distances that must be walked, specific weight amounts to be lifted, atmospheric conditions such as secondary smoke, and so on. Figure 9.4 is a sample job description for a blackjack dealer.

Prior to the interview, in addition to reviewing the resume and application, the hiring authority needs to review the job description to ensure that there is a consistent frame of reference for requisite job skills. Large hotel/casinos rely on the human resources department, which uses the job description to screen out applicants who do not meet the minimum job qualifications and then to rate those who will be given an interview with the hiring authority. These prescreening ratings are numerically based on such criteria as appearance, quality/quantity of previous employment, and customer service skills. Mirage Resorts prescreened and eliminated nearly 50,000 job applicants when recruiting for their Mirage and Treasure Island hotel/casinos based on the fact that these individuals demonstrated unacceptable customer service skills (e.g., did not extend a hand when a handshake was offered by the screener, did not make eye contact, etc.). The MGM Grand Hotel/Casino and Theme Park hiring process includes a theatrical skit for every job applicant (referred to as cast members by the MGM). The MGM's philosophy is that every employee is "on stage" and is giving a performance for its guests. A well-designed job description can emphasize these salient components of a job.

Interview Plan

The second success component of an interview is working from an interview plan. The plan helps the interviewer organize thoughts, creates a smooth flow to the interview, and provides a consistent, nondiscriminatory question bank. Figure 9.5 illustrates an interview plan.

Casinos use a numerical rating system to score the interview, and some casinos will weigh the responses to certain questions more heavily.

It is important to remember that the selection process is a two-way decision. Many employers believe the choice is a unilateral decision made exclusively by the company. Ideally, both sides need to choose each other, much like a marriage with two willing partners. The question before the employer is, Do you want this job applicant to merely take this job until a better offer comes along, or are you looking for someone to choose your team with a long-term commitment in mind?

Date

Position   **Blackjack/Twenty-One Dealer**

Reports to   **Twenty-One Floorperson.**

Job Summary   **(A brief synopsis of the job.) Deals the game of blackjack/twenty-one.**

Essential Functions: **(May be listed by priority; may list duration or percentage of time doing each function.)**

1. Deals cards to customers using a shoe or by holding one or multiple decks of cards.
2. Shuffles one or more decks of cards.
3. Accepts wagers from customers.
4. Collects losing wagers from customers.
5. Pays off wagers won by customers.
6. Explains rules of the game.
7. Signs for table fills and table credits.
8. Maintains high standards of customer service.
9. Protects integrity of the game.

Nonessential Functions

1. Occasionally trains new break-in dealers.
2. Periodically may be required to sort used decks of cards.
3. Waits at dead games for customers.

Job Specifications

1. Prefer dealer with one year prior dealing experience.
2. Ideal candidate can also deal craps, roulette, the Big 6, pai-gow poker, pai-gow, Caribbean stud poker, mini-baccarat, Let It Ride, and/or Red Dog.
3. Must possess strong customer service skills.
4. Able to work under game pressure, have good mathematical skills, make accurate payoffs, and deal one hand every 73 seconds.
5. Must be able and willing to work any shift, handle multiple guests at one time, and stand for long periods of time, with exposure to secondary smoke, loud noises, and crowded working conditions.

Wage Rate: $5.95/hour plus tips. Tips are part of a tip-pooling arrangement.

Figure 9.4
Sample Job Description for a Blackjack Dealer

PRE-INTERVIEW:

1. Have you reviewed the resume and application form?
2. Is there any pre-employment testing required such as passing a dealing audition; leadership instrument exam?
3. Have you listed questions that need clarification based on your review of the application form or resume?
4. Have you cleared your calendar and set aside sufficient time without interruption for the interview?
5. Are you avoiding any preconceived ideas or biases about the person or position?
6. Are your questions open-ended in style and geared toward determining behavioral patterns? Open-ended questions are preferred to close-ended questions since they allow for free thinking and insights. A close-ended question on customer service would be framed, "We think customer service is extremely over-rated in the gaming industry; what do you think?" The interviewer has stated a company position, and the applicant, wanting to say the "right thing," may simply agree or think it's a "trick question." The open-ended version of this question would be, "What is your philosophy about customer service in the gaming industry?" No signals have been sent; no preconceived ideas have been conveyed. The interviewee now has an opportunity to frame his or her own thoughts.

Interview Guideline:

1. Start with a handshake, introduction, and your business card.
2. Make the person feel welcomed, relaxed, and comfortable.
3. Ask questions about the person's previous employment, experience, and skills. The goal is to determine the quantity and quality of experience (i.e., does a person have five years of management experience or one year of management experience five times!); how relevant the experience is to the current position; competency levels; knowledge of current trends; leadership or team member capacity; growth potential; communication skills; attitude toward your values; management style or philosophies on such topics as customer service.
4. The next series of questions deals with the person's educational background, including any specialized training. Obviously, the employer is seeking to determine the intellectual abilities of the candidate as well as the breadth and scope of their training. Questions may be framed around school-related team projects to determine the person's philosophy about teamwork.
5. Applicants can then be asked about their interests or community involvement to determine their vitality, other illustrations of leadership or teamwork, and multicultural/societal diversity and interaction experience.
6. Conclude the interview on a positive note, and let the applicant know when a hiring decision will be made.

Figure 9.5
Interview Plan

THE HIRING PROCESS

Having selected the "best" employee, the casino must now complete the paper-work necessary to bring the new team member on board. Casinos covered by federal and state employment laws are required to complete certain forms by law and additional forms in alliance with the HRM system. Most of this processing is completed by the HR department. The HR department is often characterized as the source of the "dreaded paperwork" associated with employee processing and retention. In reality, this department is an extension of the casino, merely helping the various department managers with staffing needs. Therefore, the HR department must be viewed as an integral part of the success formula.

Following is a list of forms needed to initially process a new employee, followed by a listing of additional forms used during the post-processing period. From a review of these lists it becomes apparent that there is an extraordinary amount of time, effort, and money involved in the process, which amplifies the need for a good selection, since failure to choose the best employees will lead to needless turnover and expense. Secondly, managers and supervisors in the gaming industry will be required to either initiate, review, or approve these forms. Thus, the managing of a successful casino department requires attention to a great deal of financial *and* personnel administration forms.

Initial Processing Forms

1. Application form

2. Employee Requisition form. This form is given to the HR department by the requesting department indicating a job opening in the department. Normally, casinos use a one-for-one replacement policy (i.e., a department only hires someone as a replacement for an employee who has quit, is going on vacation, etc.). Any increases in staff are usually approved by the casino manager, the chief executive officer, or the chief financial officer. Some new managers, in an attempt to impress upper management, arbitrarily reduce staff seeking to lower their payroll. This may result in a serious mistake if the remaining staff is overworked, leading to job burnout and poor customer service. Therefore, understaffing can be just as serious a violation as overstaffing.

3. Hire Slip/Personnel Action form. This form is completed by the hiring department, approved by the department manager, and given to the HR department. The form indicates the new hire's start date, rate of pay, shift to be worked, and days off.

4. I-9 form. As required by the U.S. Immigration and Naturalization Service, this form is to be completed for all new hires, and employers must verify the person's eligibility to legally work in this country.

5. Sheriff's/police card. States, in an attempt to keep unsavory and criminal elements out of gaming, mandate criminal background investigations for new hires. If the person is approved, the sheriff's or police department will grant a gaming card if the new hire will be working in the casino or a nongaming card if this person will be working in a noncasino department.

6. Employee badge. Employee badges have multiple uses: If the casino uses a time and attendance computer system for tracking payroll, the employee badge replaces the time card and is used by workers to clock-in and clock-out for work and breaks. Badges many times will list the employee's hometown or state, and this serves as a customer marketing tool. Some casinos use different-colored backgrounds behind the employees' photos on the badges to designate the employees' department, and this helps security to quickly identify employees who should not be in restricted areas of the casino. Badges can be used to access turnstiles in the employees' dining room or shown by the employee to the dining room manager as authorization to eat in the room. Payroll checks are not issued to employees unless they produce a valid badge. Casinos frequently arrange discounts for employees with local merchants, with the retailers requiring an employee badge to be shown as verification of current employment.

7. Payroll forms. These include the IRS W-4 form used to determine the amount of federal tax to be withheld for each paycheck, and possibly a tip compliance agreement. The U.S. Internal Revenue Service recently reached agreement with a significant number of casinos to ensure fuller compliance with employee tip-reporting requirements. Employees at these casinos have agreed to tip compliance, reporting amounts that are deducted from their payroll checks by the casino.

8. Targeted Job Tax Credit forms. Employers may receive a break on employee payroll taxes by hiring individuals identified by the federal government as low-income recipients or within a group with a potential or history of long-term unemployment (e.g., exfelons), through a federally sponsored program known as the Targeted Job Tax Credit (TJTC).

9. Health insurance forms. Although most casinos require employees to wait 90 or 180 days to be eligible for company-sponsored group health insurance, the initial enrollment often takes place during the initial processing. Employee insurance plans range from a basic wraparound plan (i.e., medical, hospital, dental, and vision) to those with multiple options, each carrying an added cost for employees. Employees are also notified of their rights under the Consolidated Omnibus Budgetary Reconciliation Act (COBRA), which entitles discharged employees and their dependents to continued health insurance, with the codicil that employees must pay the monthly premium payments plus a 2 percent administration fee.

10. Employee handbook. Employee handbooks, which contain all the casino's rules, policies, and procedures, are distributed during the initial processing or at the employee orientation session. In either case, employees are required to acknowledge receipt of their handbook by signing an employee handbook receipt. Employers use this receipt as documentation that there was a mutuality of knowledge regarding performance expectations and disciplinary procedures. Employee handbooks should meet legal requirements such as policy statements on sexual harassment and employee rights under the Family and Medical Leave Act.

11. Uniform/key authorization. Employees who will be issued a uniform from the employer or a key for the employee dressing room may receive a clearance slip from the HR department indicating that they provided all necessary paperwork and may now report for work.

12. Orientation notification. A final document given employees at the conclusion of processing is an orientation notification which specifies the time, date, and location of the next new employee orientation session. The orientation session is now *mandatory,* as employees are talked through the company's rules, policies, and procedures including the HR mission statement; customer service expectations; payroll procedures, including how overtime is authorized; sick call procedures; the company's group health insurance policy and coverages; courtesy to other team members and the casino security department's authority; how the employee badge and uniforms are to be worn; disciplinary situations; vacation and holiday policies; location of employee parking; the casino's policy on sexual harassment as well as the desire for a drug-free workplace; safety standards; and a multitude of other topics of importance and interest to workers. Larger casinos incorporate a tour of the property as part of the orientation, and an introduction to the new employee's team members.

13. Miscellaneous other documents. Other legal documents such as an Alcohol Awareness Certificate may be required for cocktail servers and bartenders. Restaurant and kitchen workers in various states or counties are required to have a health card or health certificate. The HR department will require a Social Security card, and if the casino employs minors in its restaurants, these workers will need a work permit.

Post-Processing Forms and Procedures

Once the employee has completed the initial hiring process, casino supervisors and managers, working through and with the HR department, will be completing numerous other forms and reports for employees. These reports include vacation notices, leaves of absence forms, overtime authorization, disciplinary notices, employee accident reports, and completed employee/supervisor employee form.

TRAINING

Casinos have made great strides in training their employees. At one time, formal training was nonexistent and casino workers were either required to have the requisite employment skills at the time of hire or learn their jobs via on-the-job training. Today, workers are afforded numerous opportunities to improve their abilities. Following is a cross-section of training areas in formal programs being offered by casino operations in the United States:

1. Technical skills training. This may involve dealer training or teaching/enhancing computer skills.

2. Leadership/management development skills. Currently, some casinos such as Harrah's and the MGM Grand Hotel/Casino and Theme Park have a well-developed, internal program for executive development much like a corporate university. Other casinos either outsource the training or offer only a portion internally. A typical leadership training program would involve:

    a. Identification of one's leadership style through a test or instrument

    b. Strategic planning skills

    c. Problem-solving paradigms

    d. Effective decision making

    e. Concepts in employee motivation

    f. Conflict management and positive discipline in the workplace

    g. Case studies and situational analyses

    h. Developing budgeting and forecasting abilities

    i. Enhancement of financial analysis skills

    j. Exercises involving delphi analysis or other futuristic assessment programs

    k. Effective time management

    l. Coaching and mentoring procedures

    m. Problem and underage gambling tendencies

    n. Special assignments designed to address a company's particular needs (e.g., developing a corporate culture, designing a critical path for opening a new casino)

3. Sexual harassment awareness and sensitivity

4. Business and ethical behavior. Training in this area focuses on such topics as avoiding a conflict of interest and maintaining the confidentiality and integrity of company records, methodologies, and the like.

5. Legal training. This incorporates training required by state or federal law, including alcohol awareness, hazardous chemical communication training, and bloodborne pathogens training and awareness. This program is often expanded to include a review of state and federal employment laws, wage and hour laws, laws dealing with discrimination, and regulatory requirements, including cash reporting in compliance with Title 31 of the Bank Secrecy Act and state-required internal control procedures.

6. Team-building. As more casinos realize the importance of effective teams, team-building has become a top priority. Some casinos are developing team-based compensation incentives to increase productivity and create a more significant esprit de corps.

7. Safety. Casinos normally create a safety committee consisting of employees from various departments who are trained to look for potential fire hazards, conditions that might cause an accident (e.g., wet/slippery floors), and unsanitary conditions.

8. Energy management. Energy management training teaches employees more effective and efficient use of electricity, water, and so on, with a desired outcome of reduced energy costs.

9. Customer service. Perhaps the most frequently offered training, customer service educational programs focus on paradigms or models of excellence and benchmarks for customer service. This training features employee role-playing and case studies in customer service.

10. Community awareness training. Casinos often bring in local charitable organizations to make employees aware of their need for volunteers.

11. Communication. Communication training incorporates public speaking, improving writing skills (e.g., how to write a concise and effective memorandum), and may also deal with language skills.

12. Wellness programs. These training sessions help employees with weight management and reduction, stopping smoking, stress management and so on.

13. Drugs in the workplace. Although most casinos now require pre-employment and post-hiring drug testing, it is imperative that all workers be trained and remain vigilant regarding drug use in the workplace. Employees under the influence are a threat to themselves, coworkers, and customers. They also represent a potential legal liability for negligent hiring or negligent retention lawsuits, which are often based on a lack of ordinary care by the casino.

14. Cultural diversity. Basically, cultural diversity training helps workers understand other workers' culture and background, which leads to a more empathetic working relationship. Further, some casinos have expanded cultural diversity training to include patron cultural nuances.

The above training programs are representative of the educational steps casinos are taking to create a more effective, efficient, and cohesive workforce. The gaming industry must remain vigilant and proactive with training since education has been and always will be the trademark of progressive and successful organizations.

DISCIPLINE

Perhaps more than any procedure, casino managers must be able to properly discipline employees and document the corrective action taken. The concept of discipline must take on a positive connotation; the goal of discipline is to correct a job-related deficiency (a positive managerial step) and not to punish employees. Therefore, discipline is corrective, remedial, and designed to educate and adjust work performance or attitudes. It is understood that all discipline begins with a mutuality of knowledge, with supervisors and managers (and the employee handbook) clearly explaining job expectations and goals to their employees. Absent a mutuality of knowledge, employees cannot reasonably be held responsible for mistakes or falling short of expected goals. There are two types or methods of discipline: progressive discipline and immediate discharge.

Progressive Discipline

Progressive discipline is used when there is a minor transgression such as being late for work or absenteeism, which, if excessive, can lead to termination. As the name suggests, progressive discipline involves a series of counseling steps taken by managers to help employees correct minor job-related deficiencies. Remember, employees are your most valuable assets and should be treated as such. With this in mind, if an employee commits a minor violation for the first time, a manager should verbally counsel the employee, explaining why the policy is important and then allow the employee due process or the chance to explain any extenuating or mitigating circumstances. At the conclusion of the counseling, both parties need to reach an agreement regarding how similar circumstances will be avoided in the future. If there is a recurrence within a reasonable period of time (90–180 days), the manager will again counsel the employee but will now prepare a *written* notice detailing the events of the latest event, with one copy issued to the employee. This notice must also advise the employee that additional recurrences will result in further disciplinary action, to include a possible suspension and, eventually, termination. As can be seen, progressive discipline is designed to give employees every opportunity to modify their behavior and remain part of the team. Employers must be fair and reasonable in their treatment of employees, and employees must be ready, willing, and able to perform their jobs. Finally, progressive discipline sends a signal to other employees that under similar circumstances, they will receive the same opportunities and consideration.

Immediate Discharge

Immediate discharge is used when there is a serious violation of the trust given to employees. Examples of this type of behavior include dishonesty or stealing, fighting on the job, blatant rudeness toward guests, willful intent to damage or destroy company property, failure to report to work without just cause, walking off the job, and being under the influence of alcohol or a controlled substance. These violations are so heinous as to demand immediate discharge; any discipline less than discharge sends the wrong message to other team members, that it's okay to steal or that you can get away with striking another employee. Discharging under these circumstances is a positive managerial step since you are removing a serious negative influence on the business. Employees guilty of willful misconduct have betrayed their team members and the organization and have manifested their lack of shared values. Casino managers are reminded that immediate discharge is to be reserved for the most severe violations, and these terminations must be supported with strong documentation based on the quality and quantity of evidence.

 ## SUMMARY

In summation, one of the greatest needs in the casino industry is a strong sense of human resources management and the need to care for and nurture employees. Employees are a casino's most valuable asset and must be handled accordingly. Gone are the days of managing employees through intimidation and fear. Successful operations now involve employees in the management process through strong communication and by empowering and entrusting employees as team members who will bring success to themselves and the organization.

 ## DISCUSSION QUESTIONS

1. Define human resources management.
2. Explain the key components to include in a mission statement.
3. What is meant by creating a human resources management system?
4. Explain why the design of an application form must be concerned with legality.
5. What is meant by the employment-at-will doctrine?
6. Outline differences between internal and external employment recruitment.
7. Indicate two tools used by gaming managers to conduct successful employee interviews.
8. Discuss several purposes of written job descriptions.
9. What is the purpose of an employee I-9 Form?
10. Explain the concept of progressive employee discipline.

10

CASINO MARKETING

 ## LEARNING OBJECTIVES

This chapter will enable the reader to:

- Understand the process used in developing a casino marketing plan.
- Discuss various marketing techniques used by casinos to draw customers.
- Review samples of advertisements used by casinos to attract potential gaming patrons.

INTRODUCTION

What makes one casino different from all others? Why should customers choose your casino? What do you have to offer customers? How do you develop customer loyalty? What segment of the market is best suited for your property? How do you tell people about your product? The answer to these questions lies in your marketing plan. A casino may have the best table odds in town, the most exciting dice action, or a million dollars in decor, all of which will be a well-kept secret without a proper marketing plan. Although the nuances of marketing can be very complex, the basic concept is simplistic—you need to tell people who you are, what you offer, and how to find you. A restaurant menu is an excellent example of a marketing tool. Customers cannot go into the kitchen to see the food selections, so the menu must effectively

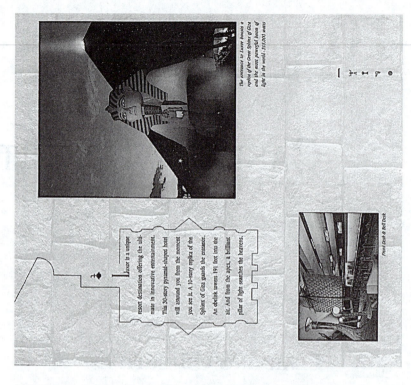

The entrance to Luxor houses a replica of the Great Sphinx of Giza and the most powerful beam of light in the world - 315,000 watts

Luxor is a unique resort destination offering the ultimate in innovative entertainment. This 30-story pyramid-shaped hotel will astound you from the moment you see it. A 10-story replica of the Sphinx of Giza guards the entrance. An obelisk towers 191 feet into the air. And from the apex, a brilliant pillar of light searches the heavens.

Front Desk & Bell Desk

LUXOR
LAS VEGAS

THE NEXT WONDER OF THE WORLD

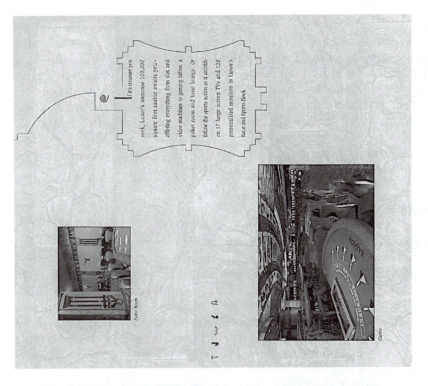

If it's treasure you seek, Luxor's immense 100,000-square-foot casino awaits you – offering everything from slot and video machines to gaming tables, a poker room and keno lounge. Or follow the sports action as it unfolds on 17 large screen TVs and 128 personalized monitors in Luxor's Race and Sports Book.

Poker Room

Casino

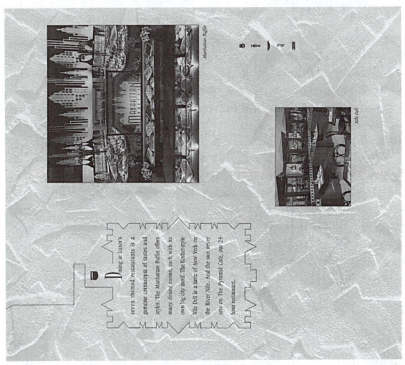

Dining at Luxor's seven themed restaurants is a genuine cornucopia of tastes and styles. The Manhattan Buffet offers many dining rooms, each with its own big city motif. The Rochester-style Nile Deli is a taste of New York on the River Nile. And the sun never sets on The Pyramid Cafe, our 24-hour restaurant.

Manhattan Buffet

Nile Deli

Rack Brochure *(Courtesy of Luxor Las Vegas)*

and succinctly sell the product. The use of descriptive, mouth-watering terms, artistic design, and visual displays market the product without a word being vocalized, and it is well established that the more effective the menu, the higher the impact on sales. Marketing a casino, like a menu, requires careful planning and understanding and effectively describing the product via the proper media venues. Marketing can be accomplished internally and externally, inexpensively or through huge media campaigns; it can be clever, subtle, direct, or even subliminal. In the final analysis, a successful plan, based on a clear understanding and conveyance of the product, will result in effective market segmentation, customer retention, and brand loyalty.

SLOT MARKETING

Casino marketing strategies focus on three primary objectives: to attract patrons to the facility; to offer inducements for patrons to stay and play while in the facility; and to provide a gaming entertainment experience resulting in their return. Why do more than 100 million Americans visit casino destinations annually? What is the profile of a gaming patron that results in billions of dollars annually to the casino industry? Why has slot revenue become the highest casino revenue generator, exceeding the combined revenue of table games? Answers to these questions provide the reader an insight into marketing objectives and strategies.

Although Chapter 1 discussed a number of reasons why casinos attract customers, it is important to revisit this issue and expand on the rationale.

1. Casinos are exciting. Lavish decor, interior and exterior ambiance, surging crowds, name entertainment—and all that money! To a great number of individuals, this atmosphere offers a psychological "high"—a pulsating excitement that, in itself, offers an entertainment experience.

2. Many visitors simply enjoy the excitement of gambling, whether they win or lose. Pitting one's skills (with the hope that Lady Luck is smiling) against the turn of a card, the roll of the dice, the spinning roulette ball, and the whirling slot reel is a memorable gambling experience.

3. The lures of "that one big hit," "the dice will stay hot," "someone has to hit the big jackpot—why not me?" are certainly indicators of a visitor's basic desire—to win money. And a casino is possibly the only opportunity for individuals with strong fantasy drives to realize this ambition.

4. As a vacation destination or for just a few hours of relaxation, casinos offer a getaway from the stress and daily routines of one's lifestyle. Lavish guest rooms, beautifully landscaped swimming pools, sumptuous dining experiences, gala entertainment are all combined to pamper guests and afford them an opportunity to escape the rigors of the daily routine.

5. Casino promotional and customer relations policies have excelled in extending personal attention and recognition to a large segment of its patrons. Offering complimentary rooms, food, beverages, and VIP invitations all say to the customer, "You are special and recognized accordingly." These strong motivational factors serve to identify casinos as unique facilities catering to this market segment.

6. Many customers perceive a casino environment as a center for social interaction, to see and be seen, to converse about winning and losing streaks, and to make new friends.

7. Free cocktails, drawings and contests offering cash awards, two-for-one meal specials, coupon books—all are strong incentives offered to casino customers; these promotions have proven highly successful in attracting clientele.

There are probably many other reasons why customers flock to casinos, as well as motivational factors causing them to do so. With an understanding of why customers come, marketing strategists now turn their attention to geographic analysis to determine where customers originate. With a high density of casinos in Las Vegas, Reno, and Laughlin, Nevada, as well as Atlantic City, New Jersey, and Tunica, Mississippi, marketing efforts seek to capture a share of gaming clientele. Jurisdictions throughout the United States also vigorously compete for the market. This identification of a casino's target market typically focuses on locals, employees of competing properties, tourists, convention delegates, trade show attendees, "snow birds," invited guests, and junketeers.

A first-time casino visitor will likely be overwhelmed not only by the incessant customer activity but also with the variety of gaming options available. With choices including twenty-one, craps, roulette, money wheel, bingo, and keno (and, in the state of Nevada, race and sports books), it soon becomes obvious that the greatest amount of casino floor space is occupied with slot machines. In answer to the question "Why the intense activity with slot machine play?" the following reasons merit consideration:

Unlike table games, a slot machine does not intimidate the customer. The customer has no dealer to confront, nor is there the concern of embarrassment about making mistakes in front of other customers. Rather, it is "me against the machine." The machine is fun and easy to play. Put the money into a reel slot and the machine does all the thinking. A slot machine is seen as an exciting and fascinating device. With a wide variety of pay tables, coins crashing into a tray, a small monetary investment, and always the anticipation of "hitting the big one," it is small wonder why hundreds of thousands of patrons are attracted to slot machines.

DEVELOPING A MARKETING PLAN

Marketing is the process of notifying potential and existing customers about the goods and services available to them through your business. A marketing plan is a formalized strategy designed to identify and reach the most likely users of the goods and services based on calculated or estimated demographics, a situational analysis, or other similar types of studies and approaches.

Marketing plans can be adjusted to reach new market segments in response to product changes and modifications, or the alteration may be based on a belief that the target market has been saturated and a new customer base exists. Las Vegas serves as an example of an expanding market base that now attracts gamblers, families, conventioneers, trade show goers, sports enthusiasts, newlyweds, high-end and economy-conscious buyers, and local, national, and international tourists.

An effective marketing plan is based on a clear comprehension of the product. If you don't understand or know your product, how can you market or sell it? Existing casinos perform a situational analysis to determine market segments currently being drawn to the property. This involves intercept interviews with customers, in-house surveys, or the use of outside consultants. Assessment of the product entails a listing of all positive and negative attributes, including the number and types of casino games and slots; the types and quality of entertainment; food and beverage amenities; size and quality of any lodging facilities; parking availability; employee/customer ratio and quality of service; unique property features; value-priced items; any discount programs; and special event offerings. It is particularly important to determine the negatives and develop an action plan to offset these problems. If customer service is lacking, a plan must be implemented to correct the deficiency. If the casino cannot compare in physical size to nearby competitors, a marketing plan would emphasize the "cozy atmosphere" and personalized service.

With the list completed, a determination can be made regarding the casino's profile and the market segments most likely to be attracted. The following example illustrates how two casinos with essentially the same gaming attractions target different customers.

Property A	*Property B*
Located on the Strip in Las Vegas	Located in a suburban neighborhood of Las Vegas ten miles from the Strip

2,500 slot machines:
  1,800 video slots/reels
  400 video poker
  200 video keno
  100 other
	2,500 slot machines:
	  500 video slots/reels
	  1,400 video poker
	  500 video keno
	  100 other

Special features:
  $1, 50¢, 25¢ mega-payoff
  progressives
Slot tournaments
Slot club that awards points for
  prizes
	Special features:
	  $1, 50¢, 25¢, 5¢
	  mega-payoff progressives
	Slot tournaments
	Slot club that awards points
	  for cash

Property A	Property B

Slot denominations:
  60% 25¢ machines
  30% $1 machines
  9% $5+ machines
  1% 50¢ machines
	Slot denominations:
	  80% 25¢ machines
	  7% $1 machines
	  10% 5¢ machines
	  3% other denominations

Slot tournaments Slot club	Slot tournaments Slot club Poker, bingo, and bowling tournaments

Extensive use of currency
  acceptors on slots; limited
  number of change personnel;
  extensive use of slot hosts to
  procure slot club memberships
	Average use of currency
	  acceptors on slots;
	  extensive use of change
	  personnel; few slot hosts

Table games: twenty-one, craps,
  baccarat, Big 6, keno, roulette,
  pai-gow, pai-gow poker,
  Caribbean stud poker,
  mini-baccarat
Table limits: $5–$2,000
Baccarat often adjusts table
  limits to address six-figure wagers.
	Table games: twenty-one, craps,
	  Big 6, roulette, pai-gow,
	  pai-gow poker, Caribbean
	  stud poker, bingo, poker
	  room, mini-baccarat
	Table limits: $2–$1,000

State-of-the-art race and sports
  book occupying extensive casino
  space
	Midsize race and sports
	  book with results manually
	  entered and an ongoing
	  party atmosphere with free
	  beer and pizza

2,000-seat showroom featuring
  top-name entertainers:
    6 p.m. dinner show, $55/person
    10 p.m. cocktail show, $35/
    person
	Country/western dance hall
	  with live music/local bands:
	  No admission charge

1,000-seat showroom featuring
  Las Vegas–style production show:
  Two cocktail shows, $30/person
	100-seat lounge featuring
	  stand-up comics, live music:
	  Two-drink minimum

Property A	Property B

3,000 hotel rooms
Average room rates:
  $85–$250/night
Extensive suite accommodations
	1,000 hotel rooms
	Average room rates:
	  $45–$75/night
	Limited number of suites

9 restaurants:
  3 gourmet/French restaurants
  3 specialty restaurants
  1 coffee shop
  1 buffet, $10.95/person
  1 New York–style deli
	6 restaurants:
	  3 family-style, mid-priced
	  1 buffet, $3.95/person,
	    children under 12 free
	  1 McDonald's
	  1 hot dog stand

Extensive shopping mall featuring expensive jewelry, imported fashions, portrait artists and art gallery, hair salon, health spa	Limited shopping with gift shop, liquor store, toy store, candy store, ice cream parlor, clothing boutique
250,000 square feet of meeting and convention space. Attract top national and international conventions, groups, and trade shows.	50,000 square feet of public space for wedding receptions and parties
Wedding chapel	No wedding chapel
Two-acre pool with cascading waterfalls and poolside gourmet dining	No pool
No bowling alley Small kids' arcade	75-lane bowling alley Extensive kids' arcade with virtual reality and motion-simulator attractions
No motion picture theater	State-of-the-art theater complex
No daycare center	Daycare center for guests' children
No shuttle service	Free shuttlebus service for locals to/from casino

Property A	Property B
1 1,000-car parking garage Valet parking	2 1,000-car parking garages Valet parking
Subdued, upscale atmosphere, plush carpeting, chandeliers, use of marble throughout	Loud, brightly lit atmosphere, country/western theme
Concierge service	No concierge service
No recreational vehicle park	Extensive recreational vehicle park

It can be seen that although both properties offer gaming and entertainment, they are profiled for different market segments. Property A is obviously aiming for the high-end tourist segment. Its slot mix is geared more toward tourists who prefer reel/video slots and will play high-end denomination machines more readily than locals. Baccarat is another game for high-rollers and tourists, especially international visitors. Table limits also are an indicator, as are the type and pricing of entertainment, restaurants, and the shopping mall; the appeal is definitely geared toward the "big spender." The pricing structure of hotel rooms and the suite offerings do not appeal to the economy or family shopper. Finally, the property has extensive convention and meeting space, which likewise appeals to national/international groups.

Property B is a "local" casino attempting to primarily attract people residing in the city and the more economy-minded tourist. Although this property cannot compete with the size and elegance of Property A (a perceived negative), it offers a different, "down-home," cozy atmosphere. The family can find a full range of activities, including motion pictures, value-priced meals, a premiere fast-food/service restaurant catering to children, a toy store, a daycare center, a massive bowling complex, and an extensive kids' arcade. The recreational vehicle park appeals to family vacationers and retirees. Locals are additionally drawn by the slot mix (the locals prefer video poker) and lower-denomination machines, a poker room, and bingo, not to mention the free shuttle service. The casino has discovered that there is a long-time social encounter that exists between a significant number of their regular customers and the change personnel, which enhances the social interactivity appeal of this property. Part of Property B's marketing plan is to offer all of the attractions of a Strip property minus the traffic, congestion, and long lines for the restaurants, shows, and so on. The plan involves advertising many of the features found on the Strip such as slot tournaments, a slot club, valet parking, megajackpot slots, and a large selection of slots. The message is, "Why fight the traffic and crowds when you can have the same gaming experience right in your own backyard?!"

Choosing the Right Marketing Vehicle

Marketing can be done through a myriad of media approaches such as television, radio, newspapers, trade journals, airline magazines, direct mailers, billboards and signs, travel rack brochures and travel agency packages, booths at trade shows, sales representatives making presentations to groups, sponsorships such as special events or community/charitable events, and other promotional and advertising vehicles. Budgetary considerations, targeted markets, and desired impact all factor into the marketing plan decisions. Las Vegas prefers groups with a gaming propensity, and some casinos have rejected groups that would occupy a significant number of hotel rooms but did not have a positive gaming profile.

Marketing Techniques

The figures in this section are offered as examples of techniques used by casinos to draw customers. Note the variety of the products and amenities offered and the market segment targeted.

Figures 10.1a and 10.1b are marketing pieces for keno. Figure 10.1a is an example of external marketing, as this advertisement appeared in a newspaper,

Figure 10.1(a)
Keno Promotion (Courtesy of Sam's Town Hotel & Gambling Hall, Las Vegas)

Figure 10.1(b)
Marketing Keno (Courtesy of the Sheraton Desert Inn, Las Vegas, an ITT Sheraton Resort & Casino)

while Figure 10.1b represents a rack brochure distributed internally to guests by the Sheraton Desert Inn Resort and Casino (which may also be used externally since the property's address and phone number appear on the back page).

Figures 10.2, 10.3, 10.4, and 10.5 are all gaming marketing promotions. Figure 10.2 projects "loose slots" with validation through the average number of daily royal flushes. Some casinos list the year-to-date total of jackpot payouts, which is usually an extremely impressive number. Other casinos advertise payback percentages such as 99.2 percent paybacks. Figure 10.3 illustrates a multipurpose, direct mail marketing piece promoting the 50th anniversary of Harvey's Hotel and Casino, Lake Tahoe, Nevada. Figure 10.4 entices players with single-deck blackjack and 10x odds on craps. Note the message at the bottom of this advertisement: "Where *locals* bring their friends." Figure 10.5 really uses three messages: (1) bingo as a gaming attraction, (2) free food, and (3) Mother's Day as an incentive. Figure 10.6 promotes a craps tournament with a $25,000 grand prize.

Figures 10.7 and 10.8 use food to attract potential gamblers. The marketing samples found in Figures 10.9, 10.10, and 10.11 all profile the excitement

Figure 10.2
Slots Promotion (Courtesy of the Fiesta Casino Hotel, Lake Mead)

Figure 10.3
Mulipurpose Direct-Mail Marketing (Courtesy of Harvey's Resort Hotel/Casino, Lake Tahoe)

Hoppin' Good Times

Microbrewery Tasting & World Music Festival
July 23 at Harveys

These ain't your average suds. Instead, they're seriously fine beers from around the world. And you can enjoy them while the vibes of *Queen Ida and her Zydeco Band,* as well as *Sukay and the Music of the Andes,* fill the summer air. A $17.50 donation (the fundraiser benefits the Valhalla Boathouse Theater and Festival) includes admission, beer, souvenir glass, and continuous music.

A Festive Fourth!

Independence Day Fireworks Displays

What's more beautiful than Tahoe's quiet waters? For one thing, seeing the vibrant reflections of one of the West Coast's largest fireworks displays in those same waters. On July 4th, Tahoe's skies will burn with a brilliant burst of color in this custom-made pyrotechnic show. Highlights of the show include music, Japanese aerial shells, computer-choreographed fireworks, and what's been dubbed "the world's absolute best double petal chrysanthemums." That's not your average firecracker. And this is by no means your average Fourth of July.

Harveys Party Gras!!!
June 17 - September 18
$50,000 in Cash! More than $100,000 in prizes!

If you're game for good times and great chances to win fabulous prizes, then play at the Party -- Harveys Party Gras. How? Simple. Every Thursday, Friday and Saturday we'll throw

Suprise Parties throughout the casino. You could win $100 cash and other prizes like T-shirts, drink tokes or dining credits just for playing. Weekly Party Gras Package Winners - three lucky people will win $750 cash, a night in one of our beautiful Lake Tower rooms and 2 tickets to "Anita Mann's A Blast from the Past" in the Harveys Emerald Theater. All Party Card holders are welcome to enter once a day by swiping a party card at the Party Card Center. The drawing will be held every Sunday evening. *The Party never ends! Join us for Monday Night Sports Parties, Party Tuesdays, Goofy Golf Thursdays and Conga Fridays.*

Attention Sports Fans!

Harveys Race & Sports Book is in full swing this summer with some of the year's biggest events, including the Preakness, Indy 500, Stanley Cup, NBA Finals, World Cup Soccer and a variety of golf and tennis championships. Catch all the fun on big screens right here at Harveys!

HARVEYS RACE & SPORTS BOOK

The Ultimate Party Package

Register to win our fabulous
50th Anniversary Party Package

Prize includes transportation in our corporate jet*, limousine, 2 nights in a luxurious Lake Tower suite, dinner for 2 at Llewellyn's and $1000 cash. The drawing is September 18. Just show your Party Card and register to win at the Party Card Center or the KHRV Booth.

*Corporate jet provided for a limited area, commercial air service provided outside area.

HVY After fifty years as a privately owned company, Harveys Casino Resorts went on the New York Stock Exchange, February 15, 1994 at $14.00 a share under the symbol HVY.

Tom Yturbide, President and CEO, described it as a *"very positive step forward for the company. Being a publicly traded company gives us an opportunity to raise money for new development and expansion."*

Harvey Casino Resorts is expanding into the Colorado and Southern Nevada gaming markets with construction of properties in Central City, Colorado and Las Vegas, Nevada, currently in progress.

Figure 10.3
(Continued)

The 1994 Lake Tahoe International Dragon Boat Festival

In the final week of August, sightings of Tahoe Tessie are expected to run rampant. But rest easy, what you see dashing across the waters aren't serpents. Instead, they happen to be a colorful armada of the world's swiftest Dragon Boats competing off Zephyr Cove Resort at Lake Tahoe.

What started out as a Chinese racing ritual nearly 2400 years ago has grown to become one of the world's most popular and unique racing events. On August 26, 27 and 28, teams from over 20 countries will vie for the top prize here at Lake Tahoe.

The fast-paced and exciting ritual of Dragon Boat Racing.

But what makes this event complete is the culture and activities that will surround it. Many of the folk customs – such as singing, dancing and cooking – will take center stage. You'll find arts and crafts, international entertainment, poetry, and all the myth and magic that has long surrounded the fast-paced and exciting ritual of Dragon Boat Racing.

It's Tahoe's maiden voyage into this event. Please join all your friends from Harveys in making this an event you'll anticipate for years to come.

> **FOR INFORMATION ON THE INTERNATIONAL DRAGON BOAT FESTIVAL, CALL 1-800-HARVEYS.**

Deal-icious! Great food and great prices are cookin' up throughout Harveys.

El Vaquero has drink specials 5 - 6:30 pm Monday through Friday during "Fiesta Hour." The Seafood Grotto features fresh seafood entrees. The Buffet features themes nightly: Monday - Mexican; Tuesday - Barbecue; Wednesdays - Pasta; Thursday - Continental; Fridays - Seafood; Saturday - Prime Rib; Sundays - Steak. The Carriage House is open 24 hours with daily specials. Llewellyn's has nightly dining, a fabulous Sunday Brunch and lunches Wednesdays through Saturdays. The Sage Room, our classic steak house since 1947, offers unforgettable food in an authentic western atmosphere. Classic Burgers is the place for incredibly thick shakes and big juicy burgers. The Pizzeria has a variety of unique toppings and the lake's best gourmet pizza.

Cash In A Flash
Harveys Check Cashing Privileges

Tahoe's no place to be caught short on cash. And with Harveys check cashing privileges, that's not a problem. You can cash personal (and most payroll) checks. Apply for check cashing privileges with your Party Card today at the Main Cashier, Party Card Center, Race and Sports Book or by calling us toll free, **1-800-HARVEYS.** We'll be happy to fax or mail an application to you.

As an added bonus, you'll receive free drinks, just for filling out an application and mentioning the Party Line.

Charles Barkley's Coming For Tee

An All American Line-Up at the 1994 Celebrity Golf Championship
July 5 - 10

Sir Charles, along with the likes of Joe Namath, Dan Marino, Mario Lemieux and more than 30 other great athletes from today and yesterday will take to the links at South Lake Tahoe's championship Edgewood Golf Course from July 5 through 10.

The 54-hole medal play tournament is serious business. The classic, now in its fourth year, will be telecast live by NBC. For a close-up look at the game and the stars competing, plan to be here at Harveys.

> CALL 1-800-HARVEYS FOR CELEBRITY GOLF PACKAGES.

Keno Tournaments Galore!

Each month, Harveys throws a special Keno Tournament. The Keno player who accumulates the highest point total during each quarter of the year receives a $1000 bonus. In addition, you can play Harveys Party Keno Special where you can win $10,000 for only 25 cents. Call 1 - 800 - HARVEYS for more information.

SUPER SUMMER SPECIAL
If you visit us this spring for just $89, you'll LOVE to revisit us this summer!

And to make sure that you come back to enjoy all the fun and excitement at Harveys, including "Party Gras" which includes over $150,000 in cash and prizes, we'll give you $50 off your return hotel stay.

> **FOR RESERVATIONS OR MORE INFORMATION ON THIS OFFER OR ANY OF OUR 50TH ANNIVERSARY VALUES CALL 1-800-HARVEYS.**

Figure 10.3
(Continued)

Entertaining Ideas.

Big names are coming to the Big Party!

Harveys Summer Celebration

A series of six themed concert events are being held in Harveys Outdoor Amphitheater. Tickets will be on sale at Harveys Box Office or at all Bass Outlets June 13. Amphitheater gates open at 7:00 pm and all shows start at 8:30 PM.

New Countryfest - August 14
Collin Ray, Sammy Kershaw, Carlene Carter

Jazzfest - August 21
Al Jarreau, David Sanborn

Latin Salsafest - August 28
Selena, Emelio Navaira

Rock n' Roll Revival - September 11
Fabian, Little Anthony & the Imperials, The Coasters, Freddie Cannon and Papa Doo Run Run

The Beach Party - September 16*

Country Hunkfest September 18
Billy Ray Cyrus

*Artists to be announced / schedules subject to change.

For more information, call 1-800-HARVEYS

Harveys $100,000 WAGON WHEEL Slot Tournament
June 5 & 6, 1994

Our slots will be smokin' hot this July. With $500 entry fees, you're in on Tahoe's top slot tourney, with 1st place taking $20,000. Second place wins $10,000, 3rd – $5,000, 4th – $2500, 5th – $1200, and the balance will be distributed between 6th and 10th place players. In addition, entrants will be treated to a lavish awards buffet, complimentary cocktails during their stay and a tournament gift surprise.

Call 1-800-HARVEYS to register.

HARVEYS PARTY Line Calendar

JUNE PARTY

May 23 - June 5	French Open Tennis
June 3, 4, 5	Larry Wilson's Superheros of Comedy appearing in the Emerald Theater
June 5 - 6	50th Anniversary Slot Tournament
June 6 - 19	Eddie Dunbar and CA Cowboys appearing in the Emerald Lounge
June 9 - 13	45th Annual Wagon Train Festival
June 10	"A Blast from the Past" rocks the Emerald Theater (indefinitely)
June 11	Belmont Stakes
June 16 - 19	U. S. Open Golf Tournament
June 17 - July 17	World Cup Soccer
June 17	Harveys Party Gras Summer Promotion Kick-off
June 18	Harveys 50th Anniversary Celebration - Burying the Time Capsule
June 20 - June 26	Lip Service and Reta and The Wizz Kids appearing at the Emerald Lounge
June 20 - July 3	Wimbledon Tennis
June 24 - 25	Keno Tournament
June 27 - July 10	Art Vargas and Two Sweet and Inside Out appearing at the Emerald Lounge

JULY PARTY

July 1,2,3,4	Danny Marona appearing in the Emerald Theater
July 4	4th of July Fireworks at South Lake Tahoe
July 5 - 10	5th Isuzu Celebrity Golf Tournament at Edgewood, South Lake Tahoe
July 11 - July 24	The Zippers and Reta & The Wizz Kidz appearing at the Emerald Lounge
July 14-17	British Open Golf Tournament
July 25 - July 31	Sweet Louis/Checkmates and The Act appearing at the Emerald Lounge
July 29 - 30	Keno Tournament
July 31- Aug. 2	50th Anniversary Slot Tournament

AUGUST PARTY

August 1 - 14	Louis Fontaine and the Fabulous Chevelles appearing at the Emerald Lounge
August 11 - 14	PGA Golf Championship
August 14	Collin Ray, Sammy Kershaw and Carlene Carter appearing Outdoor Theater
August 15 - Sept. 4	Mirage and Stinger appearing at the Emerald Lounge
August 21	Al Jarreau & David Sanborn jazz up the Outdoor Theater
August 26-28	Lake Tahoe Dragon Boat Festival at Zephyr Cove
August 26 - 27	Keno Tournament
August 28	Selena and Emelio Navaira "salsa" at the Outdoor Theater
August 29 - Sept. 11	U.S. Open Tennis

SEPTEMBER PARTY

September 2,3,4,5	Danny Marona appearing in the Emerald Theater
September 9 - 25	Madison Ave and Tommy Bell appearing at the Emerald Lounge
September 11	Rock 'n Roll Revival at Harveys Outdoor Theater
September 16	Beach Party at Harveys Outdoor Theater
September 18	Billy Ray Cyrus appearing at Harveys Outdoor Theater
Sept. 25 - Oct. 9	The Zippers and Unity appearing at the Emerald Lounge

Figure 10.3
(Continued)

Figure 10.4
Marketing Gaming (Courtesy of
Sam's Town Hotel & Gambling Hall,
Las Vegas)

Figure 10.5
Bingo Promotion and
Food/Holiday Marketing (Courtesy
of Jerry's Nugget, Las Vegas)

Figure 10.6
Marketing Craps (Courtesy of Trump's Castle
Casino Resort, Atlantic City)

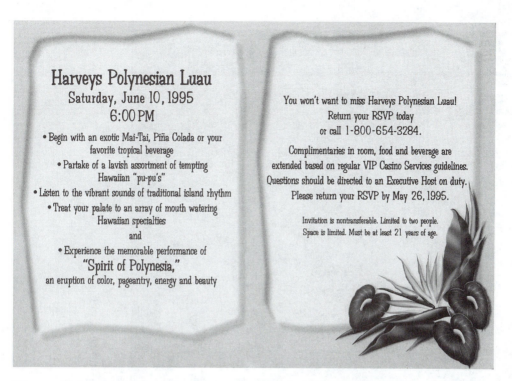

Harveys Polynesian Luau
Saturday, June 10, 1995
6:00 PM

• Begin with an exotic Mai-Tai, Piña Colada or your favorite tropical beverage
• Partake of a lavish assortment of tempting Hawaiian "pu-pu's"
• Listen to the vibrant sounds of traditional island rhythm
• Treat your palate to an array of mouth watering Hawaiian specialties
and
• Experience the memorable performance of
"Spirit of Polynesia,"
an eruption of color, pageantry, energy and beauty

You won't want to miss Harveys Polynesian Luau!
Return your RSVP today
or call 1-800-654-3284.

Complimentaries in room, food and beverage are extended based on regular VIP Casino Services guidelines. Questions should be directed to an Executive Host on duty. Please return your RSVP by May 26, 1995.

Invitation is nontransferable. Limited to two people.
Space is limited. Must be at least 21 years of age.

Figure 10.7
Food as a Promotion (Courtesy of Harvey's Resort Hotel/Casino, Lake Tahoe)

Figure 10.8
Food as a Marketing Tool (Courtesy of the Excalibur Hotel/Casino, Las Vegas, a Circus Circus Enterprise)

Figure 10.9
Excitement of Gaming/Amenities Marketing (Courtesy of Casino Magic! Corp.)

Rent a Grand Resort Chalet.
Enjoy all the comforts of home in our Grand Resort Chalets and stay close to the action. Choose between a one bedroom chalet with queen size sofabed in the living room–unit sleeps four. Or a one bedroom with bunkhouse–unit

sleeps six. Chalets come with full maid service, kitchen appliances, cookware, and dinnerware. Plus color cable TV and phone service.

Then play at Minnesota's premier casino.
There's plenty to do at Grand Casino Hinckley, whether you're six or sixty. Those 18 years old and up are welcome to play at our casino, but we haven't overlooked younger children and teens. Far from it! Our million dollar Kids Quest Activity Center and Grand Video Arcade let your kids play to their heart's content–while you play to yours.

Grand Casino Hinckley is fun for the whole family, any time of the year. With so much to offer, why not spend your next vacation right here?

For more information
call 1-800-995-GRAND
For Casino information
call 1-800-GRAND-21

GRAND CASINO
HINCKLEY

DIRECTIONS: One Mile East of Interstate 35 On Highway 48 In Hinckley, MN. Less Than 70 Minutes North of Minneapolis, St. Paul.
Grand Casino Hinckley RV Resort is a Camp Coast to Coast Host Resort.

The Mille Lacs Band of Ojibwe Welcomes You.

Grand Casino RV Resort
Where the big wheels come to play.

Grand Casino Hinckley

Stay year-round at our Grand Casino RV Resort.

Hit the road and head for Minnesota's newest vacation spot–the Grand Casino RV Resort in Hinckley. You can enjoy year-round fun for the whole family, just outside your door.

Our 50-acre deluxe Grand Casino RV Resort is fully winterized with heated water risers. We have 224 pads with full hook-ups, 30-50 amp service, hot showers, 24 hour security, and a computerized reservation system. And that's just for starters. In 1993, we'll be adding a spectacular lodge with fireplace, convenience store, RV parts department, heated swimming pool, spa, laundromat, volleyball courts, paddle tennis courts, kids' playground and wading pool, horseshoe pits and shuffleboard courts.

But the fun doesn't end there. Right next door to our Resort is the spectacular Grand Casino Hinckley–where the excitement never stops.

There's non-stop action.
No matter what your game, you'll find it at Grand Casino Hinckley. There are over 1500 loose video slot machines, including more than 400 nickel slots. We also boast the highest percentage of Progressive slots for 1,000 miles, with jackpots from $300 to more than $50,000. If Blackjack's what you're looking for, you've come to the right place. We have 52 tables with limits from $3 to $1000. For those looking for the very latest in gaming, Grand Casino Hinckley is the first casino in the country to feature Royal Ascot Video Derby, a horse racing video game that's as exciting as the real thing. Best of all, we're open 24 hours, every day of the year.

There's fabulous food.
So come hungry. There's plenty to choose from, with food for every taste. Stop by our famous all-you-can-eat Grand Casino Buffet. Or enjoy a delicious, sit-down dinner in our newest restaurant, Grand Grill Americana. In a hurry? Check out Cherries, our 24 hour snack bar, for home-made sandwiches and lighter fare. When you want a break from the action, stop by the Silver Sevens Lounge Sports Bar for great food and drinks, day or night. There's live entertainment seven nights a week, no cover charge.

There's non-stop fun.
Our child care center is kids' heaven. Kids Quest was designed for children from six weeks to 12 years old and features an indoor playground with spiral slides, tunnels, ball pits, net climbs, air bounces and lots, lots more. Kids Quest is professionally staffed by New Horizon child care professionals and is open from 9 a.m. to 11 p.m. The cost is just $3 an hour. For teenagers, we offer the largest video arcade in the area, featuring the latest video games and their favorite games of skill. The Grand Video Arcade is so much fun, don't be surprised if you see a few adults in there, too.

Figure 10.10
Excitement of Casino Marketing (Courtesy of Grand Casino Hinckley)

Figure 10.11
Excitement of Riverboat Gambling Marketing (Courtesy of Casino Magic! Corp.)

and amenities of casino gambling. Part of the message is: Las Vegas–style casino gaming right in your own backyard.

Entertainment is a popular venue for marketing. Casinos feature name entertainers, dinner shows, musical productions, broadway shows, rock 'n' roll bands, comedy shops, magicians, stage extravaganzas, country/western line dancing, kariokee singing contests, and a full spectrum of other marketing ideas to bring customers into casinos (see Figure 10.12).

Sports and race books have a wide base of appeal, and Figure 10.13 highlights not only the natural allure of betting on these gaming attractions but also the atmosphere that exists at the book. Sports and race books feature these additional promotions:

1. Season-long football contests with spectacular prizes, including new homes, cars, and huge first-prizes.

2. Super Bowl parties.

3. Parties for the Kentucky Derby, Preakness, and Belmont horse races.

4. Closed-circuit specials for championship fights.

5. Celebrity appearances, including free autographs.

Figure 10.12
Marketing Entertainment (Courtesy of the Excalibur Hotel/Casino, a Circus Circus Enterprise)

6. Live remote broadcasts for radio stations, featuring celebrities.
7. Baseball World Series, NCAA college basketball tournament, and National Basketball Association playoff parties.

Hotel/casinos use promotional pricing for their guestrooms in their advertisements and promotions, especially during slow periods for the casino. Depending on the amount of convention and meeting space, typical markets will include vacationers, gamblers, conventions, business travelers, airline crews, associations, *ad hoc* groups, incentive business or employees who have won an award from their company, trade shows, sports groups, and travel agents who can be responsible for a significant amount of business (see Figure 10.14).

Figure 10.13
Marketing the Race Book (Courtesy of Sam's Town Hotel & Gambling Hall, Las Vegas)

Figure 10.14
Marketing Hotel/Casino Rooms (Courtesy of Trump's Castle Casino Resort, Atlantic City)

Figures 10.15, 10.16, and 10.17 are rack brochures used to market individual games in the casino. Figure 10.18 is a variation on the slot tournament theme with a featured $35,000 grand prize.

Figure 10.15
Marketing Slots (Courtesy of Casino Magic! Corp., Biloxi, Mississippi)

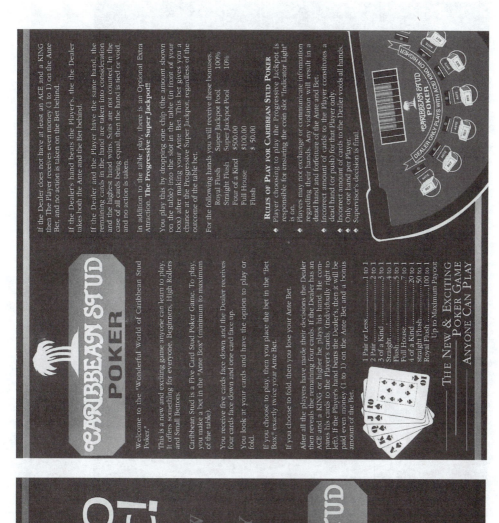

Figure 10.16
Marketing Caribbean Stud Poker (Courtesy of Casino Magic! Corp.)

Figure 10.17
Marketing Pai-Gow Poker (Courtesy of Casino Magic! Corp.)

Figure 10.18
Marketing Slots (Courtesy of the Sheraton Desert Inn, Las Vegas, an ITT Sheraton Resort & Casino)

 ## SUMMARY

An effective marketing plan results in the positioning of a casino with one or more market segments. As can be seen from the examples provided in this chapter, marketing requires imagination and a thorough understanding of purchasing habits as well as visitor demographics. In the final analysis, marketing plays a vital role in the success formula of a casino, and it is critical that operators design an effective marketing plan.

 ## DISCUSSION QUESTIONS

1. Explain the purpose of a marketing plan.
2. List several considerations that will factor into marketing plan decisions.
3. Outline key points that might be used in marketing a casino's slot department.
4. Discuss a marketing plan that might be implemented during slow business periods for a casino.
5. Discuss methods for effective use of casino rack brochures.

11

THE FUTURE

It now should be apparent that the casino entertainment industry is truly a viable business and a high-potential career path. The rapid expansion and proliferation of casinos, riverboats, and dockside operations make a cogent argument for the current stability and long-term growth potential of this component of the hospitality industry. Although no one can predict the future with impunity, there are several observations that may be made relevant to the growth of gaming.

One of the single largest concerns in the immediate future for this expanding business is trained personnel. This training needs to occur at three levels: skilled front-line employees, entry level through midmanagement, and executive level. Numerous casinos have opted for in-house training programs (e.g., dealer training) or turned to proprietary institutions such as dealer schools to meet their front-line personnel needs. Many of the large slot manufacturing companies provide training for slot technicians, and on-the-job training (OJT) frequently fills the other needs. As more casino operations realize the importance of management succession planning, they are looking externally for assistance. Universities and community colleges across the country are responding to this need with new or expanding courses, seminars, and executive development programs geared to the gaming industry. Not only are casinos seeking to address casino management issues, but they are also finding that many gaming supervisors are lacking the traditional or basic managerial skills and training. Thus, in addition to leadership enhancement classes, educational institutions will need to provide midmanagement with budgeting and financial analysis skills (e.g., profit and loss statements, regression analysis, etc.); motivational techniques; conflict resolution procedures; and other such managerial foundation building blocks.

Harveys.

Celebrating

Fifty

Years

Of

Food,

Fun

&

Fortune.

Harvey's celebrated its 50th birthday in 1994. The inset shows the original building in 1944. What will it look like in another 50 years? *(Courtesy of Harvey's Resort Hotel/Casino, Lake Tahoe, Nevada)*

Speaking of education, future managers and executives will be required to have post-secondary and graduate degrees. The casino manager of tomorrow will likely hold two degrees, and, eventually, there will likely be a national certification exam for casino executives much the same as the Certified Hotel Administration (CHA) testing program for those involved in the lodging sector. Gaming regulators, perhaps more than anyone, will need to continue their educational process. As casino financing packages become more complex, as gaming technology increases in complexity, those charged with maintaining the integrity of the business *must* stay on the cutting edge of knowledge. Training for these individuals will always remain a top-priority requirement.

Absent a major scandal that would adversely impact public opinion regarding gaming or cause shockwaves on Wall Street, the industry, as profiled in the first chapter of this book, will continue its growth. It should be noted that this growth may experience peaks and valleys and periodically stall; however, all indications are that the interest in casinos and the impact they can have on unemployment and state tax revenues will remain high. As gaming grows in the United States, the federal government will examine the possibility of and need for national regulation of gaming. This examination will focus on regulation more than on prohibition, although there is still considerable resistance in this country to legalized gambling. The industry may also face additional taxation on slots or other gaming revenue sources. Some congressional leaders may push for a federal gaming commission to oversee the industry, focusing on regulation, taxation, and problem gambling issues. Prior to any national regulation, the legal issue of a state's rights to control its own commerce versus federal authority must be resolved, and this could involve a monumental tug-of-war.

As gaming spreads, jurisdictions must examine more effective ways of addressing problem gambling. Although problem gamblers represent a small percentage of those who partake in casino-style gambling, this is a high-profile societal issue. Proactive casino operations will develop meaningful plans to meet this challenge for their customers as well as employees who display problematic gambling tendencies. In addressing this issue, a common-sense approach would be much the same approach as that taken to serve alcohol with care at bars and taverns. Finally, those who do research in this area should not only focus on the nature, causes, and extent of the problem, they *must* research solutions.

Perhaps the single greatest change facing gaming in the future is technology. The Internet is presently offering gaming via this computerized information highway. If the legal issues involved in the regulation of computerized gaming can be resolved, a whole new technological venue may emerge. The technological changes in slot machines have been dramatic. The electro-mechanical machines have been displaced by high-tech, interactive slots that allow players to insert coins, tokens, or currency; pull a handle or touch a button to spin the reels; and view the results on high-resolution video screens that have improved graphic displays and player excitement. Eventually, virtual reality will enhance the sight and sound experience to create the ultimate in technological slot play. Cashless and coinless systems using debit cards or account tracking systems will provide casino players with another playing option as the industry increases its trend away from strictly coin play. Some have suggested casino play-at-home as the next frontier, with television sets used to display slot machines on-line from selected casinos. Certainly this would seem the next logical step in the play-at-home scenario that has developed, with phone accounts for race and sports books. This concept will not likely succeed, since it removes the excitement of a "live" casino environment and would likely face legal or quasi-legal challenges (e.g., lack of underage gambling controls). In a phrase, this may make technological sense but may not be good common or business sense.

Las Vegas is unparalleled proof that casinos seeking to attract new customers and compete in the expanding gaming industry must constantly work to improve their product. Vegas went from a series of gambling halls to megaresorts featuring "must-see attractions" to a full entertainment experience. It is granted that Las Vegas is not the appropriate model for every gaming jurisdiction, but the lesson for the future must be learned: Gaming operators cannot rest on the tried and true; they must change and experiment with new and exciting concepts. *Research and development* are the watch words for the future, and those who fail to face and succeed in this challenge will face a shrinking share of the market or maybe elimination. Competition, much like in any business, will also cause some business failures. This should be expected as a norm and not as a sign that "the newness has worn off" likely to be charged by the "I-told-you-so" opponents of the industry. Business failures are likely to occur from overexpansion or venturing into jurisdictions where politics or lack of a strong public policy on gaming can cause ruination.

The current trend of creative financing of casinos and joint ventures will continue into the future, and more companies will go public as a means of financing expansion or new projects. Industry analysts estimate that the majority of states in America will have some form of casino-style gaming shortly after the year 2000. We will likely see new, nontraditional players enter the gaming arena (e.g., Sega Corporation).

As stated previously, more universities and colleges will offer casino management courses, representing a marked change in attitude for academia. Prior to the explosion of gaming, only a few universities offered casino courses; in fact, the University of Nevada Las Vegas was the first to offer these classes in 1967 and was virtually alone until gaming was legalized in New Jersey. Today, approximately thirty colleges or universities in the United States offer or are seeking to offer gaming courses, and all indications are that this number will rise dramatically in the very near future. Gaming has become a legitimate course of study, and students see the casino industry as an excellent career choice. We will also witness more top executives leaving the gaming industry for the classroom as educational institutions see the value in offering faculty chairs to attract industry leaders. Years from now, some of the technological breakthroughs or revolutionary management concepts for the gaming industry will emerge from our campuses.

As interest in the business heightens, more books and trade journals will appear. This heightened interest will further result in more gaming conferences and trade shows, both on a national and regional basis. Entrepreneurialism will abound, and the industry will witness numerous small to medium-size businesses trying to carve a niche. This will be especially evident with new game concepts and ancillary services.

Look for Wall Street and investment banks to continue a cautious association with gaming. Because of the rapid expansion and in some cases overexpansion, normal business failures could cause knee-jerk reactions from investors. Gaming must remain stable for an extended period of time and initially cannot afford any major setbacks. Unfortunately, gaming is under closer scrutiny than other businesses and therefore will be subjected to a much higher expected success rate during this growth period.

Demographically, women will rise to the top of the casino management ladder. Historically, when gaming started in Las Vegas, women were excluded from key managerial positions, but over the years they have been mainstreamed into all supervisory levels. Those in management will hopefully continue the trend toward friendly customer service. For too many years, employees were not permitted to interact or even speak to players at table games. Traditional proponents of casino management advocated or professed an adversarial relationship between dealers and players (i.e., the dealers were attempting to beat the players). If casino gaming is to continue to flourish, it must be a full entertainment experience to include the best in customer-employee relations.

In summation, the future of gaming is positive at all levels. It represents a lucrative return for most investors, an excellent career path for those seeking an exciting and expanding business, a venue for continued technological change and challenges, and an exciting form of entertainment for our guests.

CASINO JOB DESCRIPTIONS

The job descriptions featured in this appendix serve as examples of the basic functions of employees found in a typical, full-size casino. Although they are reflective of the general job responsibilities described in the various chapters of this text, there are some variations by design since these job descriptions are to be regarded as a general overview or thumbnail sketch and an additional study guide.

By comparison, some casinos have multipage descriptions with extensive details on the physical and mental requirements of each job (e.g., the exact amount of time a dealer must stand during a normal shift; the precise math skills required by slot change personnel). Smaller casinos do not employ many of the workers listed in this section or utilize combination jobs. Therefore, this appendix merely serves as a foundation for job descriptions and is not a definitive occupational resource.

The variations in the format of the "Essential Functions" and "Job Specifications" (e.g., some descriptions specify the years of experience required and others do not) are intended to suggest the numerous types of issues that may be addressed or included in a job description.

In the interest of reducing excessive duplication, not all public area employee descriptions specifically refer to "excellent customer relations skills" even though it is clearly understood that this is an essential job requirement across the board. Many in-house job descriptions contain salary information; this information is not included in this appendix due to the wide variances from jurisdiction to jurisdiction. The reporting relationships noted in the job descriptions may have some variances from property to property, based on special needs or desires or because they are mandated.

Date

Position	**Casino Manager/Director of Casino Operations**
Reports to	**Owners/General Manager/CEO**
Job Summary	**Responsible for all casino operations, including table games, card games, slots, keno, bingo, poker, sports and race book operations.**

Essential Functions

1. Responsible for all casino department heads and operation of departments in accordance with prescribed operational procedures, internal control procedures, and regulatory requirements.
2. Reviews daily gaming reports (i.e., Master Game Report) and verifies win/loss from all gaming revenue centers, as well as all other casino revenues.
3. Has final authority to settle customer gaming disputes.
4. Has input regarding odds adjustment or game rule modification (e.g., 10x odds on craps).
5. Authorizes staffing levels and gives signatory approval for hiring and termination decisions.
6. Requests investigations into possible gaming misconduct by employees or players.
7. Has full comping authority, including complimentary rooms, food, beverages, and airfare/transportation costs.
8. Establishes comping procedures for other gaming executives and supervisors, and reviews rationale for comped players.
9. Refers credit requests to the credit manager.
10. Has authority to raise table game limits as requested by high-stakes players.
11. Meets with casino marketing department to establish an effective marketing campaign.
12. Establishes an environment in the casino that creates an enjoyable, entertaining experience for guests and employees. Promotes maximum customer service strategies.

Job Specifications

1. Eight to twelve years' experience in management/casino operations.
2. Demonstrated knowledge in all casino games.
3. Strong financial analysis ability.
4. Highly effective communicator, motivator with excellent customer service skills. Able to develop a team concept with employees.

Date

Position   **Assistant Casino Manager/Assistant Director of Casino Operations**

Reports to   **Casino Manager**

Job Summary   **Assists the Casino Manager with the day-to-day casino operations.**

Essential Functions

1. Handles the normal day-to-day activities of the casino, allowing the casino manager to focus on strategic planning, customer development, etc.
2. Runs casino operations in the absence of the casino manager.

Job Specifications

1. Seven to ten years' experience in casino operations or administration.
2. Exceptional knowledge of casino operations, more so than administration.
3. Ability to plan, organize human resources/employees, and create excellent customer service standards.

Date

Position   **Casino Shift Manager**

Reports to   **Casino Manager/Assistant Casino Manager**

Job Summary   **Runs gaming operations on assigned shifts.**

Essential Functions

1. Coordinates all gaming activities occurring during assigned shift.
2. Ensures that all games and other gambling activities are done in accordance with the casino manager's policies and procedures as well as in compliance with applicable federal/state laws and prescribed internal control procedures.
3. Makes all necessary decisions relating to the casino in absence of the casino manager or assistant casino manager.
4. Maintains an ongoing assessment of casino win/loss and reports same to the casino manager upon request.

5. Maintains close scrutiny of high-stakes players and reports their gaming activity to the casino manager.

6. Remains in contact with pit managers relative to gaming activity at the table games.

Job Specifications

1. Six to nine years' experience in management/casino operations.
2. Demonstrated knowledge in all casino games.
3. Strong communication, motivation, and customer service skills.
4. Excellent financial assessment ability.

Date

Position	**Blackjack/Twenty-One Pit Boss/Pit Manager/ Pit Supervisor (one per pit)**
Reports to	**Casino Shift Manager**
Job Summary	**Direct-line supervision of assigned twenty-one pit gaming activities, floorpersons, and dealers.**

Essential Functions

1. Supervises and observes floorpersons to ensure compliance with game rules and internal control procedures.
2. Assigns tables to gaming personnel and handles staffing logistics.
3. Opens/closes pits based on business activity.
4. Maintains gaming activity log, including account of large bills played, ongoing win/loss.
5. Issues and removes decks of cards for games and maintains deck inventory and supply.
6. Handles customer disputes referred by floorpersons.
7. Requests investigation or surveillance when there is reason to believe the integrity of a game is being jeopardized.
8. Handles employee disciplinary situations involving floorpersons and dealers.
9. Interacts with players, maintaining high standards of customer service.
10. Signs pit transaction-forms.
11. Auditions new/prospective dealers, or assigns this function to floorpersons.

12. Is aware of casino internal control procedures, state gaming laws, bank secrecy act requirements.

Job Specifications

1. Five to six years' experience as twenty-one dealer or equivalent training.
2. Knowledge of all games being played in the pit, including twenty-one, pai-gow, pai-gow poker, roulette, the Big 6, Caribbean stud poker, mini-baccarat, Red Dog, and Let It Ride.
3. Excellent attention to detail and good problem-solving skills.
4. Excellent customer relations and employee relations skills.
5. Comprehensive understanding of internal control and gaming regulatory procedures.

Date

Position   **Blackjack/Twenty-One Floorperson**

Reports to   **Twenty-One Pit Boss**

Job Summary   **Direct supervision of the game of twenty-one.**

Essential Functions

1. Directly supervises four twenty-one games.
2. Ensures that game rules, internal control procedures, and state/federal gaming laws and procedures are followed.
3. Accounts and signs for table fills and credits, and verifies amounts.
4. Rates player gaming activity.
5. Settles customer disputes referred by dealers, and refers unresolved disputes to the pit boss.
6. Frequently refers customer credit requests to the credit manager.
7. Is aware of cash transaction requirements under the Bank Secrecy Act.

Job Specifications

1. May be required to periodically work as dealer in the dual capacity of floorperson/dealer.
2. Knowledge of all games being supervised, including twenty-one, pai-gow, pai-gow poker, roulette, the Big 6, Caribbean stud poker, mini-baccarat, Red Dog, and Let It Ride.

3. Ability to focus on game details amid noise and other sources of interruption.

4. Ability to identify and handle customers who have disputes involving the game, those with compulsive or problem gambling tendencies, and those "under the influence."

5. Strong supervisory and customer relations skills.

6. Excellent math skills.

7. Ability to spot cheating scams.

8. Excellent human resource management skills.

Date

Position   **Blackjack/Twenty-One Dealer**

Reports to   **Twenty-One Floorperson**

Job Summary   **Deals the game of twenty-one.**

Essential Functions

1. Deals the game of twenty-one to guests seated at the dealer's table, maintaining an average number of hands per hour as established by the casino.

2. Sells chips and tokens to players for currency and slips currency through slit in table into the drop box.

3. Pays off winning hands in accordance with payoff schedule established by the casino.

4. Collects losing wagers from players, inserting these chips and tokens into the chip rack.

5. Explains the rules of the game using personal, customer relations skills.

6. Refers customer disputes to the supervising floorperson.

7. Counts and verifies table fills and credits and signs for same.

8. Accepts tips from players in accordance with internal control procedures.

9. Shuffles deck of cards in accordance with established casino procedures.

10. Is aware of internal control procedures, state gaming laws, and the Bank Secrecy Act requirements.

Job Specifications

1. Ability to deal multiple games, including twenty-one, pai-gow, pai-gow poker, roulette, the Big 6, Caribbean stud poker, mini-baccarat, Red Dog, and Let It Ride.

2. May be required to work a combination job of dealer/floorperson.

3. Strong mathematical skills and ability to make accurate payoffs in a timely manner.

4. Ability to work under stressful conditions, noisy atmosphere, with exposure to secondary smoke.

5. Ability to pass a dealing audition.

6. Ability to deal a single and multiple deck, either hand-held or from a shoe.

7. Ability to effectively protect the game and spot cheating scams.

Date

Position	**Craps Pit Boss/Pit Manager/Pit Supervisor (one per pit)**
Reports to	**Casino Shift Manager**
Job Summary	**Direct-line supervision of assigned craps pit gaming activities and pit personnel.**

Essential Functions

1. Supervises and observes craps floorpersons, boxpersons, and dealers to ensure compliance with game rules and internal control procedures.

2. Approves all gaming equipment used in the pit, including the use of a micrometer to inspect dice.

3. Assigns gaming personnel to various craps tables and handles staffing logistics.

4. Opens/closes pits based on gaming activity as approved by the shift manager.

5. Maintains gaming activity log and advises shift manager of high-roller activity win/loss.

6. Handles customer disputes referred by floorpersons.

7. Requests investigations when there is reason to believe an employee or customer is cheating the game.

8. Handles employee disciplinary situations involving floorpersons and dealers.

Job Specifications

1. Four to six years' experience as a craps dealer and boxperson.

2. Excellent attention to details.

3. Knowledge of cheating scams used during a craps game.
4. Ability to work under pressure amidst noise and high-action gaming activities.
5. Comprehensive understanding of internal control procedures, gaming regulatory requirements, and the Bank Secrecy Act cash transaction requirement.
6. Strong customer relations skills.

Date

Position   **Craps Floorperson**

Reports to   **Craps Pit Boss**

Job Summary   **Direct supervision of the game of craps.**

Essential Functions

1. Supervises two craps games, ensuring that game rules are being properly followed.
2. Refers requests for additional customer credit to the pit boss or credit manager. Verifies existing credit for players.
3. Rates players' action for the purpose of extension of complimentaries.
4. Handles customer disputes.
5. Ensures that pit paperwork is properly handled.
6. Watches for cheating scams.
7. Ensures compliance with casino internal control procedures, state gaming regulations, and the Bank Secrecy Act.

Job Specifications

1. Three to five years' experience as a craps dealer and boxperson.
2. Knowledge of craps cheating scams.
3. Ability to handle high-action, fast-paced games in a loud and often smoky casino environment.
4. Ability to focus on game details and numerous bets.
5. Exceptional customer relations skills.
6. Excellent human resource management skills.

Date

Position   **Craps Boxperson**

Reports to   **Craps Floorperson**

Job Summary   **Immediate game supervisor and money manager of the game of craps.**

Essential Functions

1. Sits at the craps table (aka "sits box") watching the handling of the dice, wagers placed, and dealer/customer game conduct.
2. Has the authority to challenge and/or remove dice from the game.
3. Maintains physical protection of the casino chips, that are stacked in front of him/her.
4. Inserts currency into the table's drop box.
5. Verifies table fills and credits.
6. Handles customer disputes.
7. May be required to deal the game of craps.
8. Is aware of cash transaction requirements of the Bank Secrecy Act.

Job Specifications

1. Three to five years' experience as a craps dealer.
2. Ability to main focus amidst intense noise and game wagering.
3. Knowledge of craps cheating scams.
4. Excellent customer service skills.

Date

Position   **Craps Dealer/Stickperson (3/game + 1 relief)**

Reports to   **Craps Boxperson/Floorperson**

Job Summary   **Deals the game of craps.**

Essential Functions

1. Three dealers work one game of craps, with one dealer designated as stickperson.

2. The two dealers flanking the boxperson (aka "inside dealers") accept and pay off wagers placed at their respective ends of the table; they also "talk-up" proposition bets.

3. The stickperson, through the use of a croupier's stick, controls the dice by passing the dice to the shooter and retrieving tossed dice.

4. The stickperson monitors wagers placed in the middle of the craps layout.

5. The stickperson can call "no dice" and negate an errant throw of the dice by the shooter.

6. The inside dealers mark the established point by placing a puck on the number.

7. Understands the cash transaction requirements of the Bank Secrecy Act.

Job Specifications

1. Ability to handle multiple transactions amidst loud noise and multiple conversations.

2. Excellent math skills.

3. Ability to spot cheating scams.

4. Ability to pass a dealing audition.

5. Excellent customer service skills.

Date

| **Position** | **Roulette Dealer** |

Reports to   **Twenty-one Pit Floorperson**

Job Summary   **Deals the game of roulette.**

Essential Functions

1. Deals the game of roulette by spinning the roulette ball and calling out the winning number.

2. Accepts currency from guests for roulette chips.

3. Collects losing wagers.

4. Pays winning wagers.

5. Protects the game from cheating scams.

Job Specifications

1. Ability to spin the roulette ball by snapping the ball into the wheel rim.

2. Ability to spot cheating scams.

3. Enthusiasm in creating an exciting/entertaining gaming experience.

4. Ability to pass the dealing audition.

Date

Position   **Roulette Mucker**

Reports to   **Twenty-one Pit Floorperson**

Job Summary   **Helps deal the game of roulette by collecting/mucking the chips.**

Essential Functions

1. Works in conjunction with the roulette dealer and clears losing wagers from roulette layout by swiping chips into a muck apron.

2. Stacks collected chips by color.

3. May alternate with roulette dealer as needed.

Job Specifications

1. Ability to quickly gather chips from table and stack by color designation.

2. Knowledge in cheating scams, rules of the game.

3. Excellent customer service skills.

Date

Position   **Big 6 Dealer**

Reports to   **Twenty-one Pit Floorperson**

Job Summary   **Spins the Big 6 money wheel.**

Essential Functions

1. Deals the Big 6 game by spinning the money wheel.

2. Accepts currency or chip wagers placed by customers.

3. Collects losing wagers.

4. Pays winning wagers.

5. Protects the game from cheating scams.

Job Specifications

1. Ability to spin the money wheel without losing attention from the table layout.
2. Excellent customer service skills.
3. Ability to spot cheating scams.
4. Ability to pass the dealing audition. Ability to also deal twenty-one, pai-gow, pai-gow poker, roulette, Caribbean stud poker, mini-baccarat, Red Dog, and Let It Ride is usually required.

Date

Position	**Baccarat Manager**
Reports to	**Casino Shift Manager**
Job Summary	**Responsible for running the game of baccarat.**

Essential Functions

1. Ensures the efficient staffing and running of the baccarat room.
2. Maintains a list of quality, high-stakes players; solicits and retains their business.
3. Initiates requests for investigations into possible cheating scams.
4. Relays requests for increased table limits to casino manager.
5. Does financial analysis of gaming revenues; extends complimentaries.
6. Participates in baccarat marketing strategy.
7. Understands and complies with the cash transaction requirements of the Bank Secrecy Act.

Job Specifications

1. Five years' experience as baccarat shift manager.
2. Ability to create a list of quality baccarat players.
3. Excellent knowledge of cheating scams.
4. Superior financial analysis skills.
5. Business managerial and human resource management skills.
6. Superior customer service skills.
7. Ability to work as a team player.

Date

Position   **Baccarat Shift Manager/Assistant Baccarat Manager (1 per shift)**

Reports to   **Baccarat Manager**

Job Summary   **Assists baccarat manager/runs baccarat shift.**

Essential Functions

1. Operates the baccarat room in the absence of the baccarat manager.
2. Assists with hiring and personnel administration.
3. Opens/closes baccarat tables as dictated by business.

Job Specifications

1. Two to five years' experience as baccarat floorperson.
2. Excellent customer and employee relations skills.
3. Ability to identify cheating scams.

Date

Position   **Baccarat Croupier, Caller, Pole, or Stick (dealer) (1 of 3 game dealers)**

Reports to   **Baccarat Shift Manager**

Job Summary   **Deals/calls the game of baccarat.**

Essential Functions

1. Using a croupier stick, receives cards from players and calls out point values.
2. Arranges dealt cards on baccarat table for players to see.
3. Explains rules of game and makes sure all rules are followed.
4. Required to act as a baccarat "base" dealer.

Job Specifications

1. Ability to pass dealing audition.
2. Extremely professional appearance.
3. Ability to spot cheating scams.

Date

Position	**Baccarat Base Dealer**
Reports to	**Baccarat Shift Manager**
Job Summary	**Helps deal the game of baccarat.**

Essential Functions

1. Secures lost wagers.
2. Pays winning wagers.
3. Marks the "vig"/commission on bank winners.

Job Specifications

1. Ability to deal game as croupier.
2. Ability to spot cheating scams.
3. Superior customer service skills.
4. Excellent professional appearance.

Date

Position	**Baccarat Shill**
Reports to	**Baccarat Shift Manager**
Job Summary	**Game starter.**

Essential Functions

1. Acts as a "player" in order to stimulate or start the game.
2. Plays with house money but does not keep winnings.

Job Specifications

1. Understanding of the game rules and betting procedures.

Date

Position   **Director of Slot Operations**

Reports to   **Casino Shift Manager/Chief Financial Officer**

Job Summary   **Runs the slot department.**

Essential Functions

1. Responsible for the selection and placement of all slot machines. Authorizes movement of machines as needed.
2. Monitors slot revenues and other pertinent data via a slot tracking system.
3. Negotiates purchase/lease of slot machines from slot manufacturers.
4. Final hiring/termination authority for slot department personnel.
5. Responsible for slot marketing, slot club enforcement, and complimentaries.
6. Investigates alleged slot cheating scam and calls gaming control board to assist with investigations.
7. Ensures that all departmental employees adhere to maximum customer service standards.
8. Extends "comps" to qualified slot players.
9. Ensures compliance with the Bank Secrecy Act.

Job Specifications

1. Knowledge of all types of slot machines, slot computerization, slot tracking/auditing systems, and newest marketing concepts.
2. Strong analytical ability, especially with slot computer and financial reports.
3. Team leader and innovator relating to marketing concepts.

Date

Position	**Assistant Director of Slot Operations/Slot Shift Manager**
Reports to	**Director of Slot Operations**
Job Summary	**Assists director of slot operations with management of slot department.**

Essential Functions

1. Typically handles day-to-day activities, including personnel paperwork (vacation requests, disciplinary notices, etc.), scheduling, interviewing.
2. Recommends policies or policy changes to slot director.
3. Assists with slot club/slot marketing concepts.
4. Reviews labor and revenue reports with director of slots.
5. Operates slot department in absence of director.

Job Specifications

1. Strong organizational and planning skills; ability to handle numerous logistical concerns.
2. Positive motivator of employees/team builder.
3. Excellent financial skills.
4. Knowledge of all aspects of slot operations.

Date

Position	**Slot Floorperson**
Reports to	**Director of Slot Operations/Assistant Director**
Job Summary	**Front-line supervision of slot change persons, booth cashiers.**

Essential Functions

1. Directly manages change persons, slot booth cashiers, and slot carousel attendants.
2. Clears currency jams in slot bill acceptors.
3. Performs hopper fills on slots.

4. Verifies hand-paid slot jackpots and waits while change person makes jackpot payoff to customers.

5. Assists with personnel administration, including scheduling and discipline.

6. Verifies change persons', booth cashiers' and slot carousel attendants' opening and closing banks.

7. Answers guests' questions relating to problems with slots, tournaments, and/or promotions.

Job Specifications

1. Excellent employee and customer relations skills.

2. Ability to handle multiple requests for guest/slot services.

3. Excellent math skills.

4. Ability to work in crowded, loud environment.

Date

Position	**Slot Booth Cashier**
Reports to	**Slot Floorperson**
Job Summary	**Dispenses rolls of coins/tokens to customers; redeems jackpots for slot customers.**

Essential Functions

1. Working from inside a slot booth on the casino floor, dispenses rolls of coins/tokens to slot customers.

2. Receives buckets of coins or racks of tokens from slot customers and exchanges these for currency.

3. Receives currency from change person making "coin buys" and exchanges for currency.

4. Receives and issues banks to change person and slot carousel attendants.

5. Bags coins and turns over to hard-count team.

6. Has financial responsibility for booth game and accountability to casino controller for bank overages and shortages.

Job Specifications

1. Superior math skills; ability to work 10-key calculator, computer, and coin jet-sorter.

2. Ability to lift 20-pound bag of coins.

3. Excellent clerical skills.

4. Exceptional customer service skills.

Date

Position	**Slot Carousel Attendant**
Reports to	**Slot Floorperson**
Job Summary	**Sells tokens to customers playing slots at the slot carousels.**

Essential Functions

1. Standing inside an elevated configuration of slots, sells tokens to slot players.

2. Accepts "racked" tokens from players and redeems for cash.

3. Balances cash/bank drawer.

4. May announce over the public address system any jackpots that have been won.

5. Initiates conversations with customers playing slots at carousel.

Job Specifications

1. Excellent math skills.

2. Ability to initiate conversations with customers.

Date

Position	**Slot Change Person**
Reports to	**Slot Floorperson**
Job Summary	**Dispenses/sells coins to slot players.**

Essential Functions

1. Roving throughout casino, sells rolls of coins to customers playing slot machines.

2. Announces "change" while circulating throughout casino.

3. Notifies slot floorperson of hand-paid jackpots.

4. Notifies slot floorperson of coin/currency jams.

5. Pays customers with hand-paid jackpots in cash.

6. "Celebrates" jackpots with customers.

Job Specifications

1. Ability to carry 20 pounds or more and push a change cart with 100 pounds or more of coins.

2. Superior customer service skills and ability to create relationships with good customers.

3. Good math skills; ability to verify payout amounts.

4. Ability to spot counterfeit currency/tokens.

5. Ability to spot slot cheating scams.

6. Ability to balance cash drawer/bank.

Date

Position   **Slot Club Agent/Representative**

Reports to   **Director of Slot Operations/Director of Casino Marketing**

Job Summary   **Redeems slot club member prizes.**

Essential Functions

1. Working at a counter, meets prospective slot club members and explains benefits of club membership.

2. Enrolls new slot club members.

3. Distributes/orders "earned gifts" won by slot club members.

Job Specifications

1. Superior customer relations skills.

2. Excellent written and oral communication skills.

3. Ability to focus on multiple detailed assignments.

Date

Position   **Slot Host**

Reports to **Director of Slot Operations/Director of Casino Marketing**

Job Summary **Solicits memberships in the slot club.**

Essential Functions

1. While circulating throughout the casino, solicits slot players for membership in the casino's slot club.
2. At the direction of the slot monitor, goes to a "hot slot" being played by a customer who has not inserted a slot club card into the slot machine.
3. May work at the slot club counter helping to enroll new slot club members.

Job Specifications

1. Superior customer relations and sales skills.
2. Ability to work in noisy, crowded casino atmosphere.

Date

Position   **Slot Monitor**

Reports to **Director of Slot Operations**

Job Summary **Monitors slot activity.**

Essential Functions

1. Sitting in front of a computer with a slot tracking system, monitors slot activity.
2. Directs floorpersons to machines with malfunctions, jackpots, etc.
3. Detects any abnormal activities (e.g., slot door opened without a pass key or card; excessive number of fills on a particular machine, etc.).
4. Tracks "hot players" and directs slot club host to those machines.
5. Reports theoretical and actual win on each slot to director of slot operations.
6. Reports on "hot" and "cold" machines, which assists with slot floor arrangement.

Job Specifications

1. Superior computer skills.
2. Ability to keep track of multiple transactions and direct workforce.

Date

Position	**Slot Mechanic/Technician/Electrician**
Reports to	**Director of Slot Operations/Chief Engineer in a hotel/casino**
Job Summary	**Repairs slot malfunctions and verifies that each slot is working properly.**

Essential Functions

1. Repairs machines that are broken or are experiencing malfunctions.
2. Tests the accuracy of a slot machine that has hit a major jackpot prior to the money being given to the winner.
3. "Wires" new machines or machines that have been moved.
4. Replaces broken belly glass on slot machines.

Job Specifications

1. Strong electrical, mechanical experience.
2. Complete knowledge of computers and computer technology.

Date

Position	**Keno Manager**
Reports to	**Casino Shift Manager**
Job Summary	**Runs the keno department.**

Essential Functions

1. Responsible for the daily operations of the keno department.
2. Establishes jackpot limits/amounts for keno games.
3. Works with director of casino marketing on keno promotions.
4. Handles all personnel administration matters for the keno department.

Job Specifications

1. Knowledge in all aspects of keno operations, including computer/electronic technology.
2. Extremely strong administrative and financial skills.
3. Ability to build an effective, customer-service-based team.

Date

Position	**Assistant Keno Manager/Keno Shift Manager**
Reports to	**Keno Manager**
Job Summary	**Assists in the day-to-day operations of the keno department.**

Essential Functions

1. Usually handles the critical day-to-day keno functions, including employee scheduling, employee discipline, etc.
2. Operates the department or shift in the absence of the keno manager.
3. Has access to sensitive areas.

Job Specifications

1. Thorough knowledge of all jobs in the keno department.
2. Excellent customer relations skills.
3. Excellent human resources management skills.
4. Superior financial analysis skills.

Date

Position	**Second/Third Person/Assistant Keno Supervisor**
Reports to	**Keno Manager/Assistant Keno Manager/Shift Manager**
Job Summary	**Calls the game of keno/supervises keno writers and runners.**

Essential Functions

1. Initiates each game of keno, and may call each keno number drawn.
2. Closes each keno game.
3. Verifies large keno ticket winners.
4. Supervises activities of keno writers and runners.

Job Specifications

1. Good managerial skills.
2. Knowledge of keno writer/runner jobs.
3. Superior customer relations skills.

Date

Position	**Keno Writer**
Reports to	**Assistant Keno Manager/(2nd-3rd person)**
Job Summary	**Writes keno tickets for customers in the keno lounge.**

Essential Functions

1. Working at the keno counter found in the keno lounge, "writes" or electronically validates hand-written tickets from customers in the keno lounge presented at the keno counter.
2. Retains one copy of every ticket played on each game and returns one copy to the player.
3. Accepts hand-written tickets given to keno runners by keno players, records/"writes" these, and issues a copy back to the runner.
4. May "call" the game of keno in smaller casino operations.
5. Redeems and pays off winning keno tickets.

Job Specifications

1. Excellent math skills.
2. Attention to numerous details and detailed work.
3. Ability to write tickets quickly and accurately.
4. Ability to make accurate payoffs and handle keno ticket wagers.
5. Superior customer service skills.

Date

Position	**Keno Runner**
Reports to	**Assistant Keno Manager/(2nd–3rd person)**
Job Summary	**Promotes the game of keno throughout the hotel/casino.**

Essential Functions

1. Circulates throughout the casino, restaurant areas, lounges, etc., soliciting keno play, and announces "keno" while "running" tickets.
2. Accepts hand-written keno tickets and wagers from customers, takes these to the keno counter in the keno lounge, and returns validated tickets to customers.
3. Pays off winning keno tickets.
4. Asks players if they want to continue playing.

Job Specifications

1. Physical ability to "run" tickets throughout the hotel and casino in an extremely timely manner.
2. Ability to accurately make change, accept wagers, return keno tickets to proper customers, make payoffs on winners.
3. Extraordinary customer service skills.

Date

Position   **Director of Bingo Operations**

Reports to   **Director of Casino Operations/Assistant Casino Manager/Shift Manager**

Job Summary   **Runs the bingo department.**

Essential Functions

1. Responsible for the daily operations of the bingo room, including the number and style/type of games and jackpots.
2. Assists with the marketing of bingo.
3. Handles all personnel administration issues, including hiring, scheduling, vacations, etc.

Job Specifications

1. Six to eight years' experience in bingo operations.
2. Knowledge in marketing and advertising.
3. Ability to build a team-oriented department focused on customer service.

Date

Position   **Bingo Shift Manager**

Reports to   **Director of Bingo Operations**

Job Summary   **Assists manager with day-to-day operations of the bingo department (only used in larger operations).**

Essential Functions

1. Helps run the bingo department, especially in the absence of the director.
2. Has access to sensitive areas (bingo cashier's cage, bingo office, supervisor keys, etc.).
3. Has signatory authority identical to the director of bingo operations.

Job Specifications

1. Strong administrative and human relations skills.
2. Excellent financial skills.

3. Good problem-solving skills.

4. Knowledge in all aspects of bingo.

Date

Position   **Bingo Agent/Caller**

Reports to   **Director of Bingo Operations/Bingo Shift Manager**

Job Summary   **Sells bingo cards and calls the game of bingo.**

Essential Functions

1. Sells bingo cards to customers.
2. Rotates to the position of "caller" and calls the game of bingo.
3. Working as a game verifier when not selling cards or calling the game, walks around bingo room and verifies winning cards.

Job Specifications

1. Strong customer service skills.
2. Excellent math skills.
3. Ability to call the game over a public address system.

Date

Position   **Director of Sports and 10r Race Book**

Reports to   **Casino Shift Manager**

Job Summary   **Runs the sports and race book.**

Essential Functions

1. Responsible for the daily operations of the sports and race book.
2. Makes or posts daily odds on sporting events or games.
3. Posts information on racing events at national/international racetracks.
4. Handles all personnel administration issues for the sports and race book.
5. Ensures compliance with the cash transaction requirements of the Bank Secrecy Act.

Job Specifications

1. Knowledge of all components of sporting and racing events and how lines are established and moved.
2. Ability to detect betting trends and adjust operations accordingly.

Date

Position   **Race Book Agent**

Reports to   **Director of Sports and Race Book**

Job Summary   **Accepts wagers on racing events.**

Essential Functions

1. Accepts wagers on races (e.g., horse races) and issues tickets to customers.
2. Posts updates on races on the race or "tote" board.
3. Makes changes to race schedule (e.g., scratched horses).

Job Specifications

1. Understanding of various types of races.
2. Accuracy when accepting wagers.
3. Superior customer service skills.

Date

Position   **Sports Book Agent**

Reports to   **Director of Sports and Race Book**

Job Summary   **Accepts wagers on sporting events.**

Essential Functions

1. Accepts individual wagers and card (i.e., parlay card) wagers on baseball, football, basketball, hockey, etc.
2. Updates sports board with current scores from games.
3. Posts information on sporting events (e.g.,. starting pitchers for baseball, money line odds).

Job Specifications

1. Understanding of baseball, football, etc.
2. Ability to explain the various types of wagers and betting lines.
3. Superior customer service skills.

Date

Position   **Sports and Race/Book Cashier/Agent**

Reports to   **Director of Sports and Race Book**

Job Summary   **Pays off winning wagers.**

Essential Functions

1. Accepts tickets from race and sports book customers, verifies that each ticket is a "winner," and pays the wager off according to established casino odds.
2. Maintains cash bank for wager payoffs and ensures security of this casino asset.
3. Explains payoff odds/procedures to customers as requested.

Job Specifications

1. Excellent math and observation skills.
2. Ability to handle largest cash/monetary transactions.
3. Ability to maintain concentration amidst multiple transactions, loud noise, and smoky environment.
4. Excellent communication skills.

Date

Position   **Director of Casino Cage Operations**

Reports to   **Casino Controller/Chief Financial Officer**

Job Summary   **Responsible for all cage operations.**

Essential Functions

1. Ensures the efficient operation of the casino cage and maintains the integrity and security of cash, tokens, and chips on deposit in the cage.
2. Ensures proper compliance with established internal control procedures and government-specified regulation.
3. Ensures compliance with Title 31 of the Bank Secrecy Act as it relates to currency reporting.
4. Ensures the security of money or valuables left on deposit with the cage via safe deposit boxes, the vault, etc.
5. Restricts access to the cage to authorized personnel.
6. Accepts currency/token count from the slot count team and secures for deposit.

Job Specifications

1. Superior math, financial, and accounting skills.
2. Ability to work with large sums of cash and to secure the same.
3. Excellent customer service skills.
4. Strong sense of security and asset protection.

Date

Position   **Casino Cage Shift Manager**

Reports to   **Director of Casino Cage Operations**

Job Summary   **Assists in the day-to-day operations of the casino cage.**

Essential Functions

1. Schedules staff for the respective shift in the cage.
2. Handles customer disputes.
3. Corrects accounting/clerical errors made by cage cashiers and soft-count team.

Job Specifications

1. Extraordinary accounting and financial analysis skills.
2. Ability to handle a multitude of detailed items.
3. Strong employee relations skills.
4. Superior customer service skills.

Date

Position　　　　**Cage Cashier**

Reports to　　　**Casino Cage Shift Manager**

Job Summary　　**Acts as a "teller" for the casino.**

Essential Functions

1. Sells casino chips/tokens to customers for currency.
2. May redeem slot coin jackpots for customers and sell rolled coins.
3. Secures items from customers to be placed in safe deposit boxes.
4. Answers general questions about the casino asked by customers or the general public.
5. May issue/receive cash drawers for restaurant cashiers, etc.

Job Specifications

1. Extreme proficiency in handling and counting large sums of money.
2. Excellent 10-key calculator skills and ability to handle cash transactions in a loud casino environment.
3. Excellent attention to detail (e.g., ability to balance cash drawer).
4. Superior customer service skills.

Date

Position   **Main Bank/Vault Cashier**

Reports to   **Casino Cage Shift Manager**

Job Summary **Controls and issues currency and cash used by the casino.**

Essential Functions

1. Establishes cash drawers for casino and noncasino workers (especially the cage cashier).
2. Accepts returned cash drawers and counts down the bank for overages and underages.
3. Secures cash/currency to be deposited at the bank and handles transfer of funds.

Job Specifications

1. Exceptional accounting skills.
2. Experience at handling large sums of money.

Date

Position   **Pit Clerk**

Reports to   **Casino Cage Shift Manager**

Job Summary **Handles pit paperwork.**

Essential Functions

1. Through the use of a phone and/or computer, communicates pit requirements to the cage.
2. At the request of pit supervisory personnel, verifies credit of players in the pit.
3. Inputs rating data provided by pit supervisory personnel into the computer for comping calculations.
4. May do miscellaneous clerical work for the pit.

Job Specifications

1. Excellent clerical and computer skills.

2. Ability to work under pressure to serve timely and accurate information.

3. Excellent oral and written communication skills.

Date

Position   **Hard-count Team Member (One member is usually designated as hard-count team supervisor.)**

Reports to   **Casino Controller**

Job Summary   **Counts drop from slot machines.**

Essential Functions

1. Removes drop buckets from base of slot machines and moves to hard-count drop room where coins are counted/weighed, sorted, and wrapped for deposit or reuse in the casino.
2. Redistributes rolled coins to booth cashiers.
3. Accepts sacks of coins from booth cashiers.

Job Specifications

1. Ability to lift extremely heavy buckets and sacks of coins.
2. Excellent math skills.

Date

Position   **Coin Room Manager**

Reports to   **Casino Controller and/or Director of Casino Cage Operation**

Job Summary   **Supervises count team during hard count in coin room.**

Essential Functions

1. Supervises the counting of the slot drop.
2. Ensures that slot accounting machinery and equipment are in working order and recommends new technology.
3. Provides a summary accounting of the drop.

Job Specifications

1. Excellent front-line supervisory skills.
2. Ability to manage in an extremely loud and noisy environment.
3. High attention to workplace safety.
4. Excellent accounting/math skills.

Date

Position	**Soft-count Team Member**
Reports to	**Casino Controller/Casino Cage Shift Manager**
Job Summary	**Counts money from table drop boxes/slot currency boxes.**

Essential Functions

1. Opens drop boxes from each table game using drop box key and empties contents (including game openers and closers) onto count table where money chips are sorted, bundled, and stacked.
2. Completes the Master Game Report (aka "stiff sheet") and reports each game's win/loss.
3. Turns the counted revenue and stiff sheet over to the director of casino cage operations or cage shift manager.
4. Counts currency found in slot machine bill acceptor boxes.

Job Specifications

1. Ability to count and sort large sums of money and chips in a fast and accurate manner.
2. Excellent addition/subtraction skills.
3. Ability to work a 10-key calculator.
4. Ability to lift multiple metal drop boxes, often weighing up to 20 pounds.

Date

Position   **Credit Manager**

Reports to   **Casino Controller**

Job Summary   **Handles customer credit reports.**

Essential Functions

1. Receives requests for credit from casino customers or via referrals from pit supervisory personnel.
2. Performs credit background checks on customers.
3. Establishes lines of credit for customers.
4. Maintains absolute confidential records.

Job Specifications

1. Ability to give extraordinary attention to detail work and financial background information.
2. Ability to establish meaningful lines of credit for customers.
3. Sensitivity to and awareness of problem gamblers and compulsive gaming customers.

Date

Position   **Credit Clerk**

Reports to   **Credit Manager**

Job Summary   **Performs clerical functions within the credit office.**

Essential Functions

1. Performs all general, typical office/clerical functions including typing, photocopying, checking completed customer credit applications, and computer input.
2. Contacts customers' credit referral sources via telephone, facsimile, e-mail, or written correspondence.

Job Specifications

1. Able to handle all matters in a professional and confidential manner.
2. Excellent phone and interpersonal skills.
3. Highly organized.

Date

Position   **Collection Manager**

Reports to   **Casino Controller**

Job Summary   **Collects IOUs/markers owed the casino by players.**

Essential Functions

1. Manages multiple marker collection transactions and secure payment on behalf of the casino.
2. Handles negotiated settlements as necessary.
3. Conducts collections in a strictly confidential manner.

Job Specifications

1. Ability to effectively collect outstanding obligations while maintaining sound customer relations.
2. Strongly effective communication skills, both in person and on the telephone.

Date

Position   **Collection Clerk**

Reports to   **Collection Manager**

Job Summary   **Performs clerical functions within the collection office.**

Essential Functions

1. Is able to perform all general office/clerical functions to include computer input, typing, filing, photocopying, and handling external/internal written correspondence.
2. Periodically deals with customers and must handle inquiries in a timely manner.
3. Is able to handle all matters in a confidential manner.

Job Specifications

1. Excellent attention to details.
2. Able to work under pressure and stress.
3. Excellent phone and communication skills.

Date

Position   **Internal Casino Auditor**

Reports to   **Casino Controller**

Job Summary   **Audits internal control procedures.**

Essential Functions

1. Writes the casino's internal control procedures. Makes sure they are in compliance with applicable state and federal law.
2. Audits employee adherence to the internal control procedures.
3. Makes adjustments to the internal control procedures to ensure efficiency and protection of assets.

Job Specifications

1. Excellent financial and organizational (span of control, etc.) knowledge.
2. Superior writing skills.
3. Ability to conduct meaningful employee interviews and analyze work performance.
4. Superior auditing skills and knowledge of state/federal gaming laws.

Date

Position   **Director of Casino Marketing/Entertainment**

Reports to   **Casino Shift Manager**

Job Summary   **Markets, promotes, and advertises casino events.**

Essential Functions

1. Helps design, promote, and market the following types of casino events: slot tournaments, poker tournaments, championship boxing events, musical concerts, sports/race book contests, and general programs designed to bring customers into the casino.
2. Tracks results of promotions and the impact on the casino drop.

Job Specifications

1. Marketing degree or five to ten years' experience in marketing and multimedia presentations.
2. Ability to statistically track impact of casino promotions.

Date

Position   **Director of Casino Security**

Reports to   **General Manager/Casino Manager**

Job Summary   **Responsible for maintaining law, order, and safety in the casino.**

Essential Functions

1. Establishes "police" authority for the casino.
2. Establishes safety and fire prevention programs.
3. Coordinates internal control procedures for security officers.
4. Creates a crisis management program and emergency evaluation plan for the casino.
5. Expedites emergency medical treatment program for guests.
6. Responsible for procedures for handling intoxicated guests and patrons "under the influence."

Job Specifications

1. Extensive knowledge of civil and property law
2. Seven to ten years' experience in security operations.
3. Strong organizational and administrative skills.

Date

Position   **Casino Security Officer**

Reports to   **Director of Casino Security**

Job Summary   **Maintains law and order in the casino and assists with casino operations.**

Essential Functions

1. Assists with table game fills and credits.
2. Pulls drop boxes from table games and places them in casino cage. Replaces full drop boxes with empty ones.
3. Patrols casino, maintaining law and order.
4. Maintains vigilance for fire and safety hazards.

5. Acts as customer service representative for the casino.

6. Handles guest and customer emergency situations.

7. Handles lost and found items for the casino.

8. Escorts guests and employees to parking areas.

9. May be responsible for the casino's time office.

10. Restricts access to casino's hotel rooms to registered guests.

11. Removes vagrants from property.

Job Specifications

1. Excellent knowledge of the law and legal issues.

2. May be required to carry and qualify with a weapon.

3. Excellent public relations and customer service skills.

4. CPR and EMT training helpful.

Date

Position   **Director of Casino Surveillance (Eye-in-the Sky)**

Reports to   **Owners**

Job Summary   **Videotapes gaming activity.**

Essential Functions

1. Through the use of high-tech, wide-angle-lens cameras, watches table games, slots, cage, and other sensitive areas of the casino, looking for cheating scams, casino security problems such as attempted robberies, etc.

2. Videotapes all table games on a 24-hour basis and retains tapes for use as evidence.

3. Notifies casino manager of known cheaters spotted in the casino.

4. Manages surveillance staff, including selection/hiring, training, scheduling, etc.

Job Specifications

1. Absolute, total knowledge of all cheating scams that can occur in a casino.

2. Superior computer skills.

3. Thorough knowledge of all casino games.

Date

Position   **Poker Room Manager**

Reports to   **Director of Casino Operations**

Job Summary   **Administers and operates the poker department.**

Essential Functions

1. Is responsible for daily operation of poker room/department.
2. Establishes the various types of poker games to be played, house betting limits, and game protocol.
3. Oversees all poker room/department employees.
4. Extends complementaries to valued customers.
5. Approves decks of cards used in games and oversees casino chip usage and inventory.
6. Approves/stores decks of cards to be issued in the poker room.
7. Ensures compliance with internal control procedures, state gaming laws, and the Bank Secrecy Act.

Job Specifications

1. Knowledgeable in all aspects of poker room operations and types of poker games.
2. Strong operational and administrative skills.
3. May be required to maintain a list of VIP poker players and be able to attract their play.
4. Excellent customer service skills.

Date

Position   **Poker Room Shift Manager**

Reports to   **Poker Room Manager**

Job Summary   **Assists the poker room manager with administrating poker operations.**

Essential Functions

1. Assists poker room manager with the operation of the poker room/department.

2. Assists poker room manager with administrative duties to include hiring/staffing of poker room personnel.
3. Operates assigned shift and represents the casino in the poker room in the absence of the poker room manager.
4. Checks decks of cards before, during, and after each shift.

Job Specifications

1. Thorough knowledge of all games of poker.
2. Excellent human resources management skills.
3. Excellent customer service skills.
4. Ability to detect cheating scams.
5. Knowledge of financial reports.
6. Ability to assist with scheduled and related logistical matters.

Date

Position   **Brushperson**

Reports to   **Poker Room Manager/Poker Room Shift Manager**

Job Summary   **Entices play in the poker room.**

Essential Functions

1. Solicits players for poker games.
2. Explains the types of games available to potential players.
3. Announces seat availability to waiting customers.
4. Can serve as a poker dealer when necessary.

Job Specifications

1. Excellent public relations skills.
2. Strong communicator.
3. Ability to deal with various games of poker and to work as a poker dealer.

Date

Position　　　　**Poker Dealer**

Reports to　　　**Poker Room Manager/Poker Room Shift Manager**

Job Summary　　**Deals the game of poker.**

Essential Functions

1. While seated at a poker table, deals games of poker to customers.
2. Controls wagering and "the pot" while game is in play.
3. Collects casino's vig from each pot.
4. Exchanges customer currency for poker chips.
5. Is aware of cash transactions requirements of the Bank Secrecy Act.

Job Specifications

1. Must understand and be able to deal all types of poker games.
2. Must be able to handle casino chips and currency in an accurate and efficient manner.
3. Excellent customer service skills.
4. May be required to act as brushperson.

Date

Position　　　　**Poker Room Shill**

Reports to　　　**Poker Room Manager**

Job Summary　　**Initiates or stimulates play in the poker room.**

Essential Functions

1. Plays against the customers in the poker room when there are a limited number of players.
2. May double as a poker dealer.

Job Specifications

1. Must be knowledgeable about all types of poker games.
2. Excellent customer service skills.

INDEX